Marijuana Tales

John C. Krieg

Published by Ribbonwood Press
P.O. Box 390375, Anza, CA. 92539
United States of America

ISBN: 979-8-9859903-0-0

Cover Photography & Design:
Charles Sappington
© 2022

Printed in Times New Roman

© 2022 John C. Krieg

All rights reserved. No part of this book may be reproduced or transmitted in any form or by any means, electronic or mechanical, including photocopying and recording, or by an information retrieval system, without permission in writing from the author.

Other Books by Author:

Desert Landscape Architecture
Environmental Cognizance
Econation
Mobilizing the Green Revolution
Fading America: A Chapbook of Despair
Odes and Episodes: The Perilous Life of a Reckless Artist
Career in Crisis
Zingers: Five Novellas Blowing Like Dust on the Desert Wind

Officer Monkey Ears.
First appeared in Oddball Magazine

In Defense of Outdoor-Grown Marijuana.
First appeared In Wilderness House Literary Review

The Lull.
First appeared In Alternating Current – The Coil

Dedicated to Michelle Renee.
Toke it slow, honey, and
the world will stay kind.

Contents

Preface	7
Catharsis: Rectifying Forty-nine Years of Being a Silent Outcast	13
The Punitive Society and the Dismantling of the DEA	33
The Punitive Society and America's Oppressed Youth	55
Officer Monkey Ears	77
The Brotherhood of Eternal Love	87
Sloppy-Assed Drug Addicts Versus Cannabis Users	107
Cannabis: The Flagship of the New Green Economy	127
The Outdoor Marijuana Grower's Guide	151
In Defense of Outdoor-Grown Marijuana	171
The Lull	181
The Last Harvest	195
So…You Think Federal Marijuana Prohibition is Over?	215
Timeline of Events Relating to Marijuana	229
Bibliography	265
Author Bio	274

Preface

As an outdoor marijuana grower, 2014 was the last season that I slept relatively soundly. Legalization for California, the American epicenter for high-quality cannabis, had gone down in flames in the November 2010 midterm elections, but my medical marijuana business organized under the state-legal collective model and named "Natural Light Collective" was still intact and allowed me to move that year's stellar harvest. My financial life was at least tolerable, but there were storm clouds on the horizon. At that time, nobody knew for sure when Proposition 19 (state legalization) would come up for a vote again, but legalization occurring in Colorado and Washington two years earlier gave advocates and stoners much hope that it was just a matter of time. While I possessed a California medical marijuana card, I daily feared a Drug Enforcement Administration (DEA) invasion with local law enforcement dragged along under federal coercion whether they liked it or not, the incentive, of course, being to keep wide open the faucet of federal funding.

During the dog days of that summer, I penned *Marijuana Tales*, attempting to explain American marijuana prohibition and the insanity of our nation's ongoing War on Drugs, which was initiated when Tricky Dick Nixon formed the DEA back in 1973. In the spring of 1972 I was busted for selling two separate ounces of weed to two separate undercover New York State Narcotics Officers who had preyed on me, set me up, and nearly ruined my life just two weeks prior to graduating from junior college. This left a lasting impression upon me, and I henceforth always felt like a societal outcast. This was something that I *never* talked about as I tried to push the whole sordid ordeal back into the deepest recess of my psyche. So imagine my surprise when the best President of my lifetime, Barack Obama, openly admitted that he had smoked marijuana frequently in his youth and did indeed enjoy getting high. He seemed to laugh it off as the recklessness and tomfoolery of youth, but it didn't seem so funny to me that he could do that while I had had a much different experience, and while young men of his own race were daily paying the price for simply doing exactly what he had done. Deep down inside, I felt that he must have certainly known that marijuana is basically harmless. I looked upon President Obama as a fair and decent man, which caused me to hit upon the idea of petitioning him personally to federally legalize marijuana by utilizing his executive privilege and thus put an end to the injustice of all of this. Time was of the essence to get the book published, out into the public, and in front of Barack Obama. Unfortunately, none of that happened, and looking back in retrospect I sincerely doubt if Obama would have acted.

In July of 2015, the governing body of the town where I live, Unincorporated Riverside County, issued County Ordinance 925, which unequivocally outlawed the growing of marijuana within its confines for the purposes of resale in any form. My collective was instantaneously null and void, and I was forced to cancel my State Board of Equalization Seller's Permit, which was the vehicle by which I paid my fair share of state taxes, because to continue to use it would be to incriminate myself, for why would I pay taxes on something that was now illegal? I was now up on the high wire without a net.

Marijuana Tales languished in rejection hell, California finally did legalize (Prop 19 had morphed into Prop 64) in the fall of 2016, Obama left office, and the Mad King took over the ship of state. He then appointed Jefferson Beauregard Sessions III as our nation's 85th Attorney General. Sessions, who had stated on record that, "Good people don't smoke marijuana," signaled a return to the dark ages of marijuana prohibition in my hometown when he immediately overturned the Cole Memorandum, which was a little known (and little followed) Obama-era policy of encouraging federal law enforcement (DEA, FBI, ATF) and overzealous U.S. Attorneys to look the other way concerning marijuana dispensaries deemed to be operating legally under their respective state laws. There was nothing left to do but to try to go along to get along, so my exhaustive research effort began to see if I, as a small independent grower, could hop on the legalization gravy train. Reading through the State's initial *Adult Use of Marijuana Act* (2014) and fast follow-up *Cannabis Cultivation License Application Overview* (2017) caused me to take heart when the claim was made that the corporations would be held at bay for a period of five years, thus allowing small businesses such as mine to gain a foothold before being swallowed up, strangled, and/or otherwise left as roadkill in the ever-popular "green rush." Greed Rush would be a more appropriate term, and it is now raging. The truth be told, it's all about the corporations, and they are worming their way in everywhere.

 I and old-school growers of my ilk crossed over to being outlaws as we continued to grow, so as to eke out a slightly above substance-level lifestyle, keep a roof over our grandchildren's heads, and put food on the table. The nervous years ensued as it was generally thought that County law enforcement viewed Ordinance 925 as a "nuisance ordinance," which meant if none of your surrounding neighbors complained about your grow, you were left alone. Needless to say, I went out of my way to be a good neighbor, and to those who wanted it, a pound was annually given away as gifts, which was also illegal under the yoke of 925. This tenuous existence all came to an end on June 5th, 2019, when recently elected Riverside County Sheriff Chad "El Choppo" Bianco, with the National Guard, DEA, and FBI in tow, descended like a swarm of ravished locusts in a Kansas cornfield upon my hometown and the heretofore peaceful valley where I live.

 Make no mistake about it; California had no real intention of keeping the corporations at bay or giving the small independent growers a fair chance. Upset that they weren't getting what they viewed as their deserved cut, state government is now determined to wipe out what the squares and bible thumpers have always referred to as the "black market." Miraculously, my grow was spared (initially) but many of my friends and neighbors were literally wiped out in a matter of minutes and will most likely be moving on. The feeding frenzy of the phobic Trump-supporting local octogenarians on Face Book lauding El Choppo (who I so named because he loves to chop marijuana plants) as an avenging angel so enraged me that I revisited *Marijuana Tales*, updated it to include the events of the past half-decade, and doggedly submitted it until I found a willing publisher.

Good fortune did not smile upon me as the owner of that publishing house became gravely ill and abandoned the project and it's delivery date of June 2020 in May of 2020 thus nullifying any hope that my pleas for full federal legalization would cause the youth of America to rise up and seek nothing less than complete federal legalization, with the inalienable right to *grow your own*. It was the only way to finally end this madness. I implored them to go forth in 2020 and oust the Mad King and his lapdog Republican henchmen, for the good of the country and in homage to the drug of peace and love. Then the Coronavirus pandemic and the atrocious murder of George Floyd put the issue of marijuana legalization well on the back burner.

Even worse fortune was visited upon me when law enforcement raided my grow in October and effectively gutted me. More on that later. *Then came the presidential election.* Well…nobody in their right mind could have predicted what anarchy Donald J. Trump and his minions would unleash upon our great nation simply because they could not accept the fact that he had lost the election. The Capitol Riot on January 6th of 2021 proved to the sane among us, beyond a shadow of a doubt, that America is in real trouble and in much need of healing.

Today, July 14th, 2021, as I sit at this keyboard hammering out these words, United States Senators Chuck Schumer, Cory Booker, and Ron Wyden are embarking on the fool's errand of introducing a bill before Congress to finally federally legalize marijuana. The reason why it's doomed to failure? **Old white men.** Usually the U.S. Senate is the place where bills supporting anything good go to die because of a non-constitutional device known as the filibuster that demands 60 out of 100 votes to pass anything meaningful rather than a simple majority. The Republican minority (49 senators) has the power to hold the entire nation hostage and seem to enjoy doing it as leader Mitch McConnel delights in referring to himself as the "grim reaper," and indeed he is. In this case it isn't just the Republicans this time as several old white Democratic senators and President Joseph R. Biden are against marijuana also. Biden, in fact, mouths that tired old mantra of, "The evidence still isn't in on marijuana." This is what legalization advocates get from the leader of the free world when, in fact, the evidence has been in for over 20 years! *Marijuana is basically harmless*, and yet they cling to what was once our nation's biggest lie until Trump spewed forth with the whopper of all time. But Cory Booker et al have at least got the nation's attention, and if federal legalization can become a ballot issue in the 2024 presidential election, and if the youth turn out to support it, then perhaps the madness of this 84-year-old prohibition will finally end. I certainly hope that I live to see it.

    Know this, my weed imbibing sisters and brothers: state legalization is a mere half measure, because even if all 50 were to toss us a bone, marijuana would still be illegal on the federal level, and the DEA and publicity-seeking local law enforcement will still continue to gorge itself on this lowest of the low-hanging fruit. Demand that your voices be heard in 2024! Do this, and soon we will be free.

Catharsis: Rectifying Forty-nine Years of Being a Silent Outcast

There are holes in my life that I have never been able to fill. In 1958, when I was seven years old, my father was an Air Force National Guard Pilot who crashed his jet plane in the Atlantic just off the coast of Long Island, never to be seen or heard from again. The aircraft was never found. He was 34 years old. In 1972, my older brother by four years, apparently in defiance to his Vietnam War draft notice, went out for a walk and never came back. '72, incidentally, was my second year in junior college, and in April of that year I was busted for selling an ounce of marijuana on two separate occasions to two separate New York State undercover narcotics officers. This is the big one, the vortex that has pulled me down for over forty-nine years. I curse my stupidity for allowing myself to be set up, and I detest the punitive mentality that drives all of law enforcement. Beyond that, I curse my naivety in accepting that my plea bargain was really the end of it, for as you shall see, it was merely the beginning. At the outset, there were four felony counts against me, which because of my cooperation, were subsequently dropped to four misdemeanors, which I was told by the prosecuting District Attorney would initially be dismissed and eventually be expunged from my record after a period of two years. Come to find out - they never were. My court-appointed attorney, who was chagrined to be assigned such an insignificant and low-paying case, also wholeheartedly advised that I cooperate fully, which was a problem in-and-of itself, because I was such a small fish in what the DA considered a big pond that I literally had to make things up to assuage his thirst for drug dealer blood. And he grilled me hard, on three separate occasions. He threatened, he intimidated, and he asked the same questions, coming at me from all angles, over and over again. I was terrified and mentally exhausted while he became frustrated that I couldn't be a steppingstone in his career. He finally gave in with the usual "never do drugs again," "be cooperative at every turn with law enforcement," and "keep your nose clean." All of these demands seemed reasonable enough, but there was one more directive that seemed unusual, and perhaps beyond even his authoritarian reach. He said I couldn't continue my schooling in New York State and be a waste of the taxpayers' money. He was the District Attorney, after all, an upstanding member of the community, and the spitting image of Nixon's "moral majority." After this ordeal, fleeing New York State didn't seem like such a bad idea. I was graduating in June with an Associate's Degree in Horticulture and had already applied to schools in New York and adjoining states with programs in landscape architecture, all of which had turned me down. Not to continue my education meant that my college deferment from involvement in the Vietnam War would be null and void, and with my draft lottery number being 65, I was certain to be inducted into the service. The court granted me the conditional discharge on August 7th, and later that same month I was miraculously accepted into Washington State University's fledgling program in landscape architecture. I left skid marks leaving New York.

    The standing joke, if you could call it that, amongst my friends I left back in New York was that I was lucky to have gotten busted when I did, before Governor Nelson Rockefeller, a man who made Nixon look like Mahatma Gandhi, got his tougher drug laws instituted. And I was most certainly happy to be elsewhere on May 8th, 1973, when the Rockefeller Drug Laws went into effect, setting a minimum sentence of 15 years to *life* in prison for possession of a mere two ounces of marijuana. My miniscule bust in Cobleskill, if it had happened a year later, could have had me writing this from the state pen at this very moment. Lucky indeed - I guess.

Through the years, I have looked upon this misfortune with a sense of indignation, for I have never felt that using marijuana is wrong in any way, shape, or form. I have always felt vindicated in my actions. However, there is one thing I deeply regret, and no matter how much I rationalize my words, I cannot claim innocence in running my big mouth over something I knew nothing about. The first undercover cop, who came into my acquaintance on January 28th, 1972 by way of a recommendation from a boarding house mate (who disappeared two weeks before my bust), was a hairy hippie type who oozed counterculture cool and requested harder drugs, anything I could hook him up with. Trying to match that cool, I bragged that I was thinking of expanding my business into cocaine. I knew nothing about cocaine, save to say that I had heard that it was groovy. I had never tried it or been anywhere where it was present, so it's hard to say why I said that, but I did. Naive college kid trying to act like a big shot, I suppose. Upon some reflection, I decided that this was something I didn't want to become involved with. On February 2nd, when the second undercover cop showed up at the recommendation of the first undercover cop, I sold him an ounce of marijuana, and when he inquired about the cocaine that I had mentioned to his friend, I told him I wasn't going to deal any of it after all. When the first undercover cop came along with the arresting team (there were three of them) he didn't mention cocaine at all when he tried to break me during the ride in the patrol car to the county jailhouse. I spent six days in jail before my aunt and uncle finally relented and bailed me out. The District Attorney never mentioned the word "cocaine" during his marathon questioning sessions, but I have always wondered if it was in the back of his mind due to private conversations with the narcs. Perhaps that's why he seemed to have such a raging hard-on for me.

One thing was certain, at the time, I was sure elated to put the whole sordid affair behind me and move on with my life. I never stopped smoking weed. I never saw any harm in it. I quit drinking entirely in 1979 and was glad to have a better alternative. I'll admit that during some depressing times in my life, I've smoked too much of it; too much of anything being a bad thing. I was sure glad that my arrest had been expunged from my record and didn't give those "Have you ever been arrested?" questions a second thought on job applications through the ensuing years. But time and technology caught up with me. Advances in computer tracking and the Patriot Act came into play in 2004, when upon filling out an application to possess a firearm in California, the record search revealed that *I had been arrested.* Upon calling the presiding DA's office I was shocked at being called an out-and-out liar by whoever it was on the other end of the line. Then came my personal search to acquire my criminal record from all those years ago. I finally received a photocopy of the arrest report and court settlement and was informed that the information was so old they didn't even have it stored on any form of computer file. Under the written conditions of my dismissal, there was no mention of not being allowed to go to college in New York State. After some finagling, I got the firearm, wondering all the while that if the arresting entity didn't have a computer record, then how did it come up in the firearm record search? Such are the recent violations of our civil liberties promulgated by George W. Bush II, and forwarded by Barack Obama, and left unchanged by the Mad King. Now I was worried. Aside from smoking marijuana in the privacy of my own home, I was once looked upon as a pillar of my community. If this ever got out, I would be recognized as the low-life my ongoing, supposedly long ago expunged, court record would reveal I was. Well, nobody was going to hear it from me. I held registrations and licenses that could be adversely affected if someone wished to make the case that I had lied on my applications when I acquired them. Then, somebody did.

In July of 2007 the California Contractors State License Board (CSLB) sent out a notice that all license holders would be required to submit live scan fingerprints for the purpose of a background check prior to their issuing any license renewals. I did as requested, and was put through a succession of tribulations before being allowed to keep the seven licenses I held at the time. However, they let me know in no uncertain terms that I would not be allowed to acquire any new licenses (there are 43 classifications). I had to withdraw my applications for two licenses that I wanted at the time, and which I sincerely feel would have allowed me to survive the financial meltdown of 2008.

At this juncture, if I could impart one kernel of knowledge upon the readership, I would recommend that anyone subjected to marijuana related criminal charges needs to know to never trust law enforcement and the judicial system, and to always obtain a copy of their records.

At Washington State University I drank wholly unsatisfactory 3.2 beer, copped decent grass, dabbled in speed to withstand all-night drafting sessions in the design lab, and was overjoyed when it came time to leave.

In 1974 I returned home from Washington, moved up to Buffalo, lived in a big three-story house with a bunch of old high school friends, and got high almost every single night. The problem was that I was also drinking whiskey hard and quit my position with the architectural firm I was working for so that I could drink more of it. A brutal winter in the Big B has no shortage of drinking buddies in the bars on Elmwood, so long as you're buying. I rapidly ran out of money, self-respect, friendships, a girlfriend, etcetera. Changes were in order, and changes I made.

In 1976 I left the Western New York of my youth and relocated to Phoenix, Arizona. Not then the sprawling metropolis that it is now, Phoenix was ultra conservative, and when you got out into the rural communities, patrons with pistols on their hips in the country-western saloons left a definite impression that the west was still wild here, and it was best not to mention your state of origin. You had to be careful who you discussed scoring with, if you discussed it at all. It was better to crash parties and slide into the back "smoking rooms." Oddly, for being so close to Mexico, the weed was much worse in Phoenix than it was in New York. Perhaps the smugglers just kept going if they were fortunate enough to make it through the border crossing at Nogales. Bereft of decent grass, I increased my consumption of alcohol and my life quickly spiraled out of control. By April 9th, 1979, I was forced to choose; become a full-fledged alcoholic (as if I wasn't already) or quit cold turkey so as to pursue my career in landscape architecture. I chose the career and remembering vividly my jail experience of the recent past, I chose not to deal loco-weed so as to augment my paltry income. Marijuana was on the back burner, and now being a straight arrow, the thumpus-unendus of the disco nightclubs became more of an annoyance than an escape from work related stress. Life was numb and boring by the time the cocaine epidemic hit Phoenix in the early eighties. The first time I did coke, I must admit that I liked it, but I was fortunately able to see that I couldn't afford it. I only did coke two more times on someone else's nickel, and for that I'm mostly glad.

After achieving professional registration, I went out on my own, and by the mid-eighties had some financial success, which offered enough free time and disposable income to once again start hitting the resurgent disco bars. The entirety of the eighties was a lost period for me: I was surrounded by weak reefer hardly worth smoking, I couldn't drink, I stayed away from cocaine because I was seeing business associates lose their houses, cars, and families over it. And there was a definite lack of relationships, partly because I was married to my business but mostly because I was lower middle-class. I didn't want a wife; I wanted those party girls I couldn't get fucked up enough to relate to or converse with. The main reason why I was having such problems bagging those skimpily-clad disco goddesses I was so desirous of was my aversion to cocaine. I steadfastly insisted that I simply couldn't afford it, no matter how much the dancing damsels wanted it. This was taken as a sure sign of small potato-ism on their part, and in retrospect, I must admit they were right. I also must admit that I'm really glad they turned me down as opposed to what fate would have awaited me due to an association with them. Finally one day, that fate was visited upon me in the person of my first wife, who was a raging cocaine hound and an alcoholic as a matter of course. Naturally, I felt I could save her from herself, not then realizing my own codependent tendencies. That relationship was where I gained insight into what compulsions, addictions, and codependences really were, and it necessitated an endless procession into AA, CA, ACA, and any other meetings ending in an "A". They insisted that *any drug* led to addiction, apparently giving nicotine a hall pass, because meetings always had a cloud of smoke hanging over them, and if you looked under the chairs, you could easily see that Pfizer would have made a killing selling pills for restless leg syndrome.

 I became convinced that I was indeed an alcoholic, and just as convinced that I had no real problems with marijuana. Although all the "A" meetings said we couldn't do a relocation, I was happy to flee Phoenix just to get away from them. Relocating to Palm Springs, California, my wife and I white-knuckled it through "Overcomer's Anonymous" meetings at the church of her choosing, which were patterned after AA meetings, but with a greater emphasis on God and expensive banquets designed to be uplifting but heavy on the self-congratulatory aspects of just saying no. This, and a financial setback soon saw her leaving me, a quick divorce, and my return to marijuana of far better quality. Cali was indeed all it was cracked up to be in the world of weed. I started businesses, lost businesses, started more businesses, over-coddled quasi-step-children who grew to hate me, went bankrupt, ran out of emotional gas, and crashed and burned in a small town three degrees north of and 300 feet lower in altitude than Kabul, Afghanistan, with the added advantage of having much better soil. With all these physical similarities, and the economic meltdown of 2008, it occurred to me to submit to the dictates of parallel evolution and engage in the age-old practice of farming marijuana. So that's what I do now: write books that nobody seems interested in reading, and grow some stellar weed for a medical marijuana collective I legally organized, which the presiding governmental authority subsequently outlawed. No matter, I continue to grow and take my chances as a shadow merchant within the "black market". This wasn't my grand master plan, but it's an existence in which I take pride. I'm no man's enemy, and no one's burden, so far as I know. I just wish this final career choice wasn't so fraught with worry. Come on, Congress, federally legalize it, and let an old geezer take it easy before checking out and exiting stage left.

For those who think that I protest too much, let me assure you that I'm personally disappointed that I have protested too little. I'm fed up with sloppy-assed drunks, crystal meth addicts, cocaine freaks and self-righteous puffed-out-chest bastards disparagingly calling me a "pothead" as if I'm below them, or at least in their company. I have in-laws who don't want me talking to their adult children about my medical marijuana business. My younger sister, who I admire and love with all my heart, feels that marijuana is to blame for the many failed ventures in my life. And she's been beating that tired old drum for nearly three decades beginning with always citing the very sketchy research associated with the soon to be mentioned amotivational syndrome. Motivation most certainly was not my problem, because back then, I was working twelve hours a day at least six days a week. My local bank account(s) have been closed due to federal pressure, and some of the people working there now look down upon me as the scum of the earth. After paying expensive premiums for three years, a life insurance company unexpectedly cancelled my policy because I had admitted at the outset that I smoked marijuana. Some kind of internal shakeup in personal and/or procedures, I suppose. I keep a low profile and am reluctant to meet new friends. We used to throw an annual Halloween party, but that's gone by the wayside. The outlaw's life is defined by boredom and loneliness, and I'm glad that I learned long ago how to go for long stretches of time without outside human contact, and most of all, empathy.

I'm alive, but I'm not entirely sure that I'm living. Sometimes at night I'll roll a joint or fill a pipe and then forget to smoke it. I'll either fall asleep or just wander off to bed with the contraband untouched. Smoking weed just doesn't hold the same fascination for me that it used to, and I wonder why. One reason could be that I miss the social ritual. When I was in college, getting high was a process rife with anticipation, laugher, camaraderie, and purpose. Yes, *purpose*. That being to reach another plane, a better plane, a place that you couldn't stay at all the time, or it would lose its specialness. I could only go there for a while, and if I went there with my friends, the more the merrier. The womb syndrome, I suppose. High school and college seniors experience it every graduation season. They grow comfortable in their protective scholastic womb with its routine and familiar friends. Then the shakeup occurs; change is forced upon them whether they like it or not, the unknown looms like a hangman's noose, caps go flying in the air, and then nothing is ever the same. I could recapture that comfortable warm feeling at parties, with select roommates, or occasionally a special someone, but each passing year it grew more faint, until eventually it disappeared. Then I was getting high just to get high, and sometimes it didn't matter whether I did or not, because as the late great B. B. King would sing, "the thrill is gone."

A lot of the high can be attributed to an individual's *predisposition* prior to imbibing in marijuana. If the user is in a bad mood, expects the weed to be bad, or is in a state of spiraling negativity, marijuana can intensify those emotions rather than eradicate them. However, if the user is looking forward to getting high, relaxing, has just purchased The Kinks' *Muswell Hillbillies* CD and has an expectation of having their senses enhanced, then they are certain not to be disappointed, as the high will get them there. Marijuana can turn a bad mood into a good mood if the user goes into it with that intention. It's all about the predisposition of the expectation, and if you don't want to be uplifted, my advice would be to wait until you do before you partake; otherwise you're just throwing away good marijuana with the high. That's my story, and I'm sticking to it. There's nothing wrong with marijuana, although those who use it irresponsibly frequently give it a bad rap. Responsible behavior is to know how marijuana reacts within the body. Smoked cannabis travels to the lungs, the bloodstream, and then the brain. Its effects can be felt within minutes and may last up to four hours. Eaten cannabis travels to the stomach, the liver, the bloodstream, and then the brain. Its effects may take as long as an hour and a half to two hours to take hold, and something about this more circuitous route makes its ultimate effect much more powerful. This has caused many an amateur user much paranoia as they keep eating in anticipation of a quicker high, and when it finally does hit, it hits hard and doesn't stop, and the effects can last up to eight hours from that point in time when it was last eaten. Anyone taking any drug while not knowing reasonably well what to expect is a fool in waiting and dangerous to themselves and oftentimes others.

My freak flag has not flown for decades, and you know you're getting old when you forget to listen to the music you like anymore. Most days I'm now mainlining on televised sporting events and HBO miniseries, and smoking marijuana just to enhance the experience is a fool's payment for a life neglected, left to go feral, and internally forgotten about. Amotivational syndrome, my ass - insignificance syndrome would be a far better description of the life I'm currently living. Thank God another growing season is upon me, and for now, that's my purpose. I'm sometimes ashamed that I let it come to this. I'm also ashamed that I've accepted the tyranny of marijuana prohibition to the point where it has so adversely affected my self-respect.

What I'm most ashamed of was the way I stayed in the shadows and took it. I didn't even know who Harry Anslinger was [first Commissioner of the Federal Bureau of Narcotics (FBN) formed in 1932]. There were books aplenty that could have told me, most notably Larry "Ratso" Sloman's *Reefer Madness: A History of Marijuana* (1979). I never became involved in marijuana legalization or medical marijuana legislation. Like Nixon's unheard from "moral majority," I believe that the majority of pot smokers, myself included, are content to stay in the shadows and not rock the boat. Prohibition was born before we were, and we accepted it as a fact of life. It makes no sense, but then again, what in politics does? I was so beleaguered by the events of my second financial meltdown that I didn't even know that Proposition 215 was on the California state ballot. I would always vote in the national election, but never much concerned myself with state politics. All-in-all, as a marijuana crusader, I was pretty much non-existent, bordering on worthless. I got high on what street weed I could score and didn't even know there was such a thing as medical marijuana until 2006. I hopped on the bandwagon and got my doctor's recommendation but was shocked to learn how proud the dispensaries were of their $640 an ounce pot. Things had changed alright, and from my perspective, not necessarily for the better. I'll say it again: greed reigns supreme in the world of medical marijuana. The "green rush" has done a lot to turn those on the sidelines of the "marijuana debate" off.

As previously stated, I decided to grow my own, and that's when I started to truly learn about this drug that I had so admired for so many years, that had given me a viable alternative to alcohol, that had seen me through the worst of times. It had never occurred to me that it killed pain, but with experimentation, I learned that it certainly did. Then my research started in earnest, the most revealing fact being that the evidence for legalization had been there all along, from my arrest in the spring of '72 to this very moment. I had always had a passion for marijuana. I knew in my heart that all the derogatory things said about it was just a pack of establishment and square lies, but I didn't, for a fact, know why, and that really bothers me. What I didn't know, and was shocked by, was the depth and the breath of the lies from Anslinger on through to every president we have had since 1937. The Republicans were certainly worse than the Democrats, but they were all bad, all complicit bastards, all allowing law enforcement to traffic in innocent human flesh while they looked away and postured that they had more important things to do than worry over the fate of a few "potheads." Oh yeah, I hate being called a pothead with a passion - I'm now passionate about that.

Before California legalized in the fall of 2016, I subscribed to the medical marijuana movement because that was all I was allowed to subscribe to. Truly sick individuals worried that not-so-sick "patients" might actually cause them to lose their life-enhancing to life-giving medical marijuana privileges, and indeed, pro-federal-legalization advocates have been quick to sound the battle cry that all marijuana is medical. Unfortunately, the law doesn't see it that way at all. I will state that if the eternally suffering would've been in danger of losing their rights because of my actions, then I would've unsubscribed to the medical marijuana movement in the hopes that they could've continued to receive the relief they so desperately needed. Indirectly, they helped my cause more than I helped theirs' in that the medical marijuana frenzy did help the full legalization lobby because when the feds were capable of treating legitimately sick people so horribly, it opened up the public's eyes as to how badly they are capable of treating all people.

So now, as I rapidly approach the threshold of my seventh decade of life, have I finally found my balls? The stakes just don't seem as high now - career, business, lovers - been there, done that, and it doesn't look like I'll be doing it again. Aging, that great buzzkill that afflicts us all, has finally helped me find my voice. Those six days in jail back in '72 really caught my attention and worked just as the establishment intended them to. *Intimidation* is the stock and trade of the anti-drug establishment, who underneath it all considers marijuana users to be intellectual and social weaklings. What would they do without us to persecute? The War on Drugs is a jobs program for bullies, straight arrows, and those incapable of thinking for themselves. I sincerely doubt that even 20% of all DEA and NIDA employees even know who Harry Anslinger was, for if they truly did, how could they keep on keeping on with this heresy? They are just quasi-robotic operating units condemning, harassing, and arresting whoever the establishment fingers as criminals while they know nothing of the criminal behavior of the establishment itself. It's just a job, regardless of who winds up rotting in jail. The moral imperative is not their concern, and certainly not contained within their job descriptions.

How many times do we need to witness the feds acting like children and taking their ball and going home before we acknowledge that that's exactly what they are? They hold their breath, stomp their feet, play dirty underhanded tricks; they threaten where they can and intimidate if they can, and if something such as a medical marijuana dispensary is within their reach, they break it. They most certainly are childish, except for one thing - children don't have guns, but they do, and what a mind-fuck it must be for them to wear them and tell potheads what to do.

What does it say of our federal government's credibility that they cling so uncompromisingly and tenaciously to all their worn-out anti-pot rhetoric? Lincoln said:

You can fool all the people some of the time, and some of the people all the time, but you cannot fool all the people all the time.

I'm sick to death of marijuana texts by authors pontificating upon marijuana legalization when it's readily apparent by their unconcerned dispassionate statements that they themselves have never even smoked marijuana. They make about as much sense as a priest being a marriage or a sex addiction counselor. The Me Generation and the Millennials are taught above all else to value their own self-esteem and not to take anyone else's word on their inherent personal value. In other words, their own opinions matter the most to them. They don't much appreciate being lied to; in fact, they seem to have a keener sense to detect bullshit on their radar than previous generations did, and it has been honed sharply through the encouragement of their baby boomer parents to think for themselves. They will smoke marijuana, and they will come to their own conclusions about it. The jazz musicians of the 30's knew it, the beats of the 50's knew it, the hippies of the 60's knew it, the punks, the slackers, the rappers - they all knew it too, and so shall these younger generations coming up come to know it. *There is not a single Goddamned thing wrong with marijuana.* The truth transcends all obstacles. If pot isn't legalized in my lifetime, then perhaps it will be in theirs'. All I, or anyone else can do, is speak the truth, over and over again, until it finally sinks in and resonates. Hold steadfastly to the belief that the truth does indeed transcend all obstacles and unveil it whenever and wherever you can. Take heart, my cannabis loving brothers and sisters; someday we shall all be free.

At the end of the nineties, I completed the first in my "trilogy" of environmental books. Due to a long-running series of rejections, it didn't see the light of day until 2005, when I updated it and then bit the bullet and published it myself. Then, in rapid-fire succession, I brought out the other two prior to the end of 2006. I was sure America would benefit mightily from my insights, but I was sorely mistaken. The trilogy hardly made a ripple in a smallish pond of other environmental books, and I wound up feeling quite the fool. The biggest impression that I got from what seemed like exhaustive research was that many other authors were doing the same thing, and that there was no coordinated effort amongst any of us. Ditto for a plethora of well-meaning but underfunded grassroots environmental organizations. All want to be first, be better, and be well-rewarded for their efforts. The entity benefitting the least from these disjointed efforts is, in fact, the environment. This reminds me of marijuana legalization, and the various states with their various approaches - it's a disjointed effort that could crumble like a house of cards when the feds start blowing hard enough. We are winning battles, perhaps celebrating a little too much over that fact, growing complacent, and taking perceived federal inactivity as a sign of resignation that marijuana will eventually be legalized. Dangerous assumptions, I and anyone else who has ever spent time behind bars, due to a pot arrest, can assure you.

The ineffectiveness of the grassroots environmental organizations also reminds me of the ineffectiveness of all the grassroots marijuana organizations. I knew about NORML (National Organization for the Legalization of Marijuana) of course, but something in their approach turned me off. When you're an outcast, you sense who has street cred and who doesn't, and NORML reminded me of any number of small time attorneys clamoring for a table at the local diner with their "off work" buddies, the prosecutors from the DA's office. They're lobbyists, just like any other lobbyists. The fact that they lobby for something that I believe in doesn't change the fact that they are just too cozy with the enemy. It's a game and a salary to them, and if one thing has a stranglehold on government, it's lobbyists. For example, most sane people know that there is no need for "hunters" to possess semi-automatic weapons, yet the NRA gun lobby protects their rights to do just that, even though state hunting laws prohibit them from being used. The preponderance of public opinion laments it, and yet it continues. Lobbyists most frequently represent corporate interests unimpeded by any form of compassionate logic and fueled by greed. In mirroring their contemporaries across the table, NORML appears to be just too corporate for me.

I'm an outcast and have been an outcast since my first arrest in 1972. The reason why I so vividly remember my first arrest is because daily I fear another. I wake up with it in the morning and go to bed with it at night. Quite simply, the fear never leaves. It's a gnawing sensation upon my psyche, and what it gnaws away the most is my self-respect. Whether justifiably incarcerated or not, being put behind bars impresses upon you is that *you are in a cage* to be kept away from the rest of society. That you are unfit to comingle with the normal people. That something must be wrong with you. That you can never be like the normal people again, because this experience, despite the outcome of your eventual trial, is an experience that 90% of the rest of society will never experience. It separates you, isolates you, and draws attention to the fact that you are different from the norm, and not in a good way. All for what? What was the point of the intimidation? To what end did the experience change me? An outcast knows they are different than the norm and that they can never truly rejoin the herd. You stay on the edges of it, hoping that no one notices, but in your heart of hearts you believe that they all do. Why do I still feel this way?

No matter how you cut it, it always comes back to Anslinger, a man who had the Midas touch in reverse. Everything he didn't want to happen, happened. The more he tried to tie marijuana to violent crime; upon research into the matter by the medical community, the more ridiculous he looked. And, he was a vindictive bastard, the end result equating to that meanness was viewed as irrational by the rational. But he had gained power via the immortal words of Jock Ewing: "Nobody can give you power, power is something you take." Little by little, Anslinger became a more accomplished liar, and in an irony of all ironies, acquired the same primary talent of the drug addicts he hated so much. It was no longer an issue of right versus wrong, but of which side of the fence he was on. His incessant attempts to prove that marijuana use was more rampant than it really was turned into a self-fulfilling prophecy in that the exposure he demanded it be given to suppress it simply made people wonder what all the fuss was about and subsequently partake of it just to draw their own conclusions. The claim that it was a gateway drug into harder drugs was rarely true, except to say that Anslinger's great lie made people wonder what else the antidrug crowd was lying about. This skepticism had the net effect of removing their initial fears, which in the case of harder drugs, would have served a better purpose if they were heeded rather than dismissed. Harry was to discover that marijuana is indeed the trickster, and no matter what he and the squares expected of it, it was sure to deliver something else.

Harry had a few qualities of the trickster himself. In the 1937 Marihuana Tax Act Hearings, House Representative John Dingell (the original, the father) naively asked Anslinger:

I was wondering whether the marihuana addict graduates into a heroin, an opium or a cocaine user?

Note that since Dingell was already referring to weed users as, "the marihuana addict," that it's apparent that Anslinger had him eating out of his hands. In such a climate, Anslinger could have told him *anything* and probably would have been believed. As the self-appointed expert on the subject, he chose to state:

No sir; I have not heard of a case of that kind. I think it is an entirely different class. The marihuana addict does not go in that direction.

Twelve years later, with marijuana persecution being, by far, the Bureau's biggest cash cow (in much the same manner that it is for today's DEA), Anslinger does an about-face in an article entitled: *Traffic in Opium and Other Dangerous Drugs* in the Bureau's in-house magazine:

There has also been an increasing number of these young narcotics offenders who admit starting the use of narcotics with marihuana [he still believes that reefer is a narcotic], *then after a short while admit changing to the more powerful narcotics such as heroin, morphine, and cocaine* [a stimulant].

Again, he knows better, he simply chooses to lie, going against his own sworn testimony from 12 years earlier to achieve his ends: bigger staff, bigger funding, bigger salary, bigger reputation, and the oppression of the "lower classes" who he discriminates against. It never changes; once you're labeled an outcast by law enforcement in the United States of America, you're always an outcast. Accept your lot and move on.

Vindication will most likely not come in my lifetime. Rather than predicting the future, I'll close by looking into the past. The La Guardia Report, which was commissioned in September of 1938, was repressed for six years by Anslinger before it ever saw the light of day in 1944. When it did, Harry must have shit a brick, for it spoke the truth then as stoners know it today. In a list of 13 items which basically refuted every lie that Anslinger ever told, items 6 through 13 were particularly informative:

6.) The consensus among marihuana smokers is that the use of the drug creates a definite feeling of adequacy.

7.) The practice of smoking marihuana does not lead to addiction in the medical sense of the word.

8.) The sale and distribution of marihuana is not under the control of any single organized group.

9.) The use of marihuana does not lead to morphine or heroin or cocaine addiction, and no effort is made to create a market for these narcotics by stimulating the practice of marihuana smoking.

10.) Marihuana is not the determining factor in the commission of major crimes.

11.) Marihuana smoking is not widespread among school children.

12.) Juvenile delinquency is not associated with the practice of marihuana smoking.

13.) The publicity concerning the catastrophic effect of marihuana smoking in New York City in unfounded.

The 31-member panel of medical experts from The New York Academy of Medicine studied 77 prisoners detained on Riker's Island, a sampling Harry Anslinger found too small, although his Gore File had far fewer substantiated case studies. It's believed that the Commissioner penned this rebuttal in the April 28th, 1945 issue of the *Journal of the American Medical Association*, entitled: *Marihuana Problems*:

...*A criminal lawyer for marihuana drug peddlers had already used the La Guardia Report as a basis to have defendants set free by the court....*

The book states unqualifiedly to the public that the use of this narcotic does not lead to physical, mental, or moral degeneration and that the permanent deleterious effects from its continued use were not observed on 77 prisoners. This statement has already done great damage to the cause of law enforcement. Public officials would do well to disregard this unscientific uncritical study, and continue to regard marihuana as a menace wherever it is purveyed.

The truth being inconsequential in their world, it's entirely believable that The La Guardia Report would do, "great damage to law enforcement," of Anslinger's ilk. It's been 84-years since it was commissioned, and the majority of the police, the squares, and the normal members of the milling herd still ignore it and lean toward Anslinger's line of drivel. The Great Lie is still alive and well in America today. I went to jail for it and fear that I will go again. Narcs cling to it as they peek through keyholes and set college students up in the name of justice while paradoxically pretending to be outlaws. People are still rotting in jail for it. Former President Obama took one step forward and then two steps back, unable to distance himself from it. If ever there was a national addiction, our country is addicted to this lie. It's a narcotic in-and-of itself, for if it wasn't, we could put it down and move on. Why can't we? Dear Lord, why can't we let go of this lie?

The Punitive Society and the Dismantling of the DEA

Our federal government has a long and ignoble history of promulgating and perpetuating lies as it pertains to marijuana. Pre-twentieth Century, almost any narcotic or drug went with a doctor's prescription, and cannabis was considered so benign that users didn't even need that. The Pure Food and Drug Act enacted in 1906 did require that intoxicants appear on labels, and cannabis was included along with alcohol, opiates, chloral hydrate, and cocaine. This was reasonable enough, as users do have the right to be informed of exactly what they are ingesting. Cannabis was left off the illegal narcotics list contained in 1914's Harrison Narcotics Tax Act, which was legislation aimed at cutting in on the action of foreign (primarily Chinese) narcotics rings bringing their wares (primarily opiates) into the United States. It was debated whether or not to include marijuana in 1922's Narcotic Drugs Import and Export Act which was commonly referred to as The Jones-Miller Act, which led to the formation of the short-lived Federal Narcotics Control Board (FNCB), which was intended to crack down on opiates and cocoa. In the end, marijuana was not mentioned in Jones-Miller as a dangerous drug and was not a component of any FNCB dragnet. With alcohol prohibition still in its infancy, the predominance of federal efforts were directed there, and little was heard or expected from the FNCB. That would soon change with the rise of Harry J. Anslinger and his great lie when he was appointed in 1930 as the Commissioner of the newly created Federal Bureau of Narcotics (FBN), which was housed within the Department of the Treasury.

Anslinger, early on shaped from military and police backgrounds, made his bones during Prohibition as the Assistant Director of the Bureau of Prohibition (BOP). He advocated that much stiffer penalties be levied at the consumers of alcohol, from two to five years in federal prison in conjunction with a $5,000.00 to $50,000.00 fine for two-time losers. Perhaps his heavy-handedness lent to his being given another job in another division of government. This coupled with a widespread BOP scandal centering around padded arrest records on the part of agents in 1929, and the unpopularity of Prohibition in general, suggested that Harry's phobic passion be directed elsewhere. It's been suggested that his marriage to financier, and then secretary of the U.S. Treasury Andrew W. Mellon's niece in 1917, contributed to this ultimate son-in-law job because Mellon, along with the wood pulp, petroleum, and cotton lobbies, wanted the commercial hemp industry outlawed in the U.S. Lumping commercial hemp in with recreational marijuana is what really spelled the doom of legal reefer in America. Harry J. Anslinger was considered incorruptible, and that's the motive most supporters point to as the reason he was given the nation's first job as ipso-facto Drug Czar. He would serve as the head of the Federal Bureau of Narcotics for 32 years! During his reign of terror conducted towards marijuana users, Anslinger proved to be a malicious liar of extraordinary talent and unprecedented reach. Make no doubt about it, through a smear campaign quite unlike any other heretofore released upon the populace of the nation, Harry J. Anslinger became the father of marijuana prohibition. Don't doubt his passion. Do, however, doubt his ethics. Anslinger got out of the Bureau of Prohibition at an opportune time, as the entire institution would soon be defunct with Prohibition's repeal in 1933. Initially he didn't give much credence to marijuana as a dangerous drug, feeling that it was primarily used by Mexicans in America's Southwest. This was one fact that he got right. The Great Depression, which kicked off with the stock market crash in August of 1929, combined with sensationalistic anti-marijuana reporting contained in newspapers owned by William Randolph Hearst, combined to get Anslinger's attention. By 1932, with the Great Depression spiraling the American economy ever downward, federal budget cuts were imposed upon his Federal Bureau of Narcotics while the staffing was dramatically reduced. Anslinger feared losing his job and saw marijuana as the societal scapegoat that would enable him to keep it. He started his vigorous smear campaign against marijuana by insisting that it was an evil inflicted upon upstanding American society (translation: white America) by the lower classes (translation: African Americans, Mexican Americans, other people of color, minorities, et al) of American society. Cannabis was called and spelled "marihuana" because the Spanish-sounding spelling lent credence to Anslinger's arguments that Mexicans were trying to destroy the fabric of America with their loco-weed. Anslinger kept a "gore file" replete with newspaper reports of murders, rapes, and black men becoming so emboldened by marijuana inhalation that they would view themselves as white men. Even more derogatory newspaper reports would be forthcoming from William Randolph Hearst's newspapers across the nation, primarily because Anslinger fed older stories to new sources to fan the flames of his maniacal passion to eradicate cannabis. Anslinger basically hated Negros, jazz musicians such as Louis Armstrong in particular, to the point where he wanted the passports revoked of any jazz player convicted of a marijuana offense. Cooler heads within the Department of the Treasury prevailed. Hearst hated Mexicans, never quite getting over Poncho Villa's occupation of his 800,000-acre ranch in Chihuahua, Mexico in 1916 during the later stages of the Mexican Revolution (1910 - 1919). Villa met his end, as most revolutionaries do, being gunned down by seven assassins in Parral, Chihuahua on July 20th, 1923. For his part, Hearst would carry on his maniacal personal vendetta against all Mexicans for another 28 years until his death in 1951. That Anslinger was so cozy with a man like Hearst speaks to his bullying personality, because Hearst, never a proponent of the common man, was later known for allowing his papers to publish fascist propaganda, which he whole-heartedly supported, by Nazi German leaders in the late thirties.

Harry Anslinger was aware of the British government's 1894 Indian Hemp Commission report on marijuana, which ran into seven volumes and contained over 3,000 pages. The Commission saw no link between ganja and social depravity, and furthermore recommended taxation and tariffs as a means to lining governmental coffers. The Commission did in fact state that any prohibition of ganja would most likely lead to a rise in alcohol usage amongst their subjects. The FBN chief choose to ignore the report because nothing was going to derail his belief that marijuana was the boogeyman, or the avenue to job creation for like-minded knuckleheads, along with the added bonus of a personal salary bump to boot. So he began to ramp up his marijuana smear campaign in 1936, leaking to the press that it was his considered opinion that 50% of all violent crime committed in areas of the U.S. occupied by, "Mexicans, Greeks, Turks, Filipinos, Spaniards, Latin Americans, and Negros may be traced to the use of marijuana."

Just like today, Anslinger played the kid card to perfection, stating that marijuana cigarettes were being smoked with impunity by American schoolchildren. The youth exploitation movie *Reefer Madness,* financed by a church group and originally cut as *Tell Your Children* in 1936, was just the kind of propaganda Anslinger needed in pushing for H.R. 6385, the Marihuana Tax Act, which was passed in 1937. The theory was to tax recreational marijuana out of existence, a virtual likelihood because the tax of $1 per ounce was 50% of the price of a pound ($2.00/pound) in 1937. The Marihuana Tax Act also spelled the death of the commercial hemp industry in the United States, with the tax per ounce being too high and unrealistic to compete with other textile sources and manufacturing processes. Commercial hemp was allowed to be grown during the World War II years, as depicted in the rousing 1942 film *Hemp for Victory*, as an aid to national security, but it was quickly relegated back to the bondage of 1937 shortly after the war ended. Farmers with standing crops were forced by federal agents to literally plow them under or face criminal prosecution.

Anslinger's behavior during the Congressional Hearings of 1937 was particularly bullying and repugnant. Never a doctor, he served as the government's expert medical witness, telling the Congressional Committee that marijuana's effect was "deadly" and discrediting the testimony of the American Medical Association's (AMA) expert witness, Dr. William Woodward, who was also a lawyer. The AMA was unpopular in America at that time due to its opposition to and blockage of health coverage as a part of the newly created Social Security, and Committee members treated Woodward rudely. For his part, Woodward was particularly miffed at the lack of notice that the AMA was given to prepare a case. In fact, the AMA had to petition at the last minute to even be allowed to testify before Congress. Woodward questioned Anslinger's shoot-from-the-hip allegations that marijuana caused crime, destroyed human health, and in particular was devastating to children by pointing out that no facts, or statistics, and certainly no expert testimony had been requested from the U.S. Public Health Service, the Bureau of Prisons, the Division of Mental Health, the Office of Education, or the Children's Bureau. Additionally, Woodward wanted to know when were the newspaper reports, that Anslinger was basing his facts upon, considered any more than hearsay? He also chastised the Committee for allowing Anslinger to distort and take out of context prior AMA statements that were convenient to his position, but had little to no basis in truth. Woodward's closing statement of: "The AMA knows of no evidence that marijuana is a dangerous drug," was met with Anslinger's statement of: "I believe it to be a narcotic of some kind." Shortly after the hearings, the House of Representatives passed the bill and shipped it to the Senate, who amended it slightly, and sent it back. The House passed it through without even having a roll call. On August 3rd, 1937 *The New York Times* newspaper printed matter-of-factly: *President Roosevelt signed today a bill to curb traffic in the narcotic, marihuana, through heavy taxes on transactions*. Harry Anslinger had gotten away with his great lie, and innocent nonviolent marijuana users would suffer because of it for another 84 years, and the suffering continues to this very minute.

The disciples of Anslinger choose to believe the great lie because it plays into societal beliefs of haves and have-nots, racial superiority, intellectual dominance, class dominance, and ultimately, individual dominance. Today, we talk of "A-listers" and celebrities, of which professional athletes are a large part, as if they are gods to be worshipped due to their fame and/or economic status. If Anslinger and his ongoing disciples have taught us anything, it's that human exceptionalism of any kind frequently leads to a corruption of the human spirit. Once one man gets it in his head that he is for whatever reason(s) superior to another man, the doors open wide for the mistreatment of and dominance over that other man. This phenomenon has led to all manner of oppression: human bondage, slavery, genocides, turf wars, torture, murder, and psychological abuse - to mention but a few. With the passage of the Marihuana Tax Act, the oppressors of pot were about to step it up a notch in response to the ongoing dirge of Harry, Dick, and Ron.

The War on Drugs, credited with the Nixon Whitehouse of 1970, and his creation of the Drug Enforcement Administration (DEA) in 1973, really started with Anslinger, a man who wanted his way so badly that he would lie through his teeth to get it. It's and well-known fact that if you tell a lie often enough, you start to believe it yourself, and admirers saying that no one ever doubted Anslinger's devotion to his job are lying to themselves if they think that that is what makes someone a great man. Anslinger was a despicable man who did despicable things fraught with a genuine meanness that knew no bounds. On top of that, he felt special in his position and that he was above those laws he himself was sworn to protect. A lot of law enforcement today continue to act exactly like that.

Alfred R. Lindesmith was a professor of sociology and criminology at Indiana University who promoted compassionate views towards opiate drug addiction. Lindesmith would later go on record with two books stating that addiction could come from a variety of environmental factors, and that not everyone who used heroin was destined to become physically addicted to it. This is a position taken even to this day by Johann Hari in *Chasing the Scream: The First and Last Days of the War on Drugs* (2015). Lindesmith had the audacity to question federal drug control policies while suggesting that a kinder gentler way might be a better approach to the sickness of addiction. That addicts should be treated humanely clashed mightily with Harry Anslinger's "lock them up and throw away the key" mentality. In 1939 the FBN chief had an operative in his Chicago Bureau notify Indiana University that they had a raging drug addict in their midst. There has never been any proof that Lindesmith even used drugs. Internal FBN memos indicate that they, and later the DEA, had tapped Lindesmith's phone. Any means to an end in the world of drug enforcement. The ridiculous ran to the sublime when in 1950 Anslinger sought to repress a film produced as a training vehicle for the Royal Canadian Mounted Police. Entitled *Drug Addict*, the 34-minute documentary aligned with Lindesmith's belief that addiction was a medical and/or psychological condition and not concrete proof of a degenerate. Predictably, Anslinger sought to repress its release in the U.S. while Lindesmith fought against his actions in a letter to the *New York Times* which was published on January 20th, 1950. The American Civil Liberties Union (ACLU), the AMA, and even the American Bar Association (ABA) all spoke out on Lindesmith's behalf in a letter published by the University of Indiana University Press. Anslinger published his own rebuttal and denounced the article, and true to his bullying repressive nature, the film has never been shown on American soil.

Anslinger continued to wield his awesome punitive power, choosing to ignore the findings of 1944's La Guardia Report, commissioned by New York City Mayor Fiorello La Guardia, who had appointed a well-respected committee of scientists and doctors from The New York Academy of Medicine to study the effects of marijuana on users and society at large. The report first took issue with marijuana being labeled as a narcotic, when it was obviously a mild euphoriant. When the report stated: "Prolonged use of the drug does not lead to physical, mental, or moral degeneration, nor have we observed any permanent deleterious effects from its continued use," Anslinger stripped a gear, berating Mayor La Guardia and threatening doctors with prison terms if they continued to study the devil weed. He unabashedly continued his reign of terror, and with the Boggs Act of 1952 came mandatory sentences for marijuana possession, which was further strengthened by the Narcotics Control Act of 1956. The punishments were two to five years in prison and a fine of up to $20,000.00 Mandatory drug offense penalties were repealed by Congress in 1970, which, in essence, meant that if offenders had enough money, their lawyers might be able to get them off. Little changed for the poor, and marijuana, when it's compared against all others, is a poor man's drug.

The rules that applied to a government outsider viewed as dumb enough to question its omnipotent authority simply didn't apply to government insiders smart and ruthless enough to hide their shortcomings. Insiders like Senator Joseph McCarthy, who in the mid-fifties led his own reign of terror against those he considered closet communists, and who was himself a closet heroin addict. Anslinger, supposedly to save the government from huge embarrassment, strong-armed a pharmacy near the White House to fill a morphine prescription he personally authorized to facilitate McCarthy's supposed drug rehabilitation. The wheels of Washington have always turned on the buddy system.

The Great Depression finally played itself out, unfortunately getting an economic shot in the arm from America's involvement in World War II. In 1943 any medical products derived from cannabis parts and whole cannabis itself were removed from the U.S. Pharmacopeia, and physicians were no longer allowed to prescribe it. The dark ages ensued as the fifties came, repressed, and thankfully left. The sixties were a humongous backlash to all the parental demands and smothering that came before them. The British Invasion was the spark that ignited a cultural upheaval, and soon marijuana made the sixties roar.

Dr. Lester Grinspoon, Associate Professor Emeritus at Harvard Medical School, set out in 1967 to warn society, in particularly the young radical students he feared were too caught up in it, of the dangers of marijuana. Fueled by genuine human compassion, rather than the obligatory establishment-style hatred, and upon a thorough examination of the available evidence, the good doctor reversed his opinion, and in 1971's *Marijuana Reconsidered* stated: "There was little empirical evidence to support my beliefs about the dangers of marijuana." Today a staunch advocate of marijuana legalization, he runs two websites to achieve that end. At the time, however, American squares, much like their hero Harry Anslinger, refused to listen.

Anslinger was required to retire his office at the age of 70, and on his 70th birthday, on May 20th, 1962, submitted his resignation to President John F. Kennedy, but he was urged to stay on until later in that year when Kennedy got around to appointing Henry Giordano as the new Commissioner of the FNB. Anslinger was kept on as the U.S. Representative for the United Nations Narcotics Commission in part to tie up loose ends concerning the 1961 Single Convention on Narcotic Drugs. This International Treaty, which initially was not ratified by the U.S. because Anslinger considered its language too weak at that time, wallowed in relative obscurity while Anslinger pushed for (what else?) harsher punishments, and that cannabis be included in its highest schedule of narcotic drugs. Although officially sent into final retirement in 1964, Anslinger continued to consult with the U.N. Commission, apparently wanting to oppress marijuana users from beyond the grave, because when the U.S. did ratify the Single Treaty in 1966, Anslinger considered it the crowning achievement of his career. Although few of the pot texts researched for this work mention this treaty at all, and fewer still make any significant mention of it, Anslinger was well aware of its constitutional importance, and he had good reason to feel that he had delivered weed's final death knell. People who think they know the Constitution well remind me a lot of people who constantly misquote the Bible, the most frequent offenders being those who have never actually read either. Housed under Article VI GENERAL PROVISIONS "Supreme Law of the Land" Item 2. states:

This Constitution, and the laws of the United States which shall be made in pursuance thereof; ***and all treaties made*** *[emphasis mine] or which shall be made under the authority of the United States, shall be the supreme law of the land; and the judges in every state shall be bound thereby, any thing in the Constitution or laws of any state to the contrary notwithstanding.*

Currently, 108 countries belong to this treaty. This is not good news for the supporters of marijuana legalization, and leaves me to ponder whether the U.S. has ever broken any international treaties? The answer is, of course, yes, especially in the realm of nuclear defense. And, if you consider Indian Reservations in the United States of America to truly be "separate sovereign nations," the answer is, of course, yes - a lot. Perhaps this is why so many texts take the Single Treaty of 1961 so lightly, but I submit to you that with our government desperately trying to maintain the anti-marijuana status quo, that this is a gift-wrapped convenient excuse to 'just say no" given to us by Harry Jacob Anslinger himself, who does indeed continue to speak to us from the grave, having died on November 14th, 1975. Stoners, one and all, should pray fervently that he was buried upside down.

Then came Nixon, and it's undeniable that almost everything bad in a hippie's life can be traced directly back to Nixon. He just couldn't stand it that the youth were having so much fun, that they opposed the Vietnam War, that they had no compunction about speaking out against him and his ilk (translation: the moral majority), and that they were so cavalier about marijuana. Nixon's primary problem wasn't with marijuana per se, but rather with the people who were smoking it. Concerning the rebellious youth that so irked his ire, Nixon confided to an aide, "They're all on drugs." Such was Nixon's hatred of Mexican loco weed that he authorized "Operation Intercept" in 1969 without informing the Mexican government, and had U.S. operatives spray Mexican marijuana fields in the summer of 1970 with the herbicide Paraquat, which can be lethal to humans that ingest it, and at the very least inflict heavy damage to the pulmonary system when smoked. The irony in this drastic approach is that Paraquat does not adversely affect THC potency, and never known for their compassion, Mexican dealers harvested the compromised weed, bagged it up, and shipped it to the U.S. anyway. Likewise, never known for its compassion towards its own people, the Mexican government tore a page from Nixon's playbook and accepted the instruction of DEA agents and the assistance of U.S.-supplied helicopters and themselves sprayed Paraquat on Mexican marijuana fields in 1975, with the added kicker of spraying bullets as well as the herbicide.

Without displaying even a modicum of embarrassment from the national media exposure of "Operation Intercept," other forces were at work that would benefit Nixon's antidrug stance. The Marihuana Tax Act of 1937 was declared unconstitutional by the Supreme Court in 1970 on the basis that it violated an individual's Fifth Amendment right of not incriminating themselves. This came to light in the trial of Timothy Leary, who was busted for less than an ounce of pot at a border crossing in Laredo, Texas in 1966. Incensed that the individual that Nixon had labeled "The most dangerous man in America," had walked, the chagrined president took vigilante-like countermeasures to compensate for the death of The Marihuana Tax Act, and soon far *worse* laws took its place. The Comprehensive Drug Abuse Prevention and Control Act was the vehicle that finally overturned H.R. 6385, and the Controlled Substances Act (CSA) was the vehicle that got cannabis labeled a Schedule 1 narcotic drug, right along with heroin. The CSA lies at the heart of the "marijuana debate" because it corroborates Anslinger's great lie and has done less than he did to ever prove that marijuana is a narcotic. Schedule 1 drugs are given no medical significance and no federal funding is available to study them; in fact, it was illegal to study them. How can anyone present a case when they aren't allowed to build a case? In some select recent circumstances, there have been a few ways around the strict letter of the law, but they are few and far between.

In 1970 the FBN briefly morphed into the Bureau of Narcotics and Dangerous Drugs (BNDD) which was quickly replaced by the Drug Enforcement Administration (DEA), the lovechild of Nixon and his conservative ilk.

Heavy-handed Nixon wanted to deliver the death blow to marijuana, and felt he could do just that when he authorized The National Commission on Marihuana and Drug Abuse, colloquially referred to as the "Shafer Commission," to conduct a study as to why the youth of our great land were so enamored with marijuana. The Shafer Commission's final report unequivocally recommended decriminalization of marijuana by stating: *Unless present policy is redirected, we will perpetuate the same problems, tolerate the same social costs, and find ourselves as we do now*. The report concluded: *Neither the marijuana user nor the drug itself can be said to constitute a danger to public safety*. As a disciple of Anslinger, Nixon quashed the report he himself commissioned and sprung into decisive antidrug action by creating the Drug Enforcement Administration on July 1st, 1973. Thirteen months later, on August 9th, 1974, he resigned the oath of office and fled the Watergate scandal, stating, "I hope that I will have hastened the start of the process of healing which is so desperately needed in America." Not by a long shot for stoners. In his and Anslinger's honor, and as Nixon's legacy, the DEA has continued to carry the banner in the war on weed to this very day.

Then came Reagan and lose all hope all ye stoners who enter here. Ronald Reagan, famously dubbed "Ronnie Ray Gun" by Joan Baez at Woodstock, gained fame as a hardliner when he served as the Governor of California and sent in 2,700 of the state's National Guard to repress University of California at Berkeley students who were rioting against the Vietnam War in 1969. If Nixon was heavy-handed, Reagan's hands were made of stone. Nixon's initial DEA budget of $75 million was rapidly increased to $110 million before he left office. This was chump change to Reagan, who had increased DEA funding to $244 million by 1982; and it would continue to escalate to $523 million by the time he left office. Birds of a feather flock together, and Reagan attempted to lionize Anslinger (who died in 1975) when he stated in 1986 that "The first federal law-enforcement administrator to recognize the signs of a national criminal syndication [concerning drugs] was Harry J. Anslinger, Commissioner of the Bureau of Narcotics in the Treasury." High praise from the clueless heaped upon the corrupt. Reagan further announced that drugs would be nonexistent in America by 1995, and acted on this edict by amending the Posse Comitatus Act of 1878, which was designed to limit federal military intervention in local law enforcement issues in order to allow the National Guard to assist in state-run marijuana eradication efforts. Then Reagan sponsored The Comprehensive Crime Control Act of 1984, allowing the DEA to sell at auction the seized assets of *suspected* drug dealers and known drug dealers with the funds going to into DEA coffers. Now, as in times of old, an army could once again sustain itself on plunder, and ample incentive was put in place to further bogus drug busts. If the presiding judge ruled in the suspected dealers' favor, the DEA merely put up its hands and said, "Our bad." 1984 continued to be a bad year for democracy when the Supreme Court, in direct violation to the Fourth Amendment of our Constitution, allowed law enforcement to search private residences for marijuana without a warrant. America was rapidly becoming a police state. Reagan went over the top with 1988's Anti-Drug Abuse Act, which birthed the Office of National Drug Control Policy in 1989 and officially established its acting director as the nation's real "Drug Czar." Typical of the underhanded way that Reagan conducted his vendettas against evil marijuana, this time he wiped his ass with the First Amendment to our Constitution, because housed within the language of this Act was a little-known gag order banning the Czar from even being allowed to publicly discuss marijuana legalization. This deception was exposed to the light of day when Democratic

Representative Steve Cohen of Tennessee introduced H.R. 4046 on February 12th (Lincoln's birthday), 2014 in order to lift the gag order. The debate is ongoing.

The Reagan anti-marijuana juggernaut kept on churning across international borders. Reagan's punitive mentality knew no bounds, and when he declared war, he meant it, in spite of the causalities on either side. When it came to bullying, no one could ever one-up Reagan, who again in 1988 renewed Nixon's Paraquat-spraying program on Mexican marijuana fields, and in limited cases, also on U.S. fields. Ron Reagan - my country, right or wrong.

Acting as government shills and searching for findings a day late and a dollar short, in 1995 the Environmental Protection Agency (EPA) issued a statement declaring that, "no lung or other injury in marijuana users has ever been attributed to Paraquat contamination." Yeah, - sure.

Here is the wellspring from which the punitive mentality draws nourishment: Dominance. Might makes right. The ability to persecute others simply because you can. Bullying. Intimidation. Oppression. Meanness. Masochism. Bludgeoning the spirit of another human being for your own personal gain. Coercion of others to get them to accept your rules. Denial of freedom of speech and freedom of expression. Torture. Murder. None of these belong within the family of man, and if marijuana is to ever regain its lofty position as the drug of peace and love within this family, all of these have to go.

Power corrupts. First because the powerful come to believe that they're special and the rules that they impose upon their underlings should not apply to them. Secondly, because the powerful become so powerful that they can inflict harm on those who they view as beneath them with impunity. This is the crux of the tyranny that's rampant in the War on Drugs, and know that Anslinger, Nixon, and Reagan represent the trifecta of tyranny. They had an ingrained belief that they were right, any evidence to the contrary, because they wanted to be. Internally, they were convinced that their intellects were so elite that they didn't question their motives or their tactics. They were above and immune to the burning moral question that has eternally plagued the rest of mankind: Am I right in my actions? When any arguments were inconvenient to their predisposed beliefs and positions, they chose to ignore them, and in some cases, silenced them. This was not any form of leadership, but out and out supremacy. Before he died, George Carlin had a favorite line: "Psychotics always think they're right."

Our government's 84-year harassment of marijuana users in general, and the DEA-inspired 49-year War on Drugs has produced some unexpected backlash from some very unexpected sources, and some sane voices have arisen from the wilderness. Law Enforcement Against Prohibition (LEAP), later to become Law Enforcement Action Partnership (still LEAP) is today a member organization patterned after the Vietnam Veterans Against the War movement, which was formed on April 15th, 1967 when the "Vietnam Conflict" was officially only two years old. The hypocrisy surrounding Vietnam is quite similar to the hypocrisy surrounding marijuana prohibition.

The American government officially recognizes 1954 as the earliest date when military advisors were allowed to carry weapons in Vietnam, or for an individual to be considered for inclusion in the Vietnam Veterans Memorial. This is the year the French officially quit the region after their final defeat at Diem Bien Phu, and Vietnam splintered into two separate countries: North and South Vietnam. The U.S. continued to have diplomatic relations with both countries, primarily in a militarily advisory capacity, up until 1959 when Ho Chi Minh in the North declared a People's War in an attempt to unite all of Vietnam under his leadership. From communist Ho's perspective, this is when North Vietnam became officially opposed to the democratic United States of America. However, he managed to somehow keep this a secret for over half a decade and continued to receive U.S. assistance up until 1964, when increasing attacks on U.S. Naval vessels revealed the North's true animosity towards the U.S. On August 7th, 1964 Congress passed the Gulf of Ton-Kin Resolution, allowing the president to take all necessary steps, including using armed force, to prevent further attacks against U.S. Naval vessels and personnel. Most consider this the start of the armed conflict in Vietnam, although 3,500 marines constituting "official troops" didn't arrive at China Beach in Da Nang to join with the 23,000 existing military advisors until March 8th, 1965. It's important to note that the United States government never officially issued a declaration of war against North Vietnam. In essence, Vietnam was the war that wasn't to a government wearing blinders and unable to explain how then did it claim 58,220 American lives?

If you think our nation's involvement in Vietnam was confusing, and in the final outcome, pointless; then consider how the 5,000 former and current law enforcement officers of the Law Enforcement Action Partnership feel about their involvement in the War on Drugs. Personally, I can respect a man big enough to admit that he was wrong, or at least admit that his involvement in something he thought was right, upon exposure to its realities, turned out to be wrong. With a first-row view from the front lines of the drug war, these officers have come to see that our government's approach is all wrong. Our leaders are too proud, too disconnected, and too clueless to admit that the punitive mentality just doesn't go over with drug addicts, and simply fuels the bottom line of an emerging for-profit prison industry. They have incensed these officers, who have had enough of the hypocrisy and are willing, in fact, are insisting on trying another approach. Drug prohibition, just like alcohol prohibition before it, fuels crime, drives up street prices, and is a vicious cycle of incarceration replete with all the collateral societal damage that follows it. Einstein's definition of insanity and the colloquial definition of failure is doing the same thing the same way, and yet, expecting a different result. Anslinger's prohibition and Nixon and Reagan's ongoing War on Drugs has been an abysmal failure; something that even then U.S. Senator Barack Obama admitted in the run-up to the 2008 election. For someone who seemed so logical, he sure did a lot of illogical things. Things like allowing the DEA to oppress California's medical marijuana dispensaries even after the entire populace of the country knew full well that he smoked pot in his youth and seems to have turned out okay; that he admitted that marijuana is less harmful than alcohol; that he insisted that marijuana legalization wouldn't solve all of America's financial woes (just some of them). With such nonproductive leadership coming from the former highest leader in our great land, the officers have decided to take their message to the streets and to the people by themselves. Another thing I greatly admire - if it's going to be, it's up to me. LEAP wants to teach the people that prohibition has caused more harm to the overall populace and drug addicts than drugs themselves. Deny anything to anyone, and the "forbidden fruit" syndrome kicks in. Don't deny something, and it loses its luster. Even former U.S. President Jimmy Carter has stated that the penalties for using any given drug should not cause more harm to the user than does the drug itself. And, not-too-surprisingly, LEAP endeavors to restore the public's faith and confidence in law enforcement by not wanting to enforce laws that even they see as stupid and pointless. Serving and garnering the respect of the public, most insist, is why they chose to be policemen in the first place.

It's extremely difficult to win a fight when the other guy is willing to do anything necessary, even lie, cheat, and behave immorally, to beat you. Possessors of America's punitive mentality want to win so badly that they have never fought fairly. Given this deplorable scenario, the only logical question to ask yourself is: why is winning so important to them? The Mexican drug cartels are ruthless beyond belief, but *why* are they so ruthless? Money - the root of all evil. Take away their profit, and they would have no reason to continue, and would go elsewhere to get it. Take down one of their stashes of drugs and cash, and they simply raise the price of their next shipment to cover their current losses. They will charge what the market will bear until the market can bear it no more. But what if there wasn't a market demand? What if addicts had their drugs supplied at significantly lower cost, or get this, for free? Impossible, you say? It would be less expensive than what the country is now paying to finance the War on Drugs. LEAP wants to redefine the definition of failure. Their approach is to legalize and regulate *all* drugs. Fine upstanding, bible-thumping, self-righteous America has to come to grips with the fact that drug addicts, again, just like Christ's poor, will always be among us. America's addiction problem has always been completely blown out of proportion, if you consider it on a per capita basis. From 1914's Harrison Narcotics Tax Act, to 1937's Marihuana Tax Act, to 1952's Boggs Act, to 1970's Controlled Substances Act, to 1973's creation of the DEA, to today's "states' rights" medical marijuana conflict, one thing has remained remarkably the same - the national rate of addiction has always been less than 2%. Nothing stops it, and to date, nothing has significantly increased it. Why? Because that's the percentage of the overall population that want to be drug addicts, and if you read the First Amendment to *The Constitution of the United States of America* (1787) you just might understand their reasoning. It's within their rights, whether somebody else likes it or not. Alcoholism and drug addiction, for all the misery and heartbreak they bring, are the last bastions of freedom in America. I don't like it, you don't like it, their friends and family members don't like it, even they say they don't like it - but that's what they choose to do, and so long as they aren't taking the rest of us down with them, let them. It's their private manifestation of their own free will, even if it ultimately kills them. Don't like seeing sloppy-assed drug addicts sleeping in alleys? Stay away from alleys. Anyone who thinks they can control the will of a person that doesn't want to have their will controlled is embarking on an impossible mission of gargantuan proportions.

    The officers of LEAP have lived and breathed that futility and have come to the conclusion that it would be better to isolate the problem and regulate it as opposed to arresting it, and thus filling the jails and the pockets of the money changers while a new drug addict simply fills the spot of the one they dragged away in cuffs. The solution lies in supply-side economics meeting a limitless supply. An ignoble capitalistic system collapses when there's no incentive for the dealers because there's no profit in their dealing. We simply can't arrest everyone, even if we wanted to. We can't beat and intimidate everyone into toeing what we view as the appropriate line when our Constitution says they don't have to. And we certainly don't have to support a War on Drugs that has been a losing battle for over five decades. The officers and supporting members of LEAP have come to that conclusion, and from time spent on the front lines, they are battle weary and disappointed at the lack of progress. They have come to the conclusion that perhaps they should question the motives and ethics of those who tell them to keep fighting for something that isn't worth having.

The disciples of Anslinger have been revealed for the bullying, lying, punitive miscreants that they really are. It is the dawning of a new day in America, and if one can acknowledge that the world will never be free of alcohol and drugs, then it's a fool's errand to practice eradication or even reduction as a plausible solution to the addiction problems inherent in this nation. This was proven with the enactment of Prohibition as the 18th Amendment to the Constitution, which was ratified on January 16th, 1919. Prohibition was so colossally unpopular that it was subsequently repealed in the 21st Amendment, which was ratified on December 5th, 1933. During the nearly fourteen-year period when Prohibition existed it birthed organized crime in America, led to deaths numbering in the thousands, and merely served to make the Great Depression all the more depressing. While Prohibition unequivocally proved that the heart wants what the heart wants, the individuals possessing those hearts were dismayed to pay up to four times the previous cost of alcohol to acquire it. The punitive mentality of the nation's lawmakers served to punish the citizenry the most in their pocketbooks. In charging what the market would bear, the suppliers grew filthy rich, and whenever law enforcement did put a dent in their operations, they simply passed their costs along to consumers. This set in motion an ever-escalating cycle of increasingly expensive delivery methods, which were met with ever-escalating law enforcement expenses to stop them. How little things have changed.

In the forty-nine-year period that the DEA has been in existence, the cost of street drugs has skyrocketed right along with the consuming citizenry's appetite for them. The word "appetite" carries a heavy burden. On October 27th, 2010, Mexican president Felipe Calderon chastised the United States in a BBC interview, stating that the exponential growth of vicious drug cartels in his country could be directly attributed to the United States' appetite for drugs. In other words, supply always fulfills demand. Stated Calderon, "They (the U.S.) have a clear responsibility in this because they are providing the market for the drug dealers and the criminals. They need to do more in terms of reducing the consumption of drugs, and to stop the flow of weapons towards Mexico." Calderon attributed 28,000 drug related deaths in Mexico, since he became president in 2006. Assuming an average of 7,000 deaths per year, the fatality total could now well exceed 120,000. And the Mexican cartels are now on American soil. The DEA currently employs 10,169 persons, of which 4,924 are agents. The 2019 fiscal budget was $3.136 billion. Since 2005, the agency claims to have stripped drug traffickers of over $24 billion. With their annual profits now estimated to be a minimum of $25 billion, the cartels are obviously outspending and outdistancing law enforcement. In the final analysis, it all comes down to money - again, the root of all evil. Herein lies the answer. Remove the high profit margin from the sale of drugs by legalizing drugs. Rarity creates expense, so decrease the rarity. Big Pharma will rush to fill the void while concurrently producing better quality drugs, especially if pressured by a socially conscious Food and Drug Administration (FDA). What they lose in initial profit, they'll make up for in volume. The Mexican cartels will either have to accept lower profits or retool themselves into other forms of business. Drug decriminalization in Portugal has actually led to a *decrease* in drug addiction. Take away the forbidden fruit and it's suddenly not so attractive anymore. Again, Einstein's definition of insanity (translation: failure) is: Doing the same thing, the same way, and yet expecting a different result. Clearly, the time has come for government to abandon its punitive mentality while the citizenry protects itself by advocating for a major paradigm shift, with the dismantling of the DEA at the top of the list.

This seemingly perpetual, amoral and unwarranted oppression of nonviolent citizens based on the great lie of a bigoted man who didn't much care who got hurt so long as he got his way has to come to an end. I often wonder if the disciples of Anslinger, especially overzealous young law enforcement officers, even know of the treachery their hero has inflicted upon the nation?

Well...now they do.

The Punitive Society and America's Oppressed Youth

2013 was the watershed year that proved beyond even the slightest shadow of a doubt that racism was still alive and well in the United States of America. This was evidenced in the national media attention devoted to celebrity chef Paula Deen, pro football player Riley Cooper, and Donald Sterling, the team owner of the National Basketball Association's (NBA) professional basketball franchise, the Los Angeles Clippers. Deen had used the "n word" decades ago in her past in private conservations; Cooper got drunk at a country-western concert and ran his mouth with the "n word" and some other discriminatory remarks directed at a black security guard who was merely doing his job; and Sterling's private telephone conversations with his mixed-race girlfriend were subsequently released, revealing that yes, he was a racist, even though he never uttered the hated "n word." U.S. President Barack Obama was so incensed by Sterling's comments that he weighed in on national media, stating:

The owner is reported to have said some incredibly offensive racist statements that were published. I don't think I have to interpret those statements for you; they kind of speak for themselves. When people - when ignorant folks want to advertise their ignorance you don't really have to do anything, you just let them talk. And that's what happened here...

I will make just one larger comment about this. The United States continues to wrestle with the legacy of race, slavery and segregation. That's still there - the vestiges of discrimination.

We've made enormous strides, but you're going to continue to see this percolate up every so often. And I think that we just have to be clear and steady in denouncing it, teaching our children differently, but also remaining hopeful that part of why some statements like this stand out so much is because there has been this shift in how we view ourselves.

The NBA's Commissioner, Adam Silver, reacted within a week, coming down hard with a $2.5 million dollar fine, banning the 81-year-old Sterling from the league for life, and demanding that he sell his team. Deen and Sterling were basically crucified on the cross of public opinion, and while what they said was reprehensible, what they said was merely words, giving fuel to the childhood saying of, "Sticks and stones can break my bones, but words can never hurt me." Of the three, only Cooper's punishment fit the crime, as Philadelphia Eagles team officials showed remarkable restraint by sending him off to receive "sensitivity training." Cooper manned-up by publicly and profusely apologizing, with his most telling comment being: "Be honest with yourself and face our prejudices." - Cooper's black teammates, in particularly quarterback Michael Vick, who had previously been vilified in national media and subsequently sent to prison for dogfighting, were quick to forgive, and by midseason his acrobatic catches were receiving high fives from teammates all around. That's the trouble with America: either we are too quick to forgive, or we neglect to forgive at all. Some say that their words had deeper meaning, in that they undeniably revealed true and ugly racism. I say that they were merely unfortunate enough to be caught in the act, and racism is far from over in America.

And, their form of racism, in terms of the lasting damage it actually inflicts, is far from the damage that will be incurred by the hidden racism of the U.S. Supreme Court, who in repealing Affirmative Action programs across our great land has basically decreed that racism is a thing of the past. How nice it would be if that were actually true. In fact, however, it is very far from the truth. In actuality, the high court has simply decreed that the funding that comes to black communities, as a result of Affirmative

Action is a thing of the past. As with the Jim Crow laws of the past, and the more recent voter registration scams, this subliminal form of slavery becomes far more nuanced, but is just as amoral. In all the outrage and scuttlebutt that these three attention-grabbing social faux pas engendered, blacks, the youth in particularly, were understandably emotionally upset but not physically injured. President Barack Obama's outrage at Sterling's comments, while justified, does seem a tad disingenuous in light of the fact that he allowed far worse things to happen to those people of his own race than Deen, Cooper, and Sterling could ever inflict. Racism does indeed continue to "percolate up," as The War on Drugs is primarily a war on marijuana started by a white racist named Harry Anslinger, and it has been remarkably successful in inflicting the most causalities upon those for which it was originally intended - people of color, young black men in particular. I, for one, don't buy for a New York minute that Barack Obama was not painfully aware of this very fact. I say again that his outrage at Donald Sterling's comments seemed like popular grandstanding in light of the fact that he showed no outrage, in fact, hid behind federal antidrug mumbo jumbo, rather than ending the hypocrisy that afflicted American citizens of his race more than any other, and by a wide margin at that. America's 84-year marijuana prohibition was always racially driven and continues to be racially driven, and if Former President Barack Obama wanted to heal wounds or put an end to it, he needed to step up and do something about it. He very well could have through executive privilege; the biggest mystery being why he didn't? Why did he allow America's punitive mindset to pervade every institution in our great land?

What drives the entrenched American punitive mindset is religion, Christianity in particular, and the jealous God of the biblical Old Testament specifically. Wrongdoers must be dealt with swiftly and harshly, and that's that. But the results garnered from this belief system are sketchy at best and abysmal at worst. Zero-tolerance policies in our schools have not led to a better school system, but rather, a divided one. Homeschooling statistics have spiked, populated by those students finding it too difficult to "go along to get along." Of those falling by the wayside, there is a disproportionate number of people of color, and among those people there is a disproportionate amount of their youth entering our burgeoning prison system. On a per capita basis, America incarcerates more of her people than any other nation on earth. Big Prison is a growth industry, and those contributing the largest segment of bodies to the overall population are, again, people of color, especially young black adults. 2011 National Organization for the Reform of Marijuana Laws (NORML) statistics revealed that 1,341,000 individuals were behind bars, and of those, there were 48,000 prisoners nationwide that were incarcerated solely for marijuana arrests; and of those individuals, 39% were black, 24% were brown, 28% were of indeterminate race, and the remaining 9% were white. Blacks account for 12% of the overall American population, and it's estimated that they account for 14% of the total marijuana usage. National Bureau of Justice statistics showed that there were far more marijuana arrests as of 2014 than actual prison convictions, 5,982,152, to be exact. The most staggering statistic is that someone is arrested in the United States, simply for marijuana possession, every 42-seconds!

In New York City alone, the epicenter of marijuana persecution, 34,000 black youths were arrested in 2013 for mere possession at the height of the "stop and frisk" program, which was thankfully significantly overhauled in October of 2014. Most plea-bargained and were given misdemeanors, fined, and automatically paroled. On the surface, it appeared that the NYPD was simply paying their own salaries through this harassment of young black men. A misdemeanor is nothing more than a slap on the wrist - right? Not exactly. A misdemeanor carries the collateral damage of a driver's license suspension of up to six months or longer; being denied federal aid in the form of food stamps, assisted housing, and student loans; being denied the right to vote, serve on jury duty, or even adopt a child for a year or longer. The time period for these restrictions is even longer for a felony conviction, and in ten states they carry on for *life*. This is oftentimes stiffer punishment than that levied at murderers, rapists, and even child molesters. Clearly the War on Drugs is in actuality a war on marijuana, and most specifically a war on race. While the DEA spends over $3 billion of taxpayers' dollars a year, other state, county, and city law enforcement agencies dedicated to drug enforcement alone squander $51 billion annually. And while it's undeniable that the DEA does run up against some very rough international customers, causing agents to risk life and limb, that is rarely the case with the lower domestic agencies, especially those targeting marijuana users. One consistent argument for federal marijuana legalization is that it would free up law enforcement to go after more dangerous criminals, but I submit that many of these individuals, especially undercover narcotics agents, are where they are simply because they are pursuing nonviolent marijuana users. In other words, they are the bullies, they are the thugs, they are worst of the liars, because they are the ones most likely to feel that they are excluded from or above the very laws that they are sworn to protect. And above all else, they are the bigots enacting the kinds of arrests designed to oppress those who, for whatever reasons, they dislike the most, which virtually guarantees the perpetuation of this dysfunctional social dynamic known as racism.

Slavery was most definitely America's original sin. The passage of the Jim Crow Laws was even worse because white America purported to recognize the "rights" of the black man, but not just in the same room. Florida's "stand your ground" laws have declared open season on young black men, and nobody seems to care - except young black men. The bludgeoning of the rights of our black youth by New York City police, many in an attempt to simply score some overtime pay, is unconscionable. Why? Hatred, pure and simple; it has to be hatred. But from where did such long-lived and obviously unfair hatred come? The punitive mindset. Somebody has to pay.

Harry Anslinger hated blacks, hated Mexicans, hated anyone who wasn't the same color that he was, and of those who were, he hated anyone who didn't do and think as he did. Most of all, he hated the black jazz musicians of the 1930's, who defied conformity and knew in their hearts that marijuana was a miracle drug that did less physical harm to them than any other. In fact, they often sang of its praises, the best revenge always being to live well, and with pot, they did. This drove Anslinger wild. He retaliated by being sneaky, underhanded, lying, and unwaveringly dedicated to those ignoble traits. Do these young law enforcement "kids" with the puffed-out chests have any idea whose honor they're so zealously protecting? Probably not. And for most, nor do they care. The law is the law, and that's good enough for them.

    I was young once too, and my parents and I rallied behind a young Irish Catholic president whose most electrifying speech contained the statement, "Ask not what your country can do for you, ask what you can do for your country." Too bad he was wrong. It's understandable that the nation was riding high after winning the war to end all wars, but Kennedy was simply asking for too much. The basis of any democracy is that it's formed to represent the citizenry, which supports it through taxation, and sends its sons off to war to protect it. The citizenry has every right to expect the heads of their country's government to not only represent their interests but to explain themselves and be held accountable when they don't. How did everything get so hopelessly out of whack? Why does the predominance of today's youth see no point in voting in the presidential election? with many stating that it really doesn't matter who the president is because government is a juggernaut running on its own inertia, and if the banks were too big to fail, the government is too big to succeed in representing the individual citizen. To them, it's a runaway train, and they see the necessity to clear the track, but not to mount a plan to stop it. Good God, is this what we have become? A nation fed up with all wars, yet unable to stop the War on Drugs. What's the point? Government is so big, so uncaring, and so ineffectual that the youth feel that the only sensible thing to do is avoid it altogether. There are two Americas, alright - those who still feel that they count, and those that know they don't. It's sad; very, very sad.

The thing I wound up struggling with the most in developing this manuscript was the issue of respecting the opinions of others, because I have to admit that oftentimes I don't. They have the right to be heard, as do all Americans, without being rudely interrupted or shouted down, a phenomenon that could be witnessed nightly on *The O'Reilly Factor* and is still continuing on *Hannity*. I respect their First Amendment right to express their opinion as they see fit, but I am not obligated to respect the content of their opinion(s), especially if it makes no sense, is disproven, or bubbles up from a bottomless well of ignorance that they cling to like life itself.

I'm tired, beyond tired, dog-tired of being subjected to this blatantly racist doggerel now over 84-years old, when I know damn well that it was spawned from hate, was promulgated by hate, and is propelled into the future by hate. I hate hate, because hate hates truth. The continuing nonsensical droning of the disciples of Anslinger is like nails on a chalkboard, with one noticeable exception being that the marks it leaves upon society cannot be erased. Then came California Governor Jerry Brown, a man who I much admire, telling us that we needed to "stay alert," so much so that we should not legalize marijuana. Jesus, God almighty, "stay alert" for what? Another heaping helping of the same old bullshit we've been fed for over four-fifths of a century. His comments, when added to the Governator's "laughingstock" gibberish, is disheartening to say the least. Schwarzenegger's concerns about appearances certainly seemed disingenuous when it was revealed that he had a kid with his maid. Arnold, Elvis, and Nancy Reaga; it's always those most concerned with appearances who turn out to be the biggest freaks of all. And America's War on Drugs is a freak show like no other. Send in the clowns. No, wait, we still have the DEA.

In the late 1700's George Washington started growing "Indian Hemp" (*Cannabis indica*), presumably for its psychoactive effects, and it's well-documented that he suffered horribly from tooth/mouth pain that could have been somewhat alleviated by the drug. He much preferred its effects to rye whiskey's. The preference of the "hero of 1783" was supplanted nearly two centuries later by the totalitarianism of the boozing chump of 1973, with the formation of his hippie eradication squad known as the DEA. Yet every Republican since mouths the same one-word battle cry - freedom! What the hell do they know about the subject? Washington initially tried to waive his $20,000.00 presidential salary, but the House eventually forced him to accept it. Nixon doubled his $100,000.00 presidential salary to $200,000,00 immediately after taking the oath of office, if that tells you anything about the character of these two Americans. And George Washington was not alone as allegations persist that James Madison, James Monroe, Andrew Jackson, Zachary Taylor, and Franklin Pierce all imbibed in weed. Our past presidents were certainly a livelier and more inquisitive lot than our stick-in-the-mud current ones. Yet the disciples of Anslinger blindly follow the dictates of a leader of the caliber of Nixon and perpetually raise the annual budget of the DEA and a myriad of local law enforcement agencies to persecute nonviolent and mostly "colored" Americans because it plays into their punitive mindset. Somebody has to be the scapegoat. Somebody has to be undermining the fabric of America. They simply can't accept the fact that America is rotting from within basically because half of the country doesn't see the necessity to care about the other half of the country. No amount of imprisonments in the world is ever going to result in the type of societal empathy needed to move this country forward. And there you have it: the real reason why America isn't number one anymore.

Not that he would have known it, but there was a precedent for Anslinger's belief that marijuana was the product of the "lower classes." In Islam, the Koran specifically forbids alcohol but says nothing regarding cannabis. This has led to all manner of positive and negative interpretations. On the plus side, those Muslims favorable to cannabis argued that Allah preferred it because it didn't lead to violence the way that alcohol always did. On the negative side, those viewing it as sinful to worship Allah while high, saw the

Sufis sect as heretical because they used hashish to commune with their supreme leader. Sufism arose from the lower working-class segment of Muslim society and were viewed as opportunistic upstarts who swam against the current of the mainstream - a fitting definition of jazz musicians if there ever was one. Anything that fails to conform to the perceived norm of the upper class is reviled as crude and vulgar; if it were grade school, the cannabis and hash imbibers would be accused of having "cooties." Just like Anslinger, orthodox Muslims wanted hashish banned so as to put the Sufis in their place.

During the Holy Crusades of the mid to late 1100's, which pitted the Christian world against the Muslim world, the Christians ran up against what they considered a fanatical sect known as "the assassins." These were stealthy and dedicated killers, employing tactics that would become commonplace modius-operandi amongst twentieth and twenty-first century Islamic Fundamentalist terrorist groups. The assassins in actuality were the foot-soldiers on the sixth tier of the Nizari Ismaili branch of Islam. They were promised the kingdom of heaven if they followed the commands of their leadership literally. The assassins were ruthless cold-blooded killers who struck fear into the hearts of their Christian adversaries. Soon it was widely circulated that they were driven to their maniacal extremes by hashish, and thus their Arabic enemies referred to them as Hashshashin or Hashishiyya. Further research reveals that their marching drug was most likely an opiate, but the misrepresentation took and became fodder for a man like Anslinger eight centuries later. Like Hearst, Anslinger just couldn't resist a good story, even if it was entirely untrue. This medieval myth was equal to the depth of research Anslinger applied to all the hysteria he engendered and represented as infallible truth.

Harry Anslinger's one actual literary effort in book form, written in conjunction with Will Oursler in 1961, was entitled: *The Murderers*. It was billed as an expose on rampant drug gangs, but it reads like science fiction. The threat was not nearly as diabolical as presented, but in a not-so-comic twist of fate, it proved to be visionary in a way. What Anslinger claimed was happening in the sixties, which really wasn't, at least not nearly on the scale he presented, is most definitely happening in the new millennium. The drug violence so inaccurately depicted back then, due to policies that were birthed by Harry and forwarded by his disciples (translation: Dick and Ron), are most definitely happening today because the nation blindly took his word for things untrue and allowed marijuana prohibition to birth even more organized crime, in particularly the Mexican cartels. What was once a figment of a racist's imagination has now turned into a horrible nightmare because he was never questioned or called onto the carpet about his motives, his prejudices, and his outlandish lies. *The Murderers* was not an outstanding journalistic effort, but rather, an ominous product of fanatical hatred gone awry.

Unless you lived in the Southwest in the 30's and 40's, you probably have no idea how much many whites reviled Mexicans. I certainly didn't, until I moved from Western New York to Arizona in 1976. Wanting to know more about my new place of domicile, I earnestly started in on my research, and what I learned shocked me. Jim Crow didn't just apply to blacks; it also encompassed the brown man in an ensnaring net of humiliation designed to do nothing but keep him down. Mexicans had separate bathrooms, separate drinking fountains, ate at separate and much humbler restaurants, etcetera and ad infinitum. What they didn't have was a champion to bring their afflictions into the view of America's mainstream. The reason that they didn't initially attract much of Harry Anslinger's attention was that, being domiciled on the eastern seaboard in Washington, D.C., he quite simply didn't know much about them. When his fledgling Federal Bureau of Narcotics (FBN) started to receive a funding hit in the mid-thirties, as the Great Depression ground on, complaints from the Southwest's racist law enforcement piqued his interest concerning these troublesome Mexicans. Here was low-hanging fruit, ripe for the picking. Hardworking, family-oriented, and almost always poor, these Mexicans wouldn't know what hit them, and even after they figured it out, they didn't have the wherewithal to do anything about it. The brown man of America's Southwest was about to get a load of Hurricane Harry.

Racist law enforcement's and Harry Anslinger's first shot fired at the brown man was to colloquially change the name of cannabis to marihuana, knowing that the emphasis on the H would give it that Mexican flair, thus tying it to their culture as if they had invented the dreaded "loco weed." By 1936, Anslinger was receiving even more pressure from law enforcement, and the press was always on the lookout for a sensationalistic story or cultural phenomenon that would justify more staffing or sell more newspapers. When nothing availed itself, they made things up, such as this personal letter to the FBN Chief dated September 4th, 1936 from Floyd Baskette, the City Editor of Alamosa, Colorado's *Daily Courier* newspaper, which stated:

Is there any assistance you can give us in handling this drug? Can you suggest campaigns? Can you enlarge your department to deal with marihuana? Can you do anything to help us?

I wish I could show you what a small marihuana cigaret can do to one of our degenerate Spanish-speaking residents. That's why our problem is so great; the greatest percentage of our population is composed of Spanish-speaking persons, most of whom are low mentally, because of social and racial conditions.

In Sydney J. Harris's marvelous little illustrated book, entitled: *Winners and Losers* (1973), the author writes:

A winner *acts the same towards those who can be helpful, and those who can be of no help; a **loser** fawns on the powerful and subs the weak.*

The "loser" portion of this quote most perfectly describes Baskette and his ilk. Anslinger wholeheartedly believed that reefer was a curse undermining the fabric of WASP America, but much to his chagrin, what he lacked was solid, or merely mildly convincing evidence. Comments in a letter he wrote, dated December 23rd, 1936, and addressed to magazine publishers P. F. Collier and Son, in response to questions they had sent him concerning the effects of marihuana relating to crime demonstrate one of the few rational things he ever wrote and they are quite telling:

So far as I know, no student of crime has made any direct study of the relative percentage of violent crime which is attributed to the use of Marihuana...

However, in many cases, we are unacquainted with the previous mental and moral characteristics and habits of the persons committing crimes while under the influence of Marihuana, so it can readily be seen that a final and conclusive statement in this regard is not yet in order. In most of the cases under observation, we do not have their criminal records, we do not know whether they were psychopaths, neurotics, moral delinquents, or normal individuals.

...In the meantime, conclusions must be drawn from the facts at hand, which in themselves are enlightening, as witness the enclosed.

What was enclosed were snippets from Anslinger's ever-expanding "Gore File," which was the precursor to a witch hunt quite unlike anything that had happened in America before, except to say what was going on Salem, Massachusetts in 1692.

Anslinger was capable of believing anything his imagination could conjure up and was never averse to pushing his delusions onto others. His earliest known literary effort came on June 12th, 1926 in an article for the *Saturday Evening Post,* in which he was concerned that sharks were getting a bad rap, and that humanity's fears towards these creatures was unwarranted. Harry fingered barracudas as the true daemons of the deep, and concerning the unfairly vilified sharks, he wrote:

It may be safely stated that unless a shark is ravenously hungry he will not attack a human being, unless he is positive that the man has been drowned or is absolutely helpless. He has never been known to attack anything that is perfectly healthy.

Sadly, for stoners, Harry didn't take up snorkeling in shark-infested waters. Seafaring people from all over the world wrote into the *Post* calling Harry on his bullshit, and this time at least, he reversed his opinion in a follow-up article. Too bad the same can't be said of his opinions concerning minorities or marijuana. This does illustrate, however, that once a certain type of person gets something in their head, oftentimes there's no way to dislodge it. Bill Maher calls it "living within the bubble," but I think that's kind. Okay, I'll come right out and say it: when you cling to a belief, even when factual evidence completely disproves it, the way you're behaving is patently stupid. To illuminate upon this point, Holocaust deniers state that the whole ugly affair was just a mean-spirited publicity stunt on the part of the Jews just to gain international attention, despite the photo and film journals, eyewitness accounts, *The Diary of Anne Frank* (1947), and the bones still lying in the mass graveyards. Creationists insist that the earth is only 10,000 years old, despite carbon dating and the fossil record. With Antarctica and Greenland tumbling into the sea, and Texas in the eighth year of its worst draught on record, half the state doesn't believe in global warming, despite what 99% of the world's top scientists have to say about it. People believe what they want to believe, and Harry Anslinger grew adept at believing his own lies. What's truly amazing is the astounding number of supposedly intelligent people who have bought into his delusions hook, line, and sinker for eight decades. That's even more willfully stupid, and there are people rotting in jail cells because of this stupidity.

The Gore File, which was full of hearsay from racist Hearst newspapers, and subsequently leaked by Anslinger to other newspapers not under the bondage of the Hearst chain, contained some of the most circumstantial, purposely over-dramatized, and completely unsubstantiated reporting ever loosed upon the nation simply for shock value. It was a dark period for journalism, but not nearly so dark as it was for people of color. Here are just a few tidbits of the national dementia prevalent at the time:

Two Negros took a girl fourteen years old and kept her for two days in a hut under the influence of marihuana. Upon recovery she was found to be suffering from syphilis.

Colored students at the Univ. of Minn. partying with female students (white) smoking and getting their sympathy with stories of racial persecution. Result pregnancy.

The Commissioner's favorite go-to case, the one he wheeled out more than any other, was that of Victor Licata, a 21 year old Tampa, Florida young man who woke up one day, grabbed an axe, and proceeded to kill his father, mother, two sisters, brother, and the family dog. Naturally, Harry suspected that marihuana lay at the core of this gruesome act, a fact he felt was corroborated a few paragraphs into the city's chief detective's report, where in an investigation of Licata's mental state prior to the murders, the detective expressed his opinion that Licata had become addicted to marihuana cigarettes six months before that cataclysmic day. Off Harry went with his wild accusations, morphing them into various versions of the same story, with the tamest one being run in *American Magazine* in July of 1937, four years after the murders. It read:

An entire family was murdered by a youthful addict in Florida. When officers arrived at the home they found the youth staggering about in a human slaughterhouse. With an axe he had killed his father, mother, two brothers, and a sister. He seemed to be in a daze...He had no recollection of having committed the multiple crime. The officers knew him ordinarily as a sane, rather quiet young man; now he was pitifully crazed. They sought the reason. The boy said he had been in the habit of smoking something which youthful friends called "muggles," a childish name for marihuana.

Anslinger's earlier versions of the same story didn't even mention "muggles" at all, but upon learning that it was the favorite nickname for weed by jazz musicians such as Louis Armstrong, who had even recorded a song called "Muggles" in 1928, Harry took journalistic license and slipped the phrase in there. If the officers at the scene considered Licata "ordinarily sane," then why was he investigated for mental instability prior to the actual crime? This supposition was just another one of Anslinger's grand fantasies. While Harry would hammer home this tale for fifteen years after

Licata hung himself in his psych-ward cell at the end of 1950, he would continue to leave a few of the more sobering details out, even though he was well aware of them. Eleven days after his arrest, a psychiatric examination revealed that Licata was criminally insane and prone to homicidal hallucinations, not because of muggles, but due to genetics. His mother and father were first cousins, while two paternal cousins were institutionalized in insane asylums, as was a paternal granduncle. Insanity ran in the family, and even his murdered brother had been previously diagnosed as suffering with dementia praecox.

The national media exposure of the Licata case did birth an American phenomenon which would further clog our legal system(s) in ongoing perpetuity, that being that the traditional insanity defense now had a new cause and effect element - marijuana. Any violent criminal who wished to use it now had a new defense that negatively skewed the statistics concerning marijuana and aggression, which further helped to give weed an underserved bad rap.

For the grand finale of offensive lies, as they pertain to race, anyway, look no further than Anslinger's opening testimony in the Marihuana Tax Act Hearings of April 27th, 1937. This is a day that should live in infamy for all stoners, although most of those belonging to Generation Me and more recently, the Millennials, have no idea why. The oppressed should never forget who their oppressors are, or who came out swinging with these remarks:

There are 100,000 total marihuana smokers in the U.S., and most are Negroes, Hispanics, Filipinos, and entertainers. Their Satanic music, jazz and swing, result from marihuana usage. This marihuana causes white woman to seek sexual relations with Negroes, entertainers and any others.

The crux of the white man's fear of black men has always been that they might penetrate their white woman - and what would he ever do if the white woman liked it? At the start of the War Between the States (1861), slavery had existed in the U.S. for 242 years, and the slave population was one-third of the overall population of the Confederacy. While the white man had grown quite comfortable with the one-sided arrangement, the same could not be said of the black man. When in a position of premeditation, whenever a person wants to do harm to another person, they always conjure up ways to vilify and demonize that other person. Draconian, repressive, and masochistic laws *still* on the books of many localities in the southern states amply illustrate this dynamic. Punishments for perceived Negro wrongdoers were swift and harsh and oftentimes deadly. But the blowback of cruelty is always the fear in the back of the perpetrator's mind that it could somehow be reversed. The repression of this fear most frequently lies with being even more cruel towards those who they were fearful of, which ultimately becomes an ever-deepening vortex that sucks all involved down with it. So, while the white "masters" certainly benefitted mightily from the labors of their unpaid subjects, there was a certain poetic justice in the fact that an inherent white paranoia was always looming like a dark cloud over their heads. Scenarios abounded as to how to squash the inevitable slave rebellions, and those preparations were not that far-fetched. There was the New York City Slave Rebellion of 1712, the Stono Rebellion of 1739, Gabriel Prosser's Rebellion of 1800, the Saint John the Baptist Parish Slave Rebellion of 1811, Denmark Vesey's Uprising of 1822, and the Nat Turner Revolt of 1831. Two dynamics always availed themselves: the organizers of the rebellions and their most loyal followers were always hung, and in over half of the planned revolts, the organizers were betrayed by someone inside their organizations, quite possibly someone suffering from Stockholm Syndrome and identifying with their captors. These rebellions were always brutally suppressed, hundreds of slaves were hung, and yet as outmanned and outgunned as they were, another slave rebellion was always in the offing, leading one to believe that slaves really didn't like being slaves.

In *The Chaneysville Incident* (1981) author David Bradley exhaustively reviews the myriad of laws that were on the books during the reign of slavery in America by which a black man could work to buy his freedom. Each state had a different paradigm, and nothing was more tenuous for a free black man than crossing state lines and chancing his freedom due to a different legal interpretation in the new state. There were no protections on the federal level, and most preferred to stay put as opposed to risk their freedom. While not technically slavery, it was a glorified form of house arrest, and freedom was specific to time and place, and least appealing of all, white legal interpretation. It may not have been much of a life, but it far exceeded the alternative. When you think about it, this is pretty much the status of today's marijuana legalization, and in particularly medical marijuana legalization. Complete freedom will only come at the federal level, and anyone who states that the revised state laws are just as good is either delusional, lying to themselves, or not a fan of freedom with not a fan of absolute human rights running a close second.

The black and the brown man know all too well the hypocrisy of the loopholes in all laws, but in particularly in state laws. On the national level, Jim Crow affected them both, although unquestionably the black more than the brown. On the state level, Arizona's SB1070, the New Immigration Law enacted on April 23rd, 2010, leaves wide latitude for law enforcement to conduct search and seizures of Mexicans *they suspect* of not having proper documentation. On the city level, New York's "stop and frisk" policy allowed police to harass and oftentimes trick black youths into waiving their own rights. What did and do all these laws have in common? Mild violations of the First Amendment, direct violations of the Fourth Amendment, and gross violations of the Fourteenth Amendment of The Constitution of the United States of America. One common thread that runs through these violations, one and all, is that our lawmakers and law enforcement appear to know less and less about the laws they are sworn to protect. So, conversely, how can the citizenry of the country expect the laws of the land to protect them, or anyone else for that matter? In the summer of 2019, refugees from Central America's Northern Triangle countries of Guatemala, Honduras and El Salvador are coming to America to seek asylum from very real persecution in their homeland(s). They are unceremoniously being caged and degraded as human beings.

Parents are being separated from their children, children are being lost in "the system," quite possibly to never be reunited with their birth parents, and the Mad King states that Border Agents are doing a, "fine job, given the circumstances." Black Lives Matter, Me Too, and no less than 20 candidates who were seeking the democratic nomination to be elected president in 2020 are significant indicators of the times in which we all live. In other words, how little things have really changed in America since those inglorious days leading up to the Civil War.

Unless you're a Republican president or an agent of the DEA, there are times when the golden rule haunts your psyche, and you ask yourself, *How would I like it if I were treated like this?* That question gets put on the side burner in times of economic distress, and these new ravings about the revitalized job market are nothing more than a smoke screen designed to mask the further plunging of the remnants of our middle class headlong into the lower class. Make no mistake about it, this Next Great Depression isn't going anywhere, and while it persists, human rights issues will continue to come in second to survival issues. There is no generosity when it comes down to you or me, because I'm certain to care about me first. It's human nature. Out of this climate, the necessity for a scapegoat always arises. There has to be somewhere to place the blame, for if there isn't, we will have to blame ourselves. I'll say it again: the real problem in America today is that half the country doesn't care about the other half of the country, to say nothing of caring even less about anyone from another country. The issue of fairness as it pertains to federal marijuana legalization certainly pales when compared to these most recent human atrocities, except to say that those now in power couldn't care less about how we feel. The ugliness of this dynamic is on high display by treating the minorities as second-class citizens, and let me assure you, stoners, one and all - we are now being treated as a minority.

Donald Sterling wasn't the bogeyman, nor Paula Deen, and certainly not a drunken Riley Cooper. The bogeyman is in the racist laws we allow to continue to be written, in the government we do not hold accountable, and in the way that, deep down inside, we really don't care for one another as we know we should - for that would require sacrifice, work, and an uncompromising devotion to the personal anonymity and humility required to truly join the family of man. Who's ready to make that effort? As a backup plan, if us baby boomers and Generation Xers can refrain from expressing unfounded racist opinions upon Generation Me and the Millennials, then the coolest thing about them can continue on unimpeded. Most truly are colorblind when it comes to other human beings, and if left to their own devices, perhaps they can breed racism out of our national consciousness within a generation, or surely two. But the reality of today must be dealt with by admitting that racism is still a fact of life here in America - the land of the free and the home of the brave. So, let's be brave and get on with it.

Today's Jim Crow masquerades in patrol cars in New York City, as immigration "legislation" in Arizona, as the concentration camps masquerading as detention centers on our southern borders, and as a supposed federal "hands-off" edict to the DEA - not followed in California; and in my fear of fears, soon not to be followed anywhere else. It's a good thing our Constitution was written on hemp paper; otherwise all this ass-wiping on the part of our leadership may have obliterated it by now, which would be an event sure to have Harry Anslinger laughing in his grave. All of this is depressing, of course, and about the only way to numb the pain inflicted by this crystal-clear glimpse of who we really are at present is for America's youth of *all colors* to spark one up, and as Dylan sang:

Everybody must get stoned.

Poetic justice indeed, for this will have Harry Anslinger rolling in his grave. It may have taken over 84-years, but payback's a bitch, Harry.

2021 Update:

In March of 2020 the nation was hit with the breaking news that a killer known as the Coronavirus was on the loose. State lockdowns, school closings, and an acute gripping fear quickly followed. There were runs on food and supplies. Toilet paper became the most coveted of all possessions. America rapidly entered a tenuous period of financial freefall without a net with no bottom in sight. Under such conditions it was a country glued to the television watching the national death count rise on the crawl at the bottom of the screen when they saw the breaking news of the George Floyd murder. Being, in effect, a captive audience, more Americans saw this horrific event unfold before their disbelieving eyes than they had ever seen of any other natural or manmade disaster.

The Mad King handled the pandemic with the dexterity and political acumen with which he handles everything else: ignore it, deny its existence, acknowledge its existence but downplay its importance, and when it can no longer be scoffed at; appoint someone woefully unqualified to manage it. Or not, because when Vice President Mike Pence was named the head of the Coronavirus Task Force anyone remotely familiar with the man knew that it would be a botched effort of gargantuan proportions.

The murder of George Floyd as presented on America's eight minute and 46 second snuff film became the spark that ignited the fire of pent up frustration and righteous indignation. With the activist group Black Lives Matter leading the charge, a national outpouring of rage that needed an outlet, a pressure relief valve, or an atomic explosion – take your pick – erupted because the country just needed to vent, but that need rapidly swelled into a citizen's uprising.

George Floyd's death did not occur in a vacuum as it was the third death to occur to black people at the hands of the police in the mere span of 92 days, averaging a killing a month, and if the truth be told, there have been police killings of innocent blacks occurring at this rate for decades.

It was a perfect storm of cascading events that laid bare the very fact that there was more than one virus lying in wait to attack unsuspecting or unlucky Americans, and that virus had existed in our land for centuries, and its name is racism, which when coupled with the worst of all viruses, that being poverty, has now birthed a national debate that starts with one word – disproportionate. People of color suffer disproportionately in the clutches of the virus, at the knees of the police, and in the cells of the prison industrial complex.

George Floyd's murderer Derek Chauvin is behind bars now, which is a good place for a fellow like him, but injustices towards unarmed black men are *still* being caught on camera on a weekly basis. The Trumpers are *still* so delusional that they think he will miraculously return to the oval office in August. Republican run state legislatures are *still* repressing, or outright denying, the voting rights of the poor, the people of color, the lower classes, us. Federal marijuana legalization is *still* a myth with the Biden administration casting out staffers who were known to be past smokers, and the old white men who run things are *still* crucifying our Olympic athletes who are caught smoking it, the most recent causality being Sha'Carri Richardson who chose pot as the least damaging drug she could take to numb herself to the grief she was experiencing over her recently deceased mother. Outcries and petitions notwithstanding, she is banned from this summer's Toyoko games. That poor girl. The world's fastest woman has been unjustly grounded.

People of color are *still* suffering disproportionately, especially concerning drug arrests, which is the one area where that injustice can be righted by federal marijuana legalization

Officer Monkey Ears

Jesus, what a pair of ears! Those puppies protruded from his head like the cantilevering I-beams of a double-sided modern architectural cliffhanger. They defied gravity and logic and even anatomy because I was sure that steam was emitting from their molten red core. Immediately I thought of the name I would never dare call him to his face - *Officer Monkey Ears.*

Officer Monkey Ears was not a big man, a fact that obviously chagrined him greatly. He would have made the perfect poster boy for runt syndrome. What he lacked in physical stature he made up for in belligerent attitude sprinkled with heavy doses of sarcasm and condescension. He insulted me, my wife, and the town I live in with impunity, and relish. Appearing as puffed-up and as prickly as a blowfish unceremoniously plucked from the ocean, he seemed to be holding his breath so as not to completely exhale all the animus he was harboring towards me. But it was coming just as soon as he could string together another barrage of vilipends to machinegun towards me.

My wife and I were returning from a Halloween party down in the desert. We hadn't violated any vehicle laws. We weren't speeding. And we certainly were not drunk. But *we were high*. Not that anyone would know by our outward appearance because we both can hold our weed. Why then were those miserable intimidating blue and red lights flashing in the rearview mirror? On the outskirts of town, under the glow of the harvest moon, my wife had taken it upon herself to spark one up. She hadn't even fully exhaled her first hit when Officer Monkey Ears and the individual who would prove to be his good-cop partner set upon us. Sure, we both had our medical marijuana cards with us, but a subsequent perusal of the *California Department of Justice: Law Enforcement Policy & Procedures Manual* (2015) bore out that they wouldn't have helped us much. We weren't asked if we had them, and given the tension of the moment, we didn't volunteer that we had them. I knew that they were well within their rights in stopping us, because according to Officer Monkey Ears, the stench of the marijuana was overpowering. Just for shits and giggles, here is what the manual has to say:

452 Medical Marijuana
452.1 PURPOSE AND SCOPE

The purpose of this policy is to provide members of this department with guidelines for handling and distinguishing between claims of medical marijuana use under California's Compassionate Use Act (Health & Safety Code § 11362.5) and criminal narcotics violations.

452.2 ENFORCEMENT

Although federal law does not currently permit possession of marijuana for medical use, California has created a limited defense (i.e. no penalty) for certain qualified individuals possessing small quantities of marijuana for medical use under strict conditions.

Notwithstanding California Medical Marijuana laws:
1. California does not provide any exception for individuals driving under the influence of marijuana. All such cases should be handled with appropriate enforcement action (e.g., Vehicle Code § 23152, et seq).

So, Officer Monkey Ears and the good-cop partner had me dead to rights. Or maybe not. I hadn't taken a toke simply because we were interrupted before I could, and he had no way of proving how long it had been since I last imbibed. Not that he didn't ask, and not that I didn't lie in telling him that it must have been hours ago back at the party when I wasn't driving. An onslaught of disparaging remarks ensued, and I became more convinced by the second that Officer Monkey Ears was most certainly a rude abrasive prick.

"Give me that joint," Officer Monkey Ears asserted. Since it was clearly visible in my wife's shaking hand, I reached over and took it from her and handed it to him. He placed it in his shirt pocket. I fully expected him to command us out of the car so he could conduct a search, and I was relieved when he did neither, because I would not have consented to a search. *Never consent to a search*. Not only are you not required to, but to do so makes the cop feel that you are stupid and can be easily duped into further incriminating yourself. He will push you even harder once he knows that he can push you at all.

After the ordeal was over, and I was out of harm's way, what I wanted to know is: are inherently abrasive pricks automatically drawn to cop-hood? Or does the job turn ordinary people into inherently abrasive pricks? In fairness, it's a job where everyone you approach instantaneously assumes that you have a bone to pick with them and are on their guard before you utter your first word. Any cop that doesn't command respect, or failing that, fear, by his/her very demeanor puts themselves at a decided disadvantage because it's common knowledge that you can always become nicer with relative ease, but it is nigh on impossible to become meaner once you start out nice.

How you treat people who you don't like or respect, however, says a lot about who you are as a human being. Officer Monkey Ears obviously relished his role as cat in his cruel game of cat and mouse. But unlike the cat, whose first priority is to let the mouse think that it actually may have a chance of getting away so as to embolden him to make an even greater effort in doing just that before lowering the inevitable boom, I was in fact paralyzed by fear, wondering what this crazed and obviously deranged lunatic may delve into next: a strip search, a prolonged Billy-Club bludgeoning, further humiliating me in front of my wife, calling in backup so as to prance and chortle in front of his sick depraved buddies? He seemed, after all, capable of anything, and I was determined not to say or do anything that would set him off. Know that the *California Department of Justice: Law Enforcement Policy & Procedures Manual* (2015) is riddled with their ultimate (pardon the pun) get out of jail free card when it comes to the use of force simply by applying the word "reasonable," which you can be sure is most often only subject to their interpretation:

300.2 POLICY

It is the policy of this department that agents shall use only that amount of force that reasonably appears necessary, given the facts and circumstances perceived by the agent at the time of the event, to effectively bring an incident under control.

"Reasonableness" of the force used must be judged from the perspective of a reasonable agent on the scene at the time of the incident. Any interpretation of reasonableness must allow for the fact that bureau agents are often forced to make split-second decisions in circumstances that are tense, uncertain and rapidly evolving about the amount of force that is necessary in a particular situation.

Given that no policy can realistically predict every possible situation an agent might encounter in the field, it is recognized that each agent must be entrusted with well-reasoned discretion in determining the appropriate use of force in each incident. While it is the ultimate objective of every law enforcement encounter to minimize injury to everyone involved, nothing in this policy requires an agent to actually sustain physical injury before applying reasonable force.

"What do you know about hot-boxing, John?" he snickered. I had no idea what he was talking about, but was to later learn that hot-boxing is when a group of stoners close off all paths of ventilation in a small room so as to get even higher on the trapped secondhand smoke. "All you Anza losers are hotboxing, aren't you? That Anza is only good for drug addicts and welfare basket cases." Officer Monkey Ears ascended the ladder from abrasive prick to consummate dickhead with relative ease and I became quite uncomfortable in thinking that he was obviously capable of reaching stratospheric douche-bag heights if he so chose to.

Again, after accessing the aftermath of Officer Monkey Ears' verbal assault, I had to ask myself, where did the popular police motto: "To Protect and to Serve," originate? In February 1955, the Los Angeles Police Department, within the pages of its internally produced *BEAT* magazine, conducted a contest for a motto for the police academy. The winning entry was the motto, "To protect and to Serve," submitted by Officer Joseph S. Dorobek. "To Protect and to Serve" then became the official motto of the Police Academy. On November 4, 1963, the Los Angeles City Council passed the necessary ordinance, and the credo has now been placed alongside the City Seal on the Department's patrol cars. While society at large may think that all police departments are bound by this credo, that is a misnomer. The saying most definitely did not adorn the side doors of Officer Monkey Ears' car. In fact, if a fitting saying were ever to be ascribed to his general demeanor, it would read "To Bully and Harass." Which brings me to how we feel about our interactions with the police in general, and specifically how I feel about my interactions with the police in total. Sure, they might protect me if they have to. But serve? Give me a break. I have never known a cop who wanted to help me out of the goodness of their heart, and in particularly out of any sense of duty. Any time I called on them to put down a family squabble, they frequently told me that *I* could go to jail, and often voiced their true feelings, saying, "What are you calling us for?" The great Hunter S. Thompson said it best in stating, "Never call 911!" It simply doesn't pay in the final analysis.

When you think about it, the justice system and the banking system are a lot alike. Both are predisposed to contribute mightily to the ongoing failure of their clientele. It has been said that banks only want to lend money to people who really don't need it. The high interest rates they impose upon the others, in particularly the poor, virtually guarantees that they will default on their loans and slide ever further down the credit rating scale towards economic irrelevance or oblivion. The recidivism rate of our prison system stems from the maniacal societal shunning that comes with a felony. The inmate may pay their debt to society, but society just keeps piling on. Once a felon, always a felon seems to be their view, so why give a felon an even break? In either case, once they get their foot on their victim's throat, they will push down ever harder until the problem is eradicated. "Good riddance," they seem to collectively say.

Officer Monkey Ears' feet were most definitely itching to apply even more pressure. He was eyeballing me, leaning in and crowding any nominal definition of my personal space, menacingly jabbing his index finger at my face while shining his bright flashlight across me and directly into my wife's eyes. He was deliberately trying to piss me off, and he was succeeding in his efforts. He was goading me, the bullying little prick. It probably gave him a real hard-on. I took heart in imaging that it was probably a really tiny hard-on. I wouldn't look at him, focusing my eyes directly ahead in what could only be defined as an icy stare. "Look at me!" No, I wouldn't look at him. I averted my eyes towards the floor of the vehicle. The good cop-broke the ice, saying, "Tell the truth, and the truth shall set you free." Really? It would be that easy? "Do you have any more marijuana on you?" Officer Monkey Ears asked. I had a joint in my shirt pocket but wasn't going to admit to it. If he was going to search me, he probably would have done it by now. "No," I replied, knowing that any other answer would just invite another one of his tirades, or even worse. The last thing I wanted to do was leave the deceptively comfortable confines of the car. It was like a security blanket that I knew could be ripped from me at any moment, but until that moment came it gave me great solace. This thin layer of metal separating the deranged Officer Monkey Ears from what I felt was the cowardly me, was the only protective barrier left.

Would Officer Monkey Ears have behaved differently if the circumstances had been different? Suppose he had come to break up one of my Halloween parties that a neighbor had complained about (primarily because they weren't invited) and found me high on marijuana, but not belligerent or otherwise obnoxious. Would he have been just as incensed as he was now? I was driving after all, and I'll concede that being high is being impaired when one is behind the wheel. I *was* certainly wrong on that count. Considering the extreme he was taking it to, and the extent that the other officer would have to go to lie about it in order to refute it, I was beginning to take heart that he was simply getting his money's worth in his bullying and his badgering, and had no real interest in hauling us in.

His Napoleon Complex knew no bounds, and he would grasp at anything to exercise it. My wife, due to the stifling pressure of the moment, and her proclivity to quite literally shut down in crisis situations, lit a cigarette to ease the tension she was feeling. "Put that out!" Officer Monkey Ears exploded. "I don't appreciate that. Who said you could do that?" We weren't as of yet under arrest, and she was lighting a legally bought cigarette, so why was the hair so deeply up his ass? Perhaps he genuinely hated all cigarette smokers like many self-righteous, overly self-important people do. Cigarette smokers, after all, are people too. Most likely this was his knee-jerk reaction to something so completely unexpected that it caught him off guard and not in complete control, which was something he fought mightily to never let happen. In bewilderment and shock, she did as ordered. Now, a standoff of sorts ensued. The silence was deafening as he pondered his next insult, and I certainly wasn't going to say anything. Into the still night air, the words I was praying to hear emerged, emanating from the lips of the good cop: "Get the hell out of here!" I glanced over my shoulder and saw that he was walking back to their vehicle. Officer Monkey Ears stood firm, not twitching a muscle, with his eyes glaring and ears still glowering. I thought of asking him for his permission, and instantly thought better of it. Let them argue amongst themselves if they were going to, but I wasn't going to kick this gift horse in the mouth. I put our car in gear, took extra care not to run over Officer Monkey Ears' feet, and slowly, ever so slowly, agonizingly slowly, crept away in a show of shame and humiliation, but mostly deep relief.

When out of their earshot, my quite recently and greatly emboldened wife stated, "They'll probably smoke that joint right after they get off work." "Well, at least they'll know that at least one Anza lowlife grows really good weed. I hope it knocks them for a real loop," I replied.

In the ensuing weeks and months, I thought a lot about Officer Monkey Ears. Did he really have to be such a colossal prick? I have a healthy fear of the omnipotent power of all of law enforcement, so there was no question as to whether or not I had treated him with the utmost respect. He certainly had the power and wielded it like a Middle Eastern despot putting down a military coup. But what was his purpose? In the final analysis, it doesn't much matter now if he was right or wrong. It doesn't much matter how I personally feel about his Oscar-worthy performance, because Officer Monkey Ears succeeded in putting the fear of God in me. I never got high and got behind the wheel again.

Postscript

My browbeating at the hands of Officer Monkey Ears left a deep impression upon me. I didn't want another stoner to ever have to experience the type of demeaning harassment that I had endured. This led me to develop a list of Ten Commandments for all the members of my then active (and legal) medical marijuana collective. These are:

- Know California state Laws. Read the contents of Proposition 215 (1996) and Senate Bill 420 (2003). Card holders are allowed to cultivate 12 immature or six mature Cannabis plants, *but not both*. Card holders are allowed to possess no more than eight (8) dried ounces of medical marijuana at any given time.
- Even though doctor's issue "99 plants" cards, they usually are not recognized by law enforcement or the courts.
- Do not imbibe in public spaces.
- Do not imbibe in the presence of anyone under the age of 18 or who is not a California medical marijuana card holder.

- Do not imbibe and drive. Use California's drunk driving laws as a guide.
- Do not possess or imbibe in medical marijuana within 1,500 feet of a school or any other youth facility.
- If you want respect as a medical marijuana user, show courtesy and respect to nonusers. Let the state laws that apply to cigarette smoking be a guide for cannabis.
- Never carry more than one (1) ounce on your person away from your place of residence.
- When transporting marijuana, keep it in the locked trunk of your car, or in the back of your truck, inaccessible from an operable back window. This is to avoid "open container" laws.
- American Indian Reservations, National Monuments, National Parks, National Forests, BLM Land, and any Federal Buildings all fall under the ownership of the United States' government, and as such are subject to federal law. If you are caught with any amount of marijuana in any of these locales you will be prosecuted to the full extent of federal law. Your state medical marijuana card is not applicable in these locales. These are words to live by, if there ever were any.

May peace and blessings be bestowed upon you, Officer Monkey Ears.

The Brotherhood of Eternal Love

They were born in the middle, caught in the vanguard of the post-World War II baby boom, yet doomed to suffer their adolescent and early teen years at the tail end of the repressive fifties. Sappy sugary music promulgated by squeaky clean Anglo-Saxon white-bread singers such as Pat Boone, The Four Freshmen, Tommy Roe, Frankie Valli and the Four Seasons, et al and ad infinitum, dominated the airwaves. "Elvis the Pelvis" Presley was reviled by parental America while bebop extolled traditional values and worshipped the All-American muscle car. While the sixties loomed on their collective cultural horizon, those youths poised to become the Brotherhood of Eternal Love (BEL) were yet to experience the British Invasion, the sexual revolution, massive anti-war protests, and the proliferation of then-legal LSD (lysergic acid diethylamide). With the coming of LSD, everything changed in their lives. They started their young adult years all too willing to rock around Bill Haley's clock and rapidly matured to asking Jefferson Airplane's Alice about the pleasures of the new mood-altering, mind enhancing drugs now at their disposal. Social upheaval was thrust upon them, and once in the midst of the fray, they embraced it, stood on the cutting edge of it, and gained their everlasting fame as a result of it.

They were lower middle class all the way, many the progeny of transplanted Okies that came west during the "dust bowl" years of the thirties'. By the time the dust had settled on their future prospects, it didn't appear that they were destined to rise above the socio-economic status of their hardworking, blue-collar fathers. Some had basically dropped out and taken to the surfing scene that was beginning to define the youth's cultural angst up and down the coastline of Southern California. Surfing, by its very nature, reeked of countercultural behavior, and in comparison to the overall population, only a handful of people engaged in it. The exhilarating freedom of the tube contrasted mightily with the forty-hour workweek. Life was relatively innocent in the late fifties/early sixties, and then everything abruptly changed, and America would never be the same bastion of mom, baseball, and apple pie again.

Aw, the sixties. That decade most recognized as being responsible for a colossal social and cultural upheaval, that period of time when the hugely unpopular war in South Vietnam prompted mass protests, draft card burnings, marches on Washington, and riots elsewhere in the streets, as well as other youth-related acts of civil disobedience of which smoking marijuana was the most common. During the early to mid-forties, the Greatest Generation had returned home victorious from the wars in Europe and the Pacific Theatre, and with extremely limited competition from the other soundly defeated industrial nations, an unprecedented period of economic prosperity ensued in America. With celebratory zeal they birthed the baby boomer generation, my generation, and two decades hence the colleges and universities of our great land would swell at their seams with the ranks of the most well-educated, free thinking, and rebellious student population the nation had heretofore ever known. Some, such as myself, probably would have never seen the inside of a college classroom had it not been for the necessity of gaining a college deferment so as to avoid being sent to Vietnam and risk dying in a "conflict" so insignificant to our national government that they never got around to declaring it an actual war. I most definitely came from a middle-class background and save for turning up #65 in Richard Nixon's second (1951 and up) draft lottery, I would have preferred to stay middle class and not gone off to college. It wasn't that way for the Brothers who were almost a decade older. Initially, they were slow to adopt the hippie lifestyle, but once entrenched in its cultural mores, they became some of the most shining examples of its social constructs.

It all started for the Brotherhood back in the summer of 1966 when a group of greasers, surfers, small time crooks, street thugs, and other socially displaced young adults started congregating at founder John Griggs's home, affectionately called "the church," in Modjeska Canyon outside of Anaheim, California for Wednesday night acid dropping sessions. They viewed LSD as a sacrament that opened their stream of consciousness and the vehicle that would suffice as the catalyst for nonviolent social change. As such, it became their largest goal to turn the world on to LSD. The nation, however, did not share their views, and LSD was banned in California in October of 1966, and made federally illegal in May of 1970. Swimming against the mainstream from the very outset, such was the Brother's belief in its powers that it could cure the common criminal that they eventually held as a goal the desire to turn on U.S. President Richard Milhous Nixon. While this never came to fruition, the Brotherhood, perhaps more than any other group of drug smugglers, were most responsible for Nixon's formation of The Drug Enforcement Agency (DEA) in 1973.

The mid-sixties were ripe for the taking, and cultural, racial, and in particularly, sexual equality were issues brought to the boiling point. The late great Alvin Lee's menacing guitar picking on Ten Year's After's "Sugar the Road" (*Crickelwood Green*, 1970) served as a late-arriving anthem for young women wanting more and wanting to shake themselves loose from the shackles of demanding men expecting them to knuckle down and manifest the old status quo of barefoot, pregnant, and rustling up supper in the kitchen:

Having a good time, baby / You're having a ball / Your daddy don't dig what you look like / Don't dig it at all / ... Live like you want, let them call you a freak / You'll be a baby factory once you're married a week.

Those words pretty much said it all. Women were now going to college in record numbers, not suspecting that an education would be the best combatant to early pregnancy besides one other thing. That other thing was the birth control pill that sent seismic hormonal shockwaves through the twenty-somethings. Now men and women could fuck whoever they wanted, whenever they wanted, and fuck, they did. Sexual freedom tore at the misogynistic stereotype of the fifties female more than any other social change. The Brothers and their old ladies were not immune to the phenomenon of the birth control pills' liberating influence, and monogamy became a relative thing, somewhat hanging on the excited lyrics of Stephen Stills' "Love The One You're With" (1970). Perhaps it was because the church was just too far back in the woods, or that the Brothers were destined for bigger things, or perhaps that the lot of them needed more exposure and to be closer to the urban pulsebeat of the hippie scene in order to act upon those very changes they envisioned. Whatever the reason, the Brotherhood of Eternal Love would soon be moving on up.

Like many hippie haunts of the era, the church burned down via an unmonitored wax candle, prompting the Brotherhood to relocate to Laguna Beach, California in 1967. Most opted to live close to one another in the aging clapboard houses of Laguna Canyon in a section of town that came to be known as "Dodge City." Then the ball really started rolling. To finance their LSD aspirations, they turned to smuggling marijuana in from nearby Mexico before stepping up their game and turning to smuggling hashish in from Afghanistan. The Brotherhood of Eternal Love proved to be adept at their craft and bootlegged thousands of tons of hashish during their six-year run. Their pot and hashish was smoked during the Summer of Love, at Woodstock, at Altamont, and at their swansong concert known as the "The Christmas Happening," held in Laguna Canyon on Christmas Day 1970. This event infamously signaled the death of hippiedom, but not before BEL even more infamously dropped 25,000 doses of Orange Sunshine acid from a cargo plane onto the unruly crowd.

Shortly after the formation of their LSD ashram in Dodge City the Brothers became followers of Harvard Professor Dr.

Timothy Leary's, "Tune in, turn on, and drop out," doctrine, and they devotedly reaffirmed as a primary tenant of their existence the desire to change the world by convincing it or tricking it to use LSD. Leary, along with his Harvard colleagues Ralph Metzner and Richard Alpert (later to become Ram Dass) had already written *The Psychedelic Experience: Based on the Tibetan Book of the Dead* (1964), not-too-surprisingly liberally borrowing from many concepts housed within the Buddhist religion's *The Tibetan Book of the Dead* (circa 8th Century). The primary thrust of this book, or that which is considered most important to LSD users, is the believed void area that exists between death and rebirth. Leary and his followers referred to it as the "ego death" and firmly believed such a death had to occur while on acid before a spiritual and intellectual rebirth could occur within the user. Detractors were quick to point out that this middle realm was the province of Buddha, or whatever god an LSD user chose to believe in, and that by using LSD to navigate and/or traverse it, they were in fact declaring LSD to be their God.

    I personally tried LSD on 10 separate occasions during the summer between my freshman year and sophomore year in college ('71). I knew nothing of Timothy Leary, and even less about Buddhism. I was doing it because I had heard it was groovy. I had heard of "bad trips," but most experienced users attested that such incidents were rare. My curiosity outweighed any misgivings. For me, it was a powerful mind-altering substance, and one that I usually respected, but sometimes feared. In those days, east coast acid was frequently cut with speed, so "coming down" could be a rough teeth-chattering ride, but at its height the experience of the "trip" was largely dependent upon who I was with, and what my expectations were prior to "dropping." I usually saw the bright lights and shimmering colors; everything was more or less hazy, muted, and somewhat out of focus. Food and drink (even alcohol) didn't taste better, but music definitely sounded better. With one girlfriend there was hysterical unending laughter, and it was quite possibly one of the best nights of my life. On one particular trip I did see life from a variety of angles, or perspectives, if you will. I was able to see my aunt who raised me as she was as a child, a young woman, a mother, middle-aged, and how she would be as an old woman, although I must admit, that if I wasn't so completely self-absorbed, I probably could have seen that, anyway. But, because of that, I do see where the ego death logic comes into play. I just don't know if an occasional enlightenment is worth the overall risk. I was made aware of that risk on a bad trip when I dropped alone, basically out of boredom, and descended into a mindset of complete and utter negativity. It wasn't totally awful; it was just a massive downer. I hung out in my room for slightly over eight hours before there was a letup, and that was the end of my experiences with LSD. I considered myself lucky that that trip wasn't worse, because I could envision how it could have been. I heeded the warning, in other words. I can say that I simply don't see how anyone could become addicted to it, due to the fact that the experiences during any given trip can be so vastly different from previous trips. I can see where a group dropping together with a predisposition to find something, especially of a religious nature, could come to the conclusion that LSD did indeed help them find it.

By viewing LSD in this light, I think this is where the Brotherhood went a little off the rails, in that they found what they were looking for and assumed that others would too. Although the thought of Richard Nixon on acid is heartwarming, I have to go on record stating that I personally feel it's not okay to give anyone anything, including mind-expanding drugs, without their knowledge and consent. That's just plain wrong. It does, however, speak to a common belief that was prevalent among the hippies of the sixties: that being that their way was the right way and therefore the only way. This was dangerous territory, and that belief system sometimes persists even to this day. Not considering the positions of others, even when convinced that they are askew or even dead wrong, denigrates their intelligence and right to free will.

It's because of their hashish smuggling that I feel a type of kinship with the Brotherhood of Eternal Love. When I was young and determined to have a career in sports; that was somewhat delusional due to my lacking any size of significance and athletic ability at all, my heroes were sports heroes, but today, these guys are my heroes. They used what they made from the sale of hash and weed to finance what they felt were their altruistic attempts to bring LSD to society at large. They weren't the first young people, and certainly won't be the last, to feel that they are capable of changing the world. While definitely misguided in their zealous mission to bring LSD to the unsuspecting masses, the Brotherhood's derring-do, resourcefulness, and never-say-die attitude does present several significant talking points. What are harmful versus harmless drugs? Who ultimately has the right to procure, produce, and distribute drugs, and why? Is it right to inflict your opinions concerning the usefulness of any given drug upon an unsuspecting individual by administering it to them without their knowledge? And how do you stand up for yourself when you're being told that something is wrong when you know in your heart that it simply isn't wrong? A lot of what the Brotherhood of Eternal Love promoted cut against the fabric of the mainstream, and some of it was stupid, ill-conceived, degenerate, and somewhat corrupt. But they held to their convictions and acted on them with remarkable dedication and bravery. The battle for complete federal marijuana legalization has been waging for over eighty-four years, and such are the attributes necessary to drive it over the finish line. Their nonviolent reign over the marijuana world is truly a remarkable accomplishment that reflects the tone of the times when marijuana and hashish exploded onto the scene and into America's national consciousness. Pot, reefer, ganja, herb, mota, rope, jib, grass, or by whatever other street name it's given, it's undeniable that marijuana and its derivatives is what made the sixties roar. It functioned as the visual and olfactory beacon of free expression. It was the symbol of defiance towards the Vietnam War and lay at the underpinnings of civil disobedience. It was the "freak flag" of the counterculture and heralded in the golden age of rock and roll. It's something we loved simply because our parents hated it. We knew early on that it was less harmful than alcohol and had fewer side effects than prescription pills, and it served as the ever-constant reminder that the opinions of the establishment weren't always right, in fact, were seldom right. Amazingly, after six decades, when it comes to weed, they *still* aren't right.

While still residing at the church in 1966, John Griggs had Glenn Lynd, the only founding member of the Brotherhood with no previous criminal record, file papers for incorporation so that the group could indeed become a tax-exempt church. This blanket corporation served as the legal vehicle that allowed for the 1967 opening of "Mystic Arts World," a well-run, well-stocked head shop in the heart of Laguna Beach. The shop became a magnet for Southern California's burgeoning hippie population, causing Laguna Beach to become dubbed "Haight-Asbury South." The connection between these two hotbeds of hippie culture became more evident when there was a mass southern migration of northern hippies into the area after the failed experiment in peace and love at the end of the Summer of Love in the late fall of 1967. San Francisco would still remain the epicenter of LSD production, being the home of outlaw chemist Stanley "Bear" Owsley, who apprenticed Tim Scully and Nick Sand, the latter two perfecting "Orange Sunshine" LSD. Not everyone was enamored with it. Some felt it was more "stony" than hallucinogenic (e.g. Purple Haze, Windowpane), but for the majority of the Brothers, it became their mind-altering drug of choice. Due to the massive quantities being manufactured by Scully and Sand, it also became the most recognizable calling card of the Brotherhood of Eternal Love.

Unfortunately, it was widely circulated that Orange Sunshine was also the drug Charles Manson and his merry band of murderers were on when they broke into Roman Polanski's Hollywood Hills home and butchered pregnant actress Sharon Tate and three others on August 9th, 1969. The following evening, they murdered two other people and wrote, "Death to Pigs" in blood on a wall. Needless to say, these vile acts further served to galvanize Nixon and his fast developing "moral majority" against anything remotely smacking of the hippie lifestyle. Even with the famed Woodstock Festival embarking five days later on Yasgur's Farm in New York State, peace and love had taken an immense hit with middle America, and one that would soon send it into a tailspin. *Predisposition*, remember? The user's predisposition is everything in determining where they may end up on an LSD trip.

The Brotherhood remained unaffected and devoted to LSD. Robert Ackerly acted as the go-between and main mule for getting the drug into Brotherhood hands. The Brothers were so dedicated to LSD that their biggest dealer, Robert "Fat Bobby" Andrist, sold it for ten cents a tab and gave substantial discounts for bulk purchases. Profit was not a concern in their quest to spread the consciousness-expanding message of Orange Sunshine. Other drugs, most notably hashish, were viewed as profit centers. Griggs expected a cut from every major Brotherhood score in order to finance Mystic Arts World, and their mutual goal of buying their own island where they and their families could self-subsist. Acid was approached as a religious pursuit with personal enlightenment at its core, while hashish smuggling was viewed as a seriously professional business operation. But as professional as they would have liked to have been, at the outset at least, they were learning on the job and most frequently stumbled into success.

Travis Ashbrook and Rick Bevan were the first Americans, as well as the first members of the Brotherhood of Eternal Love, to brave bringing Afghan hash back to the U.S. In 1967, they traveled the Middle Eastern portion of the Hippie Hash Trails so lovingly and accurately depicted in Robert Connell Clarke's classic entitled: *Hashish!* first published by the Red Eye Press in 1998. Originally intending to go to Katmandu, Nepal, they received advice from a British couple they picked up hitchhiking along the way that the best hash was in Kandahar, Afghanistan.

Ashbrook, an accomplished surfer since high school, had known of John Griggs since his days as the leader of an Anaheim greaser gang known as the Street Sweepers. His personal evolution pretty much aligned with that of Griggs's who by the mid-sixties had acquired the nickname "the farmer" due to his magnetism in drawing people to him and an innate ability to cultivate personal relationships. Bevan was younger than Ashbrook and a surfing understudy to him. Ashbrook looked upon him as a little brother, but before this first hash-procuring expedition into Afghanistan was over, all hero-worship would be cast asunder, and it would take years to completely repair their relationship. Ashbrook's surfing ability transformed into a thriving surfboard shaping business at a storefront he rented on Sunset Beach. It was a perfect front for someone soon to be neck-deep in the hash smuggling life.

Ashbrook and Bevan, and those to follow in their footsteps, would come to discover that the smuggler's life was not as glamorous as it may have seemed. While ultimate success lies in well-laid plans, these were frequently cast asunder by the human factor, which all too often could lead to the random act of stupidity. Loose lips could sink ships, and yet any operation could involve a half-dozen to two-dozen participants, and that was just to bring the contraband in. After that, the distribution network could number in the hundreds, and amongst individual buyers, in the thousands. A weak link could occur anywhere along a very long chain. But the profits were immense in comparison to a nine-to-five job, the women were prettier, and the label of being an outlaw in some circles gave you instant status, or what today is called "street-cred." But it's something more that motivates the smuggler, and that something is the highest of the natural highs. Pulling it off against long odds. Succeeding at something that most men wouldn't have the balls to try. Doing it under the establishment's very noses by sometimes hiding in plain sight. Most of all, imagining the anguish/disgust/hatred the suits would feel when they got wind that more hashish was on the street and hippie freak flags were once again flying high.

For this first and subsequent incursions into transoceanic hash smuggling, Ashbrook would pay back his investors at a ratio of 10 to 1. Ashbrook and Bevan complied $10,000 for their venture. Then they plane-hopped from California to New York City, to Iceland, and then to Germany, where they purchased a small used car manufactured by Ford Motor Company known as a Taunus. After crossing the Austrian Alps, traversing Bulgaria into Greece, crossing the Bosporus Straits into Turkey, and then arriving in Tehran, Iran, the Taunus was on its last wheels. While holed up in Tehran while repairs were being made to the Taunus, they smoked hash on the streets, not realizing then that in less than a year a Canadian and some Europeans would be executed for doing the same, and then after, anyone could be executed for having hashish in their possession.

Ashbrook became sick after stopping in Mashhad, Iran's second largest city occurring just inside the border with Afghanistan. Upon arriving in Herat, in the midst of Afghanistan's western desert, Ashbrook insisted they stop at a hotel. While he convalesced, Bevan took in the sights, scored some primo hash, got fired upon by an Afghan soldier, and went back to the hotel, imploring Ashbrook to leave because the soldier had seen their car. In the ensuing days they both grew sicker, more tired, and more homesick, causing them to seriously start to get on each other's nerves. Upon arriving in Kandahar, they booked a room at the Government Hotel, the only one in town, and decided to drop acid to center themselves and at least temporarily repair their friendship. This may seem foolhardy to the lay observer. Who drops acid prior to conducting a major sore? It must be noted, however, that the Brothers were avowed acidheads. Most dropped on a weekly basis as a matter of course, and some partook daily. They had been on the road and pushing hard for nearly three weeks and had not indulged in their drug of choice during the entire time, so to them, it seemed perfectly natural to get back into the swing of things before stepping once more out of their comfort zones.

They dropped on a mountainous slope on the outskirts of town and settled into a soothing trance. The trance was broken by a shepherd who appeared to them to be like Moses. The shepherd introduced them to his chillum, the traditional Afghan hashish pipe, and smoked his primo with them while concurrently coughing and laughing with them for hours. Other shepherds on other hillsides likewise coughed and laughed and basically communed with them, as they were doing the same thing. These two Brothers had stumbled across the true generosity of Afghanistan's humble and poor indigenous people at that precise point in time when that experience was able to impact them with the all-encompassing embrace of the brotherhood of man, and if left to its own devices that brotherhood may have flourished, internationally leading to a world quite different than the one we exist in today. A world that could have gone the way of the Summer of Love and Woodstock on the one hand, or the way of Nixon's moral majority and Watergate on the other. Afghanistan at that time was a country at the crossroads of self-determination before the interference of imperialistic governments and the invasion of modern foreign fighting forces literally forced the population into splintering fractious and fundamentalist religious factions from which it may never recover. In 1967 these two Brothers were given the rare opportunity to become immersed in ancient traditions, which if they would have continued to have been respected, may have produced a far better recent history than our two nations, and the world, now has.

At sunset, they parted ways with the shepherd and silently went back to the Kandahar town square. As they both remembered it, the crowd parted and into the void walked a tall Afghan man in a turban, announcing to them: "My name is Nazrullah Tokhi. You guys want to buy some fine Afghan shit?" The Kandahar to Laguna Beach connection, which would be the main conduit by which the finest hash on earth was to reach the mushrooming hippie population of the United States of America, was poised to be forged.

Nazrullah Tokhi and his older brother Hayatullah were primed for their shot at capitalism and saw in these two emissaries of the Brotherhood of Eternal Love the avenue by which to ride on its gravy train. The following day, they did indeed roll out their very best shit, and Ashbrook and Bevan were blown away. It was, to date, the finest hash they had ever smoked in their entire lives. Negotiations quickly ensued, and the Brothers traded their Taunus for 87 pounds of hash, an extremely small quantity when you consider that these two entities would soon be dealing in *tons* of hashish. The two Brothers had originally planned on only purchasing 20 pounds and were shocked and exhilarated to learn how far their Yankee dollar could go in the third world. This Afghan hash that sold for six dollars a kilogram in-country would fetch $100 for that same kilogram in the U.S. The Brothers bought several Afghan tamboors, which are stringed instruments fashioned similarly to a sitar. The Tokhi brothers disassembled them, stuffed them with hashish, and carefully reassembled them. Hashish was also rolled inside fur coats, Afghan rugs, animal skins, and Afghan hats, and then everything was bundled into a large wooden crate that was shipped out of the recently built Kandahar airport, bound for Frankfurt, Germany via Ariana Afghan Airlines. The crate was too large for their own flight and fearing separation from the object of their highest desire, Ashbrook sewed several kilograms of the hash into a coat that Bevan wore. The hash was fresh and therefore odoriferous, but no one seemed to notice. This was before the maniacal post-9/11 airport security measures, certainly a more trusting time, and most definitely the golden age for all manner of cannabis smuggling.

Dion Wright, artist in residence at Mystic Arts World, picked them up at the airport, marveling that no one else seemed to smell what he could smell from 40 feet away. Two days later the crate arrived, and after paying $50 in duty tax as prescribed by a fake bill of sale scribbled in illegible Farsi, the airport officials helped Ashbrook and Bevan carry the crate out to their waiting car. Back in Laguna Beach several of the expectant Brothers were having a party unlike any they had heretofore ever had. They smashed the tamboors with an unbridled zeal, not realizing that stateside they were considered antiques that would have fetched much more than the hashish. Ashbrook split most of the booty into five separate thirteen-pound bundles for five separate partners in the deal. He considered Mystic Arts World one of the partners, thus delivering tribute to the entire Brotherhood in one fell swoop. That still left 22 pounds unaccounted for, and generosity ruled the day as all excess weight was distributed to other Brothers gratis. A Brother shared with a Brother; at least it was that way back then, and thus - the Brotherhood of Eternal Love. For my money, this was their finest hour, the time before Timothy Leary laid their idealism riven, before the untimely death of founding member John Griggs sent them rudderless into the jaws of capitalism, a time before one Brother eventually turned on all the others, and the time before the DEA hounded and harassed them into extinction.

Rick Bevan was as excited as Travis Ashbrook to share their new discovery with his Brothers. They both stood out in that crowd with their short hair and clean-shaven faces, done so that they wouldn't draw attention to themselves while strangers in a strange land. Now, back in familiar surrounds. the party took on epic proportions. In an interview with Nicholas Schou, the author of *Orange Sunshine: The Brotherhood of Eternal Love and Its Quest to Spread Peace, Love, and Acid to the World* (2010), Travis Ashbrook is quoted as saying:

I made sure all the Brothers got a quarter pound or a half pound each. That was everybody's introduction to primo hash, the good stuff, and the beginning of the Afghan hashish saga of the Brotherhood. From there it blossomed into a lot of people doing it. Too many people started doing it, and people started to get caught.

Several Brothers, of which Robert Ackerly (alias Chris Wheat) proved to be the best, immediately thereafter entered into the Afghan hashish smuggling business. The new tactic was to buy the iconic hippie Volkswagen Bus in Germany, and then follow Ashbrook's and Bevan's original route to Kandahar, where they were greeted by the Tokhi brothers with open arms. The VW Buses were most typically driven to the seaport town of Karachi, Pakistan and shipped home to Los Angeles. Before long there was a glut of used Volkswagen Buses for sale on the streets of Kandahar, and Brothers started flying directly into Kabul, which most assuredly caught the attention of authorities. Still, the exportation part of this plan worked remarkably well up until 1969 when increased suspicion, to say nothing of the professionalism, on the part of law enforcement, prompted searches and seizures, although remarkably few Brothers were actually arrested. Money was flowing into the Brotherhood coffers maintained by John Griggs, and it was looking more and more like they just might purchase that island they were so fondly dreaming of. Founding Brotherhood member Eddie Padilla, an infamous street tough in his youth, stated that he and many other Brothers were reading manuals on how to build their homes from scratch, how to grow crops for food, how to deliver babies, and how to subsist off the grid. Some of them were definitely into it, and some of them were completely ambivalent, but most of them sincerely believed that the island purchase was most definitely just a matter of time. Then came a self-centered, self-absorbed, totally egomaniacal ass by the name of Timothy Leary, and those island plans would shortly thereafter go up in smoke, and the well-crafted human tapestry known as The Brotherhood of Eternal Love would lose the one strand that would cause it to unravel.

John Griggs first met Timothy Leary in late 1967 under dubious circumstances. Griggs had bumped into Leary's son Jack in San Francisco during an acid procuring run. Griggs gave Jack several hundred-dollar bills to pass on to his father with an invitation to visit Dodge City and added the affirmation that there was much more to be had where that came from. Jack instead went to a Grateful Dead concert at the Fillmore and took to lighting up massive spliffs with the hundred-dollar bills. Upon learning of the irresponsible behavior of his son, Leary called Griggs to apologize, and Griggs formally invited him to Laguna Beach and to see Mystic Arts World. This wouldn't be the last time Jack Leary would cause either a good or a bad connection between Griggs and Leary. Leary showed in Laguna Beach and made an intellectual connection with Griggs. Dion Wright has since stated that he felt that Griggs paled in Leary's light, although, for his part, Leary stated that he thought that Griggs was "the holiest man ever to live in this country." This jacking off of words would lead to a Brotherhood indebtedness to Leary that defied logic and knew no bounds. Part of Leary's charisma was an acute ability in knowing who to stroke and when.

He lived for the limelight and wasn't about to move to a remote secluded island. Soon Griggs's island plans were quashed in favor of a mountain commune in the San Jacinto Mountains, a thousand feet lower and just southeast of the town of Idyllwild (elevation 6,300 feet). Leary soon became the grand poohbah in residence and the spiritual leader of all inhabitants at what came to be known as "the ranch." Not all of the Brothers were enamored with these recent developments, especially concerning Griggs's new rule that only married couples could permanently inhabit its confines. This left many out in the cold and wondering why then was Leary's girlfriend, the very attractive Rosemary Woodruff, cohabitating with him there? Dissention soon crept in within the ranks. Griggs was now married with two young children and a teenage foster daughter and apparently had adopted a more responsible stance that irked the unmarried members who viewed the commune an easy setup for a narc infiltration. Such an infiltration did indeed happen when Travis Ashbrook unwittingly led federal agents directly to the ranch. He was transporting a personal stash of hashish in a hollowed-out surfboard, a mainstay of Brotherhood smuggling for packages of lighter weight. The board had split open at the airport due to the intense summer heat, and the odor had alerted authorities, who put a tail on Ashbrook. Typical of the Brotherhood's internal code, he copped to sole ownership, seeing that none of his three companions received any jail time.

Griggs and the remainder of the commune survived the bust, but not his own newly found self-righteousness. He started a secret affair with his foster daughter Suzie Q, which was apparently ratted out by his pet beagle wagging its tail and barking at the scene of one of their trysts. Griggs's wife forgave him, but things were starting to unravel. While he was on yet another hash smuggling run in the Middle East, Rick Bevan's seventeen-year-old girlfriend Charlene Almedia drowned on July 14th, 1969 in a swimming accident in the ranch's pond. On July 21st, Griggs successfully delivered his wife's Carol's baby. The cycle of life was followed by the cycle of death on August 8th, when Griggs overdosed on synthetic psilocybin and died. Two days earlier, he had turned 26 years old.

They would take four years to manifest themselves, but other forces were already in motion to cripple the Brotherhood at the time of John Griggs's death because, inevitably, there's always that one person who feels that they've been monetarily stiffed, or underappreciated, or otherwise somehow slighted, who becomes the loose brick that causes the entire wall to collapse. In the Brotherhood's case, that person was Glenn Lynd. Upset that Timothy Leary's son Jack was fornicating with his old lady in the summer of 1968, Lynd approached Leary, who stood by his son and did nothing to stop it. Lynd took his family and left the commune with animosities still smoldering. Lynd saw sexual freedom turn to hedonistic greed, saw peace and love turn to unconcern and hurt, saw the chinks in the armor of the man he admired most, Griggs, turn to gaping holes. He saw the fallacy of what he believed in and determined to forsake it. He didn't light the match, but he might as well have burned the Brotherhood down to the ground by turning state's evidence against them in 1972. Lynd refused the federal witness protection program, moved to Grants Pass, Oregon, lived a quiet and uneventful life, and died of cancer in 2002.

After Griggs's death, the majority of the remaining brothers moved to Maui, Hawaii, which played mightily into their surfing roots. They continued their Afghan hash smuggling operations, eased up on their LSD use, and replaced it with even more dangerous cocaine. Through their breeding efforts, the potent "Maui Wowie" strain of marijuana came into being and exists even to this day. The concert scenes of the cult movie classic *Rainbow Bridge* (1972) starring Jimi Hendrix were filmed on the slopes of Haleakala Volcano largely due to BEL efforts, while all of the surfing scenes feature Brotherhood members, most notably Mike Hynson, who in 1966 had starred in the surfing movie classic *Endless Summer*, and Chuck Mundell, who had given BEL its name later that same year. The concert was rife with weed due to a 6,000-pound shipment of premium Mexican "colitas" brought in by Eddie Padilla on a near disastrous journey from Mexico on the oceangoing yacht, the *Aafje*.

Due largely to a fallout with Travis Ashbrook, Padilla abandoned his plans to sail the *Aafje* to Pakistan on yet another Afghan hashish run, and instead moved to Peru to smuggle cocaine. This ended badly, and he was sentenced to forty-five years in Lima's notorious Lurigancho Prison, then rated as the worst in the world by Amnesty International. He survived the ordeal after four years of incarceration by escaping with another American. He and co-author Paul Wood wrote a book about the harrowing experience entitled *Lurigancho* that was eventually picked up in 2013 by Flying Rabbit Press out of Pukalani, Hawaii. Ashbrook skipped bail on the ranch bust, but eventually did ten years in the federal pen.

In the spring of 1970, in tribute to the memory of John Griggs, The Brotherhood financed the escape of Timothy Leary from a Southern California prison, utilizing the services of the Weather Underground who orchestrated the daring escape and enlisted the services of the Black Panthers, who had an embassy set up in Algeria which accepted Leary as a political refugee. Then the wheels came off. Increasing sophistication in police undercover and networking operations eventually allowed them to identify individuals within the Brotherhood as major drug suppliers, and various sting operations and quick-strike busts decimated their free roaming numbers. *Rolling Stone Magazine* got wind of the phenomenon and published a piece in 1972 dubbing BEL as "The Hippy Mafia." Some members went into hiding for years and even decades. The last Brother was arrested on September 26th, 2009 and subsequently released two weeks later. So ended the legend of America's largest, best organized, and completely nonviolent hash smuggling ring.

In retrospect, just who were the Brotherhood of Eternal Love? Like a hippie commune, this hippie smuggling ring was loosely organized, with leadership being so sensitive to the membership's feelings that it would never want to appear as absolute leadership. In such a democratic business environment, it could certainly prove difficult to get things done. More than one motorcycle gang has collapsed under the weight of being equally fair to all. John Griggs most definitely was the true leader of BEL. His charisma and street smarts combined to make him the obvious choice to lead, but credit must be given to many of the other Brothers for being sage enough to realize that in order for a leader to lead, others must be willing to follow. Perhaps humility was the greatest attribute of the membership. Except in their own private company, Brothers never referred to themselves as Brothers, or as members of any such organization known as the Brotherhood of Eternal Love, for bringing attention onto themselves was just as likely to bring just as much heat. A common street maxim was that the more anyone talked up being a member of the Brotherhood of Eternal Love or being associated with the group, the more likely it was that they weren't. They resisted the trappings of wealth, preferring to live simply within the basic human dictates of adequate food, shelter, and clothing. Their one indulgence was drugs. They choose to live in invigorating temperate environments, and though not all were surfers, the inherent freedom of the surfer's mentality and lifestyle lay at the forefront of all that they did. A desire to change the world was what united them, and when it appeared that some were less dedicated to that ideal than others, that cognition is what signaled the beginning of the end.

Greed being what it is, it's highly unlikely that there will ever be another illegal or legal drug producing, procuring, and distributing organization like them ever again. The Brotherhood of Eternal Love existed at a time when there was an altruistic confluence of peace and love, and most of all, believability that our American society was at least receptive to change, and indeed a significant portion of the baby boom generation once were. But we weren't yet in power, a fact made nauseatingly apparent to us when Nixon's "tin soldiers" gunned four of us down at Kent State. Reagan tore Carter's solar panels off the roof of the White House, opened the doors to our country's mental institutions, and told the lower classes to open their collective needy mouths to receive his "trickle down" theory. Rich getting richer and poor getting poorer, in other words. It was more of the same with Bush One, and ditto with a bullet for his dimwitted kid. Barack Obama pussyfooted around, sidestepping the pot issue, and then came yet another corporation ass-kissing, war on the poor promulgating, bank-assisting, power mongering douchebag Republican to the White House known as Donald J. Trump. It could well remain this way until the day I die. Federal marijuana legalization may never come, the world may never change, and America's best chance to retain her claim of being the home of the brave and the free may have already come and gone, riding the crest of an anti-establishment cultural wave known as the Brotherhood of Eternal Love.

Sloppy-Assed Drug Addicts Versus Cannabis Users

Wherever there is alcohol there will be alcoholics. Wherever there are drugs there will be drug addicts. Human nature being what it is, the mind rules the body, and while the body desires the high, the mind craves the escape. Escape from the troubles and turmoil of life, escape from haunting memories that pull and tug at the psyche unless quashed. The paradox of the drug addict's life is that they want to make things better by constantly getting higher, yet that simply masks the reality that they are perpetually sinking lower. Emotionally, oftentimes physically, and most of all mentally, they are never in one place for very long. Psychologists and addiction counselors all sound the numbing drumbeat that all an addict has to do is hit bottom, but for some, there is no bottom. The overarching argument of the compassionate is that the drug addict is sick and that their addiction should be treated like any other illness. True enough on the surface, but there is one key difference. Almost everyone who's sick, stricken with cancer or any number of other debilitating diseases, truly desires and works to get better. Conversely, any drug addict not serious about recovery will only get worse. If it seems that they are hell-bent for self-destruction, it's because they are.
Again, where illness and addiction part ways is in the desire to heal. Talk is cheap, and if you spend any time around drug addicts, they'll talk your ears off. What keeps a drug addict in business is their ability to rationalize, which quickly blurs into their ability to lie. Police, who are adept at recognizing (and imitating) such things, will tell you that there is no better liar on earth than a drug

addict. Is it any wonder that drug addicts are accomplished liars when they practice 24/7 lying to themselves? The degree to which they believe their own lies acts as the dividing line that separates the possibly curable run-of-the-mill drug addict from the totally incurable sloppy-assed drug addict. If you're involved with a drug addict who's so determined to remain a drug addict that they've crossed the line into being a sloppy-assed drug addict, you have a problem of monumental proportions. Nothing you can do or say will change anything, and you'll wind up a dupe, a patsy, an utter fool until you run out of patience, or money, or both. Being saved is not the forte of the self-absorbed, and self-absorption defines the sloppy-assed drug addict.

Defining the ignoble parameters of a sloppy-assed drug addict's makeup is crucial to the primary argument of why America's War on Drugs, and its Keystone Cops-like goon squad known as the DEA, is a pointless exercise in futility. The incorrigible alcoholic and the sloppy-ass drug addict are the epitome of the First Amendment of The Constitution of The United States of America (1787) in that they view their own bodies as temples of free expression, even if that expression will ultimately kill them. No matter - the only thing they can completely control is what they ingest, and no one can stop them from doing that against their own free will. A multi-billion-dollar industry has grown up out of drug addiction rehabilitation. The recidivism rate for recovery facilities is staggering. If there's a new mental illness that's identified, the sloppy-assed drug addict is sure and quick to claim it. ADD, ADHD, and now the ever-prevalent PTSD are conjoined with the all-encompassing bipolar disorder to produce an individual beyond repair, recovery, and most of all, accountability. The inherent message that radiates from the sloppy-assed drug addict's very existence is: if they can't be saved, then why try? Sloppy-ass drug addicts are human quicksand, and the more you try to help them, the more helpless they become. Wouldn't time, money, and resources be better spent on conducting triage on those who are capable of being saved, and leaving those who refuse to be saved to their own devices?

The American Psychiatric Association's most recent edition of its in-house manual entitled *Diagnostic and Statistical Manual for Mental Disorders (DSM-5)* (2014) conjoins substance abuse and drug dependence into one category they term "substance abuse and addictive disorders." In the manual they provide a checklist whereby any individual meeting three or more line items is considered at risk for a full-blown addiction. These are:

- Tolerance (needing more of the drug to achieve the same high as previous use).
- Withdrawal (stopping use causes characteristic deleterious symptoms),
- Using more than intended at any given session.
- Inability to cut down on use.
- Spending an inordinate amount of time obtaining and using the drug,
- Use of the drug causes interference with work, family, and/or social functioning.
- Continuing to use the drug while knowing of its deleterious effects upon the user.

To this list I would add the "Intervention Clause": An unwillingness to listen to anyone, including family, loved ones, doctors, police, and even yourself concerning the necessity to stop using in order to save your own life. When even death does not deter the drug abuser, they have most definitely crossed the threshold from being a drug addict to being a sloppy-assed drug addict.

You can apply the 80/20 rule to any study of drug use, in particularly marijuana use; that being that 20% of the users are responsible for 80% of all the consumption of any given drug. This 20% separates recreational use from habitual use. Of this 20%, an argument can be presented that less than 5% have any real or even serious problem with marijuana. Incarceration and court-ordered rehabilitation programs in regard to marijuana are frequently ineffective because a marijuana user's life is never at risk. As stated elsewhere, no one has ever died from a marijuana overdose. In fact, cannabis's lethal-to-effective dose ratio is 40,000 to 1, while aspirin's is 10 to 1. This should quell all well-meaning arguments that marijuana users need to be saved from themselves for the sake of their own lives.

The argument for protecting someone's life by denying them their personal liberties seems to be exclusively reserved for drug users, marijuana users in particularly. People engage in plenty of death-defying acts every day: playing full-contact football, skydiving, bungee and base jumping, motocross motorcycle racing, white-water river rafting, juggling chainsaws, flying to Pamplona, Spain to run with the bulls, etcetera. NASCAR events are so popular because the predominance of the spectators are there to witness the high-speed crashes. And even with the highest state speed limit being 80 miles per hour, production cars are capable of routinely achieving speeds in excess of 130 miles per hour. Where's the life-protecting logic in that? Over 100,000 people die annually from alcohol related maladies, and over 400,000 die from tobacco use, yet these products remain on the shelves and are relatively easy to obtain. So why the disconnect when it comes to drug use? Why is it so bad and life-threatening in comparison to everything else?

There is also the procurement issue to take into account when considering dangerous and deleterious outcomes, because addicts will apply any means to an end of getting what they want, and those means frequently include robbery, theft, extortion, blackmail, and even violence; in fact, oftentimes violence. This isn't likely to change unless the desired drugs become more readily available, and their current steep prices become more affordable, or all prices are eliminated through programs of free distribution. Maintaining the same antidrug status quo assures the perpetuation of the criminal activity that has always been associated with it. The current dysfunctional business model will remain unchanged unless something is removed from its cyclical nature, or an entirely different paradigm is applied. A new paradigm is unlikely to be attempted unless society becomes willing to accept that like Christ's poor, drug addicts will always be among us.

Marijuana is the least addictive of all the mind-altering drugs, and yet it is the most accused, persecuted, and misunderstood drug in society today. It's purported 9% addiction rate amongst regular users is a padded figure because the courts oftentimes demand attendance in rehabilitation programs in lieu of jail time, and these attendance figures get applied to addiction statistics. Another reason marijuana supporters feel that addiction numbers are way below this percentage is because, despite its Schedule 1 Comprehensive Drug Abuse and Control Act (CDACA) listing of 1970, *marijuana is not a narcotic*. It's a euphoriant, the name being self-explanatory as to why the feds are apparently so upset that someone could be happy. Unlike a narcotic, such as opium, that is water-based and can be further processed with additional water, marijuana's THC and various CBD's are oil-based and do not readily mix with water. Unlike crystal methamphetamine that can be manufactured from common cold medicines and toilet bowl cleaners, marijuana is the only drug that can deliver its effects as is. That is, cannabis requires no processing, which is why users say it delivers a "natural high." THC is immeasurably better when allowed to dry and cure, due to chemical reactions that occur during this period that allow it to become more potent. Like any drug, users can build up a tolerance to marijunaa that requires more to be used to achieve the same plateau of their previous high, except to say that with disuse this tolerance level reduces on its own. This is why many growers such as myself refrain from usage for four or five months prior to their upcoming harvest in order to get a read on how good the current crop would be to a "normal" user. By the time hash is produced, all bets are off, because good hash makes any bud seem rather ordinary. It is far better to form an opinion earlier in the season. However, it should be noted that everything's better with hash.

Arguments that marijuana is just as bad as alcohol and leads to equally violent and destructive behavior are ludicrous. Alcoholics drink to get drunk, get drunk to forget, and when in that forgetful state, forget to be civil, responsible, nonviolent, and kind. Marijuana users smoke to get high, get high to have a good time and expand their consciousness, and when in this heightened state, are most frequently appreciative of their companions and their surroundings. Under normal social conditions, alcohol deadens awareness while marijuana heightens it. The jazz musicians of the thirties and forever after knew this, appreciated it for what it was, and were unfairly persecuted for simply being different in choosing a less damaging path to mood alteration.

When a woman begins her conversation concerning the "marijuana debate" with the statement "As a mother," watch out, for she has already backed well over 50% of the overall population, those who are not mothers and all males, into a corner. They couldn't possibly know what it's like to be a mother, and the vast majority (the males) never will. It's self-serving exclusiveness, for who but an asshole would disagree with a concerned mother, no matter how misinformed, opinionated, or intellectually challenged she is? But being a mother does not necessarily equate to being a compassionate human being. She could well love her kids, but what of another's? If you doubt this dynamic, I invite you to observe female parents picking up children at our local high school in their apparently indestructible gas-guzzling SUVs. They play by the traffic rules on the way in, but once their kids are in their vehicle, all bets are off as they speed away, pass other cars, and honk annoyingly at anyone or anything that gets in their path.

These mothers are not alone in their "for the good of the children" actions. Conservatives, naysayers, knuckleheads, et al, all play the "kid card" to get what they want, but I often wonder, if we are so interested in protecting our youth, why have we let them become hopelessly addicted to video games? Why have we allowed elements of our educational system to slide to number 27 in the rankings amongst the first world nations? 27! Why do we allow them to eat super-processed shit, and wash it down with sugary sodas? Why are we so reluctant to get onboard the green bandwagon and create new sustainable jobs in order to assure their economic futures? Why have we not taken a much tougher stance towards enforced birth control, especially as it concerns repeat offenders on the public dole having babies they can never take care of? Why is the subject of child molestation considered too taboo to talk about? Let's have the discussion after the event because there's never time to do the job right, but there's always time to do the job over. Why in God's name do we persist in a drug war that can't be won, spending money that could be spent on, get this, the kids? No, the kid card gets dealt whenever the garden variety forms of paroxysm fail to do the trick.

The most repugnant example of overplaying the kid card comes in the form of "amotivational syndrome" a square accusation of dubious distinction masquerading as a scientific discovery birthed in the late sixties to explain to the mainstream why hippies were a scourge upon society, and then reaching fanatical proportions during Reagan's reign of terror, which at its height subjected the nation, and in particularly its schoolchildren in particular, to Nancy Reagan's "Just say no" to drugs hysteria. Mrs. Reagan was herself addicted to prescription pills in a never-ending example of Republican hypocrisy, which fails to recognize that the only difference between illegal drugs and legal drugs is oftentimes contained in the words on a pharmaceutical label. That is what separates respectable society from the dregs of society - not the high, but the license to get high. Amotivational syndrome was the brainchild of Slikker, Paule, et al, whereby in 1968 they reported that cannabis research on juvenile monkeys compromised their development into normally functioning adults. From this, the leap was made to postulate that the same could be said of humans. Every decade since, some low-ranking physicians and psychologists, eager to develop a new young client base, dusted it off as fodder by which to cajole gullible parents into believing that they knew what was wrong with their underachieving progeny. Later studies have debunked this theory, or at least its bridge hypothesis concerning mankind. People are unmotivated and/or lazy because they have a predisposition to that behavior. When embroiled in such behavior, they naturally turn to drugs and alcohol to medicate in an attempt to brighten up their miserable lives. Adolescent drug abuse is almost always a byproduct of low self-esteem. Prohibition does not deter drug use amongst youth so inclined, but rather makes the consequences of drug use all the more devastating.

Kid-concerned anti-pot factions are just as stubborn as the dogmatic disciples of Anslinger in giving up the evil weed ghost. Their fears can be accommodated if pro-pot people were simply willing to concede that there's good reason to impose an age limit on marijuana use for the same reason that there's age-related restrictions as it pertains to premiums for car insurance policies. The insurance companies have conducted exhaustive research to back up their claims that teenagers' brains have not fully developed the ability to foresee impending negative scenarios, especially when under conditions of duress. This is not a knock against young people per se so much as it is a statement of fact. The brain's frontal lobes of the cerebral cortex, that area where discernment is conducted, do not usually fully mature until around the age of 20 or 21, which is reason enough as to why 21 is the national drinking age. Addiction counselors are convinced that if alcohol, marijuana, or any number of mood-altering drugs are extensively overused during the teen years, the permanent damage, at the very least, is that the maturation process is locked into that age at which the heavy use started. I call this phenomenon "age-lock." So, it makes perfect sense to impose an age limit on marijuana use; everyone should get that. In dealing with the kids who do get into it, logic would dictate that no higher level of chastisement be applied to that than if they had gotten into alcohol. Adolescents are naturally inquisitive, meaning that kids will be kids. Note that the above warning is tempered with the words "extensively overused," which for clarification would usually mean daily toking, and it's hard to believe that any parent serious about being a parent wouldn't notice that and take countermeasures.

I would like to dispel the notion that federal marijuana legalization would automatically increase usage two or threefold. Jonathan P. Caulkins, one of the four authors of *Marijuana Legalization: What Everyone Needs to Know* (2012) has the audacity to speculate:

My best guess is that legalizing marijuana would only double, or perhaps triple, abuse and dependence, from 4 to 8 or even 12 million people in the United States.

This is a conservative piling on because, quite simply, *nobody* has that crystal ball. Additionally, when making such all-encompassing and socially damaging statements, it's best not to guess, even if that guess is one's best guess. Where are his facts? What is he basing his best guess on? because legalization in Colorado and Washington has not produced nearly this effect. National decriminalization of all drugs in the country of Portugal has actually seen addiction levels for all drugs go down. Ditto for marijuana legalization in Paraguay. Caulkins overestimates abuse numbers and underestimates and minimizes imprisonment numbers, to say nothing of his callousness and gross lack of empathy for the quality of human life in stating:

The cost to taxpayers of imprisoning marijuana offenders is a medium scale issue - 40,000 people in prison times $30,000 per inmate-year is $1.2 billion.

Smug, very, very smug. This mindset speaks for itself and is ample reason to believe that conservative America will succeed in its quest for a for-profit prison system; to hear Caulkins tell it, it's bound to be a growth industry. This is an extremely short-sighted and one-sided mathematical equation if one considers the collateral damage to society when those imprisoned are released upon the populace. Prison is nothing but a training ground for higher crime, and should be a last consideration in the event of nonviolent and victimless crimes. Caulkins goes on to use a subplot of the "no child left behind" theory to explain that if anyone is hurt in the movement, then nobody should be allowed to move forward, in stating:

In a free society there are plenty of other ways to have fun without insisting on the right to use something that becomes a stumbling block to others (p. 240).

The proclivities of the strong should acquiesce to the shortcomings of the weak. Dick Cheney's one-percent defense theory put into practice: if there's even a one percent chance that we can be attacked, we should waste no resources in making sure that doesn't happen. Sounds good in theory, but the problem is that there are limited resources and they can't be wantonly spent on low-probability occurrences, otherwise there won't be any left for the real threats. With the 9% addiction rate, pumped up by court-ordered substance abuse counseling, the remaining 91% of people who enjoy marijuana should abstain out of consideration for those with an inability to cope? This is utter naivety directed at a paradigm that is insane. The heart wants what the heart wants, and it isn't going to allow other hearts that could become broken to stand in its way.

The most reasonable argument for not legalizing marijuana has at its core at least an element of compassion, and goes like this: with so many legal chemical and alcohol dependency problems rampant in our society today, why allow even just one more? I get that logic, and respect the empathy it contains towards the family of man, but as a bleeding-heart liberal, I simply can't accept that anyone has the right to tell anyone else what they can and can't put in their own body with the caveat of: so long as no one else gets hurt. Pregnant women, for example, should be held accountable for endangering the lives of fetuses through the use of drugs, cigarettes, and alcohol.

Coming from a family of alcoholics, it's no mystery that I had my problems with alcohol. I spent time in Alcoholics Anonymous (AA) and can state unequivocally that there's veracity in one of the program's mottos: "It works, if you work it." AA has aided countless individuals in achieving sobriety and going on to live productive useful lives. There's something inherent in the individual stories (they call them testimonies) that seems to run as a common thread through each and every individual, in particularly the women - low self-esteem. With the men it's any number of things, but with the women, it's always one thing - sexual molestation. Somewhere in their background there was a father, a stepfather, a grandfather, an uncle, a cousin, a family friend, or an opportunistic predatory male that took advantage of them sexually and ingrained deep-seated feelings of shame, worthlessness, and most of all, guilt within their psyches. Internally, they feel guilty for allowing it to happen, that they somehow did something to cause it to happen, that underneath it all, that it was their fault. This is the stock in trade of the serial child molester, the ability to turn on the tap that causes an outpouring of these depreciating feelings. Anyone serious about addressing the problems of alcoholism and drug addiction needs to get serious about addressing the scourge of child molestation, and I would suggest that that's where a dismantled DEA budget, and the oftentimes misdirected but undeniable zealousness of its officers, should be directed. That would actually be good for America.

I parted ways with AA because of their insistence that any compulsion, whether it leads to drug use or not, is bad, that a 12-step program can always be applied to any perceived case of the misuse of anything, that complete abstinence from all euphoriants and intoxicants is the only way to a tenuous "cure." Different types of alcohol, and different types of drugs, affect different types of people differently. Like their fingerprints, every individual's psyche and body chemistry is different. AA's abstinence program encompasses all mood-altering substances, but while I submit to you that while abstinence may in actually be the best approach, it is not always the most practical one. For individuals who are going to use something just because they are, some things are better than other things. Here the issue isn't no harm, but less harm, and even the vast majority of people who are against marijuana legalization, for whatever reasons, will readily admit that marijuana causes less harm than alcohol; it's a provable fact that most rational people don't even bother to argue anymore.

While I run the risk of being accused of a mass self-serving rationalization, I will submit to you that I am okay, perhaps not great, but okay with pot, and know in my heart that a return to alcohol would be the end of my life. The primary factor that drives this belief is the issue of cravings. It used to be daily, then it was weekly, but now it's about once a month that I think about drinking, I dream about drinking, I wake up horrified that I have taken a drink. Working in my garden on a hot summer's day I can still feel the taste of a cold Heineken in a frosted mug on my lips. Sometimes at Thanksgiving or

Christmas gatherings the noise of the crowd goes to a dull background drone and I feel like having some Canadian Club and ginger ale. I can literally hear the bubbles popping in the glass. Who would know, and who would care - right? I would know, the people who know me would be terrified, and grandchildren who have never seen me drink would be confounded by the tension in the air. My "sobriety date" for alcohol is April 9th, 1979. I no longer have my AA chip(s) because I believe that their members would take what I'm saying here as utter heresy, and if total abstinence works for them - God bless them. For me personally, I never crave marijuana like that. I used to tell the guys on my construction crews that if they couldn't wait until the 5:00 p.m. quitting hour to drink or get high, that they had a real problem, and consequently, *we* had a real problem. I felt justified in throwing down this gauntlet because there were times during my period of alcoholism that I drank straight whiskey in the mornings before work, at the lunch hour, and immediately after work. I knew deep down inside that I was cheating my employer and myself, but that guilt couldn't stop me from drinking. I managed to keep it somewhat together during the weekdays and the Saturday workday, routinely averaging 80 billable hours a week, but I was a total mess by late Saturday night, oftentimes experiencing blackouts of such a nature that I woke up lying in my open doorway, not knowing how I had gotten home or what I had done. And that was the worst of it; hearing stories from friends and dinking "acquaintances" of things I had done, and not being able to remember or refute them. That humiliation is what finally caused me to stop drinking. However, as noted above, I have never stopped wanting to drink. Honestly, it's not that way with marijuana. I'll concede that I don't know everything, especially as it pertains to another's psyche and body chemistry, and it's conceivable that it could be that way for a select few people on marijuana, but it is most definitely not that way for me.

 Big Pharma and the alcohol lobby have opposed marijuana legalization at every turn. Big Alcohol's "Please Drink Responsibly" campaign is one of the most disingenuous smoke screens ever released on the populace because they are well aware of the 80/20 rule; in fact, a case could be made that they created it, and they most definitely are not going to make a serious attempt to derail their most lucrative customer base.

Martin A. Lee in his extremely well-written *Smoke Signals: A Social History of Marijuana - Medical, Recreational, and Scientific* (2012), laments the rigidity of big Pharma's mindset, stating:

Drug-war strategists were playing a waiting game; they assumed that Big Pharma would eventually develop synthetic cannabinoid products with greater therapeutic efficacy than the herb. Modern medicine was all about controlled doses of single-molecule compounds. Federal regulators sought to discredit cannabis by harping on the difference between the "crude" botanical and the "pure" pharmaceutical. "You want to get as pure a medication as you can to minimize side effects," explained NIDA director Nora Volkow.

Of course, pure, single-molecule meds cause terrible side effects, but unlike cannabis they withstood "the rigorous scientific scrutiny of the FDA approval process," or so the authorities claimed. Some drug policy critics suspected the FDA frowned on marijuana because synthetic pharmaceutical makers stood to lose billions if they competed against cannabis on a level playing field.

The scientists just can't stand that they can't control everything. This lies at the heart of Big Pharma's isolationist theory. If they can't isolate, identify, and replicate each individual component of a natural drug, then it's purposeless to them. It's childish, in a way, because they simply have to be in control, or nobody can be. This mentality has kept cannabis languishing on Schedule 1, which isn't drug limbo, but drug hell. Good enough for it, the intolerant scientists think; if it defies them, then it deserves to be driven into extinction. For such smart people, they really are simpleminded. Marijuana in its natural plant form works synergistically, meaning that the components of THC, various major cannabinoids, various minor cannabinoids, terpenes, etcetera interact and play off one another to deliver varying degrees of various highs and various healing effects. Synergy, similar to teamwork, means that the sum of the parts working together exceeds the total of the individual parts tallied separately. A scientist just can't tolerate the notion that the more they try to manipulate Mother Nature in their own image and likeness, the more she comes right back around and proves to them that she had a better plan all along.

A person's body chemistry, just like their fingerprints, is ever so slightly different from everyone else's. In the world of chemistry these slight, ever so subtle differences can have huge impacts. This is where Big Pharma misses the boat entirely. Their one-size-fits-all mentality doesn't take into account that everyone is different from everyone else. Any given strain of marijuana will affect each individual differently. Even identical twins do not have identical fingerprints.

Nutritionists have been telling us for years that the closer to the plant source we eat, the better the nutritional benefit. Eat the banana, not the banana cream pie. Eat the orange, don't drink the orange juice, and definitely not the orange soda. Eat the strawberry, not the strawberry shortcake. The more any food is broken down and/or *processed*, the less beneficial it becomes, sometimes (some say oftentimes) to the point where it actually becomes detrimental to those who ingest it. Although red meat is bad enough, processed meats are much worse. As a plant product, natural cannabis can be viewed as akin to a fruit or a vegetable, and as such, its dried buds can be smoked or eaten whole. The synergistic chemical benefit is at its highest at this point of consumption. Beyond this, the issue of overall benefit lies in the cocktail of chemicals any given strain delivers. Marijuana is not only benign, it's benevolent. Some call it God, some call it a higher power, some call it sheer random luck, but one thing is certain: mankind has been given this great gift, and all it can think to do is tinker with it and mindlessly try to improve upon it, or failing that, outlaw it and develop a law enforcement/prison/industrial complex to profit in any way possible (even amoral ways) from its existence. Precious few of us seem capable of simply accepting it for what it is. And now here comes wax and shatter, approaching 60% and 80% THC levels, requiring specialized paraphernalia to smoke it, and endangering the strongest tenet of the fading peace and love movement as it pertains to traditional marijuana uses, that being (again) that no one has ever died from a marijuana overdose. I suggest that if you need a blowtorch to adequately ignite your preferred drug of choice, then perhaps you should strongly reconsider your preferred drug of choice. Additionally, wax and shatter are derived from butane extraction processes that present the double whammy of either blowing oneself up due to the volatile nature of butane, or making end users extremely sick if all the excess butane is not properly purged from the end product. This is amateur hour at its darkest, and hydroponic shops are morally wrong to be selling butane in bulk to untrained and unlicensed wax and shatter makers. I advise newcomers to cannabis use in raw bud form that they can get pretty high on 12% THC, and outrageously high on readily available strains that run at 22% to 24% THC. Hash routinely has 35% to 40% THC, and that's as far as I'll take it. Wax and shatter could well ruin things for all cannabis users, and I sincerely believe that shatter in particularly could well lead to the first death from marijuana usage; not from THC per se, but from the intensity of the hit causing a full-blown heart attack amongst older users. Claims of "extreme purity," while true, are also nonsense because properly prepared hash and bud are plenty pure enough. Other claims that wax and shatter require less of a dosage could well be true enough, but I witness young people honking on it until it's gone and then wanting even more, which, as much as I hate to say it, is the exact behavior of common drug addicts. I have no use for these products, and fear that they will make any claims to peace and love a thing of the past. Similar to the proof restrictions on alcohol, the Green Rush has to address capping THC levels, or it could very well end with extinction.

 In mankind's dealings with Mother nature, through eradications, manipulations, and in particularly, introductions, have we not by now learned a powerful lesson about Mother Nature's better, albeit infinitely more complex plan? In fairness, scientific experimentation has led to some amazingly beneficial discoveries that have immeasurably aided mankind. Perhaps this is what still drives some of Big Pharma, but the profit motive has predominately become the underlying engine that now pushes it forward. If they can't do any better than the plant itself, then they can't charge the populace who can grow the plant themselves for the products they produce. The collective brains of this gargantuan corporate douchebag are exploding at this notion, and this is why Big Pharma pays lobbyists staggering amounts of cash to keep cannabis on Schedule 1. Surely some other corporate douchebag can profit from marijuana. Just wait until Big Agri throws its hat into the federally legal pot ring. It's the American way, according to Gordon Gecko; "Greed is good" - at least for him and his ilk. Free cannabis surely threatens the freedom of the ruling class, diminishes the beneficence of the so-called job creators, and undermines the fabric of capitalism.

Every dog has its day, however, and Big Pharma simply hasn't figured out how best to manipulate the marijuana debate for their own ill-gotten gain. It sits back, licking its corporate chops, letting small grassroots organizations do the heavy lifting required to move cannabis from Schedule 1. When that finally does occur, they will lock arms with their largest and most powerful traditional ally, the U.S. government, and determine how to best utilize patent #6,630,507, filed in 2003, in order to lock down the lucrative position of being first in line to ride on the legal cannabis gravy train. Incredibly, the patent was filed by the United States government! The language of the patent, compiled by the National Institute of Health, states that cannabinoids are helpful in treating and even preventing autoimmune diseases, preventing strokes, relieving trauma symptoms, and alleviating the symptoms of Parkinson's, Alzheimer's, and HIV-induced dementia. They didn't mention its lessening the frequency of epileptic seizures, most likely because that research was in its infancy over a decade-and-a-half ago. The patent is assigned to the U.S. Department of Health and Human Services, and one has to wonder why the DEA hasn't yet raided them to destroy the evidence that marijuana is indeed useful to mankind. The bastards! The duplicitous lying bastards! They just won't give up Anslinger's ghost, and what do they plan on telling the other members of the Single Convention?

Cancer patients are fond of saying that without cannabis that they are dying of cancer, and that with cannabis they are living with cancer. The divide between those two diametrically opposed situations balances on the thin line of hope. For a drug that has eased so much human suffering through the centuries, humans of recent centuries sure have caused it to suffer. White-collar bullies and thugs of Anslinger's ilk can repress, and lie, and force others to toe their line, but they most certainly can't tell anyone that the relief from the pain they feel is imaginary, unimportant, or amoral. People do have the right to relieve their pain, despite what the uncaring, the unimaginative, and the uncompromising may think of it. These oppressors simply have to be right, even when they're wrong, the supposed divine providence of tyrants, dictators, and despots worldwide. They said it, so therefore it is. Nations go to war and lose their sons over such power-mongering diatribes. Others rot in jail cells, have their basic rights as citizens revoked, and become looked down upon as the scourge of societies, that in reality, are the scourge of them. If they let go of their power to tell their underlings that they cannot use cannabis, then all the other unfairly exercised power they inflict upon the masses will come into question, and they simply can't have that. The whole house of cards could collapse down upon them. Better to maintain a lie, that any rational person can see is a lie, than to admit to lying in the first place. The problem with lies is that they always beget more lies in an effort to suppress the truth that would expose them. Truth is the enemy of the powerful, for it begs the question of those below them: "Why him, and not me?"

Consider this: the less the profiteering of drugs on the part of nations hostile to the United States, and terrorist groups in particularly, the fewer armaments they can purchase to wage war against us. Above all else, war is costly; remove the funding, and strangle the war. And then there is the ingrained cultural mores of a society to consider. People do what they have traditionally done, despite what relatively new laws may or may not say is legal or illegal. The U.S. telling Afghanistan to outlaw hashish is like Afghanistan telling the U.S. to outlaw beer.

There is much debate as to whether or not marijuana is really still the cash cow of the Mexican drug trafficking organizations (DTOs) that many claim it to be; some bandying about figures as high as 60% of all DTO revenues. That's a highly doubtful statistic considering the increase in home growing north of their border, catering to a more discerning consuming American public with an acquired taste for high grade sinsemilla and a far larger profit margin in heroin, cocaine, and even crystal methamphetamine, which is much easier to smuggle due to decreased package sizes per pound of product. According to Robert J. MacCoun and Peter Reuter, the authors of *Drug War Heresies* (2001), a better estimate would be that weed accounts for around 20% of all Mexican DTO profits. With crystal methamphetamine use now rampant on U.S. soil, it's doubtful that all of it is being manufactured by small clandestine labs in the U.S.

Its production in Mexico would tend to decrease the cartel's dependence on marijuana sales, which take longer, are harder to manage, and are less profitable. This trend alone speaks for the need for complete legalization of all drugs in America. It's not often talked about, but it is certainly worth noting that the Mexican drug gangs have become so well financed as an outcome of the War on Drugs that they have diversified into extortion, kidnapping, carjacking, child prostitution, and the other standard fare of organized crime. Marijuana prohibition did for them what alcohol prohibition did for America's Mafia. At least there would be parallel and vastly more meaningful jobs for the law enforcement officers of the beleaguered DEA if it were to be redirected, downsized, or dismantled. At least they would be fighting the kind of crime(s) that a majority of Americans could agree on as being unconscionable in nature.

As stated above, there are at least one dozen assertions in *Marijuana Legalization* that marijuana legalization will automatically lead to enough increased marijuana use to make a supporter ill. What everyone needs to know is that this assumption has no statistical, to say nothing of logical, basis. The closest case study, within American society at least, was when alcohol prohibition ended in 1933. There is no conclusive evidence that alcohol use thereafter increased at all. There was a phenomenon that occurred then that is just as likely to occur now if marijuana is federally legalized. Usage could initially appear to increase simply because closet users would no longer be afraid and could choose to no longer stay in the shadows. I have plenty of professional friends who shun acquiring a medical marijuana card, and who have others procure their marijuana for them or buy it on the street themselves as they have in the past. They fear the federal government, fear the rebuffs or revocations from the professional organizations they belong to, fear the social stigmatization and ostracization that could occur if they were ever seen going into a medical marijuana facility. Additionally, parents with minors in their households fear the Nazi-like incursions of Child Protective Services (CPS) that have already occurred in several medical marijuana households. All state that they don't want to be "in the system" should any of the proverbial shit hit the proverbial fan. Legalization may or may not draw them out of the closet, but it's a fair assumption that initial numbers reflecting an increase in usage could in reality be numbers propped up due to a decrease in existing fear.

America's ongoing national phobia concerning the fate of sloppy-assed drug addicts determined to be exactly what they are has driven our society to the brink of ruin. The oppressors of pot almost always perceive themselves as tough guys and gals who are disgusted with and intolerant of weak drug users. The greater percentage are hard-drinking, law abiding (since alcohol is legal) citizens desirous of riding society (those who count, anyway) of sleaze-bags, stoners, and addicts. Compassion doesn't figure into their mindset, and they really strip a gear at the thought that anybody might be getting "high." Drunk is perfectly acceptable, but high is a sure sign of a degenerate. They have their collective noses so far up everyone else's asses that they can never smell the stench of their own shit - which is a mighty powerful odor inflicted upon the rest of rational society. Many enter politics, and incredibly, a lot of them get elected. In truth, there isn't much to choose from, but that should never be used as an excuse not to choose. The only way stoners are ever going to reclaim their self-respect and reclaim the true intent of our Constitution will be to root them out, expose them for the simplistic morons they truly are, and utilize our democratic system of government to elect saner individuals to government offices. Without this, America will continue on in its downward spiral, massive amounts of money will continue to be spent on stupid things, and the delusional will continue to run the lives of the apathetic.

Cannabis: The Flagship of the New Green Economy

I have personally written and paid to co-publish with my own hard-earned money, three books concerning the environment, and what I personally feel are the best methodologies to see that it is saved. Forget for the moment all the external threats and consider that America's ever-expanding wealth disparity between the richest one percent and the rest of us is in reality the primary inward threat to national security. The conservative Republican-based Tea Party, the Freedom Caucus, the gun lobby, Mitch McConnell, and in particular our Mad King have hijacked our basic sense of fairness towards our fellow citizens, and I personally hate to see how some Americans are treating other Americans. There are two fundamental truths that we as a country have to come to grips with concerning the workplace: the overall quantity of jobs are diminishing, and worker productivity has dramatically increased within those job markets that still exist. In short, fewer people are needed to perform fewer jobs. This is not a viable formula for increasing Gross Domestic Product (GDP), and certainly not a formula for generating economic growth. The obvious solution is to create new labor-intensive jobs, but with ongoing downsizing and outsourcing, this seems to be an extremely low priority. Aside from the bump in worker efficiency, the Trump Administration appears to be facing the very same problems that were facing the Franklin Delano Roosevelt Administration. Roosevelt swung into job-creating action through the formation of his now famous "alphabet agencies," which were the worker bees of his progressive "New Deal" style of government. Former President Barack Obama hinted at job creation through new green industry in the run-up to the 2008 election, but that notion faded to a distant memory seemingly before he even took his first oath of office. The Mad King promised to bring back formerly displaced American manufacturing jobs, as well as the dirty jobs of the coal industry, all the while alluding to something as ridiculous as "clean coal." Then he embarked on spraying terrorizing tariffs around the world like bullets from a Tommy gun, the net effect being that he now jeopardizes many of the jobs he promised to bring back and many of the businesses he promised to strengthen, in particularly those in agriculture. He is the living breathing embodiment of a king alright: King Midas with his golden touch working in reverse.

Generation Me and the Millennials took exception to corporate greed in the summer of 2012, and there was hope among us supposedly socially conscious baby boomers that something would come of the "Occupy Wall Street" movement, but it soon turned into a Woodstock-minus-the-music type melee that temporarily elevated our national consciousness, but ultimately didn't accomplish anything. The kids had the right scent, but they were tracking the wrong animal.

Corporations will never play fair or do anything to increase payroll, for that simply isn't in their nature. What can anyone expect from any entity given human-like qualities except to say that they never die and don't have a beating heart? Corporations don't create jobs; politicians like Roosevelt do, and while Obama had talked the same talk, in the final analysis, he was no Roosevelt. About the best we could've expected from him was to step up and legalize marijuana through executive privilege, but of course, he didn't. Don't look to the Mad King to be of any help in this area because he's too busy fiddling with the fate of his unwelcomed subjects, much as Nero did while Rome burned. If a Democrat does ascend to the office of the Presidency in 2020, the issue of federal marijuana legalization may be brought to light again. If that were to happen, then cannabis could well become the flagship industry leading the nation, in particularly Generation Me, the Millennials, and all of the soon-to-be twenty-somethings into a new and flourishing green economy. The Bureau of Alcohol, Tobacco, Firearms, and Explosives (ATF) could easily incorporate cannabis (C) and become the ACTF. Administrative and inspection-type jobs could easily be filled with employees from the DEA, which could then be downsized or eliminated. Obama had publicly said that the legalization of marijuana wouldn't solve all of the nation's economic problems, incredulously ignoring that it would obviously help solve *some* of the nation's economic problems. Income through taxation statistics coming in from Colorado and Washington, where marijuana has been legal for over half a decade, are very encouraging. This is substantiated by statistics coming out of Oregon, Alaska, and the District of Columbia, which legalized shortly after Colorado. Pot does create revenue and is so popular that Colorado on occasion has temporarily been out of weed.

Government's paradigm for creating income has historically been to charge the producer usage and operational fees and tax their profit, and most definitely to tax the end consumer. Setting all of this up takes time, of course, which is something the economy can suffer the least. I would suggest that the federal government legalize marijuana and charge every individual user a one-time use fee of $100.00 to acquire a federal marijuana card, just to get the ball rolling until a better administrative procedure is put in place. Conservative estimates count frequent marijuana users at over 30,000,000, which when multiplied by $100.00 equals $30 billion right out of the gate. $100.00 is a small price to pay to assure freedom from incarceration and police harassment, and I'm of the opinion that users would happily pay that until a more permanent system can be put in place. Instituting this program could be as easy as checking a box on your income tax return. This initial economic shot in the arm could fund other green and/or restorative industries. Our nation's infrastructure has continued to rot away ever since Ross Perot called national attention to the threat during his 1992 presidential campaign. It seems like the citizenry has forgotten about that fact faster than it has forgotten about him. Our electrical grid is of the same quality as a third world nations. Research to decrease our dependence on foreign oil has stalled, and it's an accepted fact, at least among environmentalists, that procuring natural gas through fracking is not a viable long-term energy solution and is in fact an extremely environmentally detrimental energy solution. Even though millions continue to deny global warming or climate change, depending upon your point of view, corporations in Russia, Norway, Greenland, and Canada are all vying to drill for even more oil in the once frozen but now navigational waters of the Arctic. And then there's our decaying National Park system, aging hydroelectric dams, and alarming rates of wind and water erosion of topsoil, water purification, solid waste disposal, shoreline and fishery restoration, combating the effects of climate change, ad infinitum.

Many environmentalists feel that the most grassroots and productive of Roosevelt's New Deal "alphabet agencies" was the Civilian Conservation Corps (CCC). Created on March 31st, 1933, in its nine-year existence it offered a base wage, job training, meals, and barracks-style housing for over 3,000,000 young men. The CCC's stated purpose was to build roads, plant trees, provide flood control, and initiate a myriad of other conservation projects. Run like a quasi-military operation, members did indeed wear surplus World War I uniforms and utilize tents and other equipment from that era. Retired officers were employed as directors and young men volunteered for service. Sound familiar? Men and equipment are coming and will continue to come back in droves from Iraq and Afghanistan. The agency was disbanded in 1942, mostly due to the need for the able-bodied young men that made up its ranks to join the World War II effort. The Civilian Conservation Corps has now been defunct for 80 years. With the myriad of environmental calamities now facing America, there is only one thing left to do: Bring it back, Jack! And not a moment too soon. An argument has been presented that the Job Corps is basically the same thing, but this is a huge misnomer. The Job Corps, though well-intended, is an underfunded, disjointed effort wallowing in ineptitude at the state level. Most of its ranks are populated by disadvantaged youth given it or time in jail to choose from. It does not attract the best and the brightest, but rather is a warehousing effort gone awry.

Desperate times call for desperate measures, and who but a blind man couldn't see that America, now entrenched in its eleventh year of this Next Great Depression, is indeed about as desperate as it gets. Forget the Mad King's endless ravings about the "great economy," because it is only great for him and his ilk. Escalating positive job statistics fail to mention that they are largely made up of minimum wage jobs that the corporations will replace with robotics just as soon as they can. Improving unemployment statistics are only improving because so many people are simply falling off the rolls and have given up even looking for a job. What's needed is a whole new approach to job creation with the well-being of the working classes being more highly emphasized than the well-being of a lucky few elite.

Mounting a federal effort to lift the nation from its environmental, infrastructural, financial, and political maladies is exactly what's needed to provide the impetus for private industry to jump on the green bandwagon. Instead of demonizing marijuana, let's put it to work. The country simply has to go green to maintain some semblance of a capitalistic system, or it will erupt from within. The time bomb is ticking, and yet the populace turns upon one another rather than seeking viable and sustainable economic solutions. That Republican lovechild known as the DEA imprisons our youth - our single best hope for a way out of this hideous mess, and yet we allow it to continue to exist, Big Agri offers mass production despite the environmental costs, Big Alcohol offers a diversion from the hardships of life despite the violence that comes right along with it, Big Pharma offers better living through chemistry despite the side effects, and Big Prison offers protection from ourselves, despite the fact that we are all Americans. Darwin has taught us that every species, including *Homo sapiens*, must adapt or die. That's the most basic law of nature, and yet we refuse to adapt. It's go green or go extinct, and the fastest way to go green is to allow marijuana to be the savior rather than the pariah.

Martin A. Lee, the author of *Smoke Signals: A Social History of Marijuana - Medical, Recreational, and Scientific* (2012), puts forth some compelling evidence that marijuana, perhaps more than any other plant in existence, is a plant of paradoxes. Along with what I've written above about it being viewed as either a savior or a pariah, consider these other areas of polarity: Loved/hated. Understood/misunderstood. Recreational use/medical use. Valued for fiber/valued for buds. Given away to friends/expensive to buy at dispensaries. Ingested by smoking/ingested by eating. *Sativa* equals a head high/*Indica* equals a body high. THC desired/CBD's desired. Federally illegal/Legal in some states. States Lee:

Marijuana's therapeutic mechanism is bimodal; it acts upon both the central nervous system and the peripheral nervous system, an unusual combination for a drug...It has been used as a curative and a preventative medicine. It is both prescribed and proscribed.

Opinions abound as to the true usefulness of hemp fiber, the most prevalent negative one being that it simply can't compete with any number of the new synthetic ones. Another one being that if hemp is so great, why then isn't it produced in significant quantities in those countries that haven't outlawed it? The problem with that word "synthetic," whether it be prescription drugs, clothing fiber, or bodily enhancements, is that they always cost more than the original. Additionally, almost anything synthetic, and especially synthetic prescription drugs come with side effects. In the case of synthetic cloth, it would be the deleterious chemicals that are disposed of after the manufacturing process is completed. It all has to end up somewhere. On a level playing field of cost basis comparisons, is rayon or nylon really cheaper than hemp fiber? Sure, the process of retting which ultimately produces hemp fiber is a labor-intensive process, but in a country desperate for jobs, even relatively low-paying ones, is that a bad thing? In comparing hemp fiber versus cotton, admittedly cotton may be preferable, but it doesn't have the plant hardiness range (hardiness determined by susceptibility to freezing) that hemp does. This is why there is little to no cotton farming done above the Mason-Dixon line, while hemp can be grown as far north as Alaska. Additionally, hemp is more drought tolerant than cotton and adapts more readily to drip emitter forms of irrigation, which is a definite advantage in regions becoming more arid as a result of climate change. In the U.S. those areas of increasing aridity are most notably Southern California, Texas, and the southern Great Plains states.

All of the 182 countries that are signatories of the Single Convention have technically agreed not to grow hemp, but a few don't take it very seriously. China, Canada, and Australia produce the lion's share of industrial hemp, and even at that, it amounts to less than 1% of all fiber crops grown worldwide, of which cotton dominates. In reality, there are only two ways for hemp fiber to compete with synthetic cloth and cotton. The first is on an environmental basis: that being that its production is the least damaging to the environment of the three. The second would be, in a world of smaller yet more diverse regional economies (which may become a reality sooner rather than later), if anyone utilizes an accounting method that factors in transportation costs, hemp could well be more cost effective in the long run. This is especially true in a world once believed to be running out of fossil fuels, but now facing the prospect that it would be patently unwise to burn all the fossil fuels it currently has due to the undesirable outcome of accelerating the rate of climate change. Alternative fuel sources and modes of transportation (e.g. light rail) are now not so much needed due to fuel scarcity as they are needed due to the issue of human survival. Hemp also beats cotton in the possibility of recycling itself. Cotton at maturity is not particularly leafy, while hemp has an abundance of recyclable leaves because hemp fiber is garnered from the stems and branches, rendering the remainder of the plant available for other purposes, of which soil restoration plays a large part. Hemp strips nitrogen from soils probably at about two times the rate that cotton does, but true to its duality of opposite purposes and uses, the recycled leaves would serve to replace it.

Jack Herer's often cited classic *The Emperor Wears No Clothes* (copyright 1973, 12th edition 2010), in which the "Emperor of Hemp" attests that hemp can save the world, has overreached, at least by the standards of today's world, while contributing author Christina Farber's discrediting the overall importance of hemp in (no surprise here) *Marijuana Legalization: What Everyone Needs to Know* (2012) is short-sighted and utterly unimaginative. The answer, as it so often does, lies in the middle.

Hempseed oil competes well with the highly refined petro-oils needed in motor housings and for fine machinery, but it won't compete economically with the motor oil used for motor vehicles, making even more of a case for electric instead of hybrid vehicles. But where does that electricity come from? Coal-fired electrical plants are no long-term solution. The world has now witnessed the sheer folly of nuclear power plants. Solar appears modestly practical for short distant vehicles, but the issue of its short shelf life when attempting to store solar energy has always been its fatal flaw. What the solar world still needs more than anything else is a better battery.

It's the cruelest of ironies that just about the time the information highway is spanning the globe, that information is indeed about the only thing that can travel on it. The world may be getting bigger from an informational standpoint, and in terms of the unified global acceptance of the diversity of all races and all cultures of people, but the methodologies for physically reaching out and touching one another are growing fewer and fewer. Climate change has us grounded and will soon have us handcuffed. About the only power that doesn't in one way or another negatively impact the environment is manpower. And this revelation arrives at that exact point in time when Generation Me and the Millennials of America have come to disdain physical work.

It's no stretch to say that for the foreseeable future, the value of cannabis will be determined primarily by its recreational and medical properties.

Albert Einstein once said that, "No problem can ever be resolved by the same consciousness that created it." Therefore, entities traditionally hostile to examining any viable purpose for marijuana are not very likely to dream up ways to now make it useful to society. In many cases they simply have too much distaste for the product to ever view it in a favorable light, for that would simply cut against their grain. In other cases, the trouble with reversing the stubborn mindset of the disciples of Anslinger lies in their immense pride. Nobody wants to think, much less admit, that they have devoted their professional and working lives to an ideal that was flawed from the beginning, or in defense of leadership that was likewise corrupt from the outset. That's just too much to bear. However, anyone involved in growing marijuana for any significant amount of time has, by necessity, come to learn of its awesome economic power in bartering for goods and services. This concept of bartering, along with the age-old farming tradition of lending out money or extending other forms of credit until the harvest comes in, plays itself out in any number of unexpected ways. As an example of how bartering and/or delayed payment systems can work, I'll present the following example:

I was measuring a lot for a residential client in San Jose when a city truck pulled up. Out jumped four energetic young men, and within 20 minutes they had planted two very healthy, well-staked street trees, and off they went. The owner explained that it was all part of a city beatification program that was funded by her and her neighbors' city taxes, and she was glad to have it. This got me thinking of other similar urban programs that could fund themselves, thus eliminating the need for taxation, and that some people would be thrilled to have.

I envision a city-run agency or private landscape contracting firm that sends a four-man crew out during the springtime to expertly plant six marijuana plants of an ill owner's choosing in a garden of 250 square feet with an automatic drip irrigation system, all contained in a full (including roof and floor) chain-link enclosure with a lockable gate. Where possible, the garden can be hidden from public view, and where not, the public would just have to accept that some ill people need their medicine more than they need to avoid their neighbor's indignation. Where is the compassion? Where has it been for 84-years? This same entity can return in the fall, cut and hang the colas in a safe room of the owner's choosing, remove the rootstalks, and button things up for the winter. An owner can trim the marijuana at their own pace, and if diligent in their endeavors, reap a minimum of three pounds of high-grade herb. If those three pounds of herb were sold wholesale to the corner dispensary, it would command a minimum sales price of $4,500,00 ($1,500.00/pound) for the dispensary to purchase, and if sold by the dispensary to a willing consuming public at the going price of $40 per 1/8th ounce, it would retail to dispensary customers for $15,360,00. Somewhere in the translation of these figure, say perhaps discounted at less than half of the retail sales amount, say $6,000,00 the ill owner could keep enough herb (1 pound worth approximately $1,500.00 wholesale) to make it through the year and sell the remainder (2 pounds worth approximately $4,500,00 discounted) back to the city-run agency or private landscape contracting firm on a buy-back plan that could pay off the cost of constructing the garden in the first place. With a standing garden facility, the owner's costs the next year would be considerably less, and a sustainable product delivery loop could thus become established.

Another option would be for an entrepreneurial inner-city firm operating from a protected truck to contract with ill patients to grow on their land, leave them enough cannabis to get by, and process the rest themselves, or process the whole shebang their young and healthy selves and deliver cannabis back to the ill owners on the giveback plan. No other agricultural product has this kind of economic power, and the only thing that prevents these proposed scenarios from working is the antiquated law enforced, once again, by the disciples of Anslinger. I can hear the naysayers lining up to shoot this one down as "logistically impossible." Oh really? The same business model of "grow it, process it, and distribute it" has been going on in indoor grow rooms and in outdoor guerilla grows for decades. Allow these outcasts and outlaws the opportunity to perform their expertise legally and out in the open, and any number of business models could be devised without the "aid" of Big Pharma or Big Agri, and most significantly without the fear of Big Prison. Jobs creation and compassionate health benefits in one fell swoop; wouldn't that be nice?

What exactly is a new and flourishing green economy? What is meant by "new" is an entirely different way of approaching income/profit generation. American and Eurocentric industry has always functioned on a linear one-way extractive paradigm. Find a resource, then drill it, kill it, catch it, cut it, or in one way or another use it up and move on to another locale from which to do the same, or find a different resource and apply the same extractive mentality to it. Works fine, until you run out of resources, or the environmental consequences of the extraction are just too calamitous to allow for its continuation. Contrast this strategy to a cyclical restorative paradigm that is by its very nature *sustainable* over time. The objective is to always have the resource available for consumption, basically in perpetuity. Such a resource has to be managed, which requires, above all else, that it is understood. Crop rotation, selective timber cutting, grassland management by controlled fires, etcetera. There are plenty of overused resources to begin with. Some are severely compromised, and some are on the brink of collapse, but most are capable of being restored if only mankind could abandon its extractive mentality, and the only way to do that is to convince it that the sustainable paradigm, if given adequate time to become instituted, is just as capable of generating just as much income as the extractive one historically has. The transition from the old methodology to the new one depends heavily on an ample dose of patience, given that impatience, a very close cousin to greed, is what got us into this horrible mess in the first place.

Gretchen C. Daily and Katherine Ellison were at the forefront of sustainable environmental thinking when they penned *The New Economy of Nature: The Quest to Make Conservation Profitable* (2002). Stated the authors:

This increasingly apparent decline has begun to inspire a shift in thinking for many scholars, most notably economists. To be sure, economists have long been concerned with issues of resource scarcity and limits to human activities. That's why their field was dubbed "the dismal science." Yet throughout the 1960's, the 1970's, and the 1980's, most economists clashed with ecologists. Economists accused ecologists of being alarmist about adverse human effects on Earth and of proposing costly and unnecessary measures of protection. Meanwhile, ecologists charged economists with promoting "growth" at any price and misusing partial indicators of well-being, such as the gross national product, that are blind to wear and tear on the planet.

One of Daily and Ellison's most groundbreaking concepts was that of Ecosystem Service Units (ESU's), which was a vastly different accounting method than the one extractive industries had historically applied. When the value of an undisturbed or readily restored ecosystem is studied and measured, its estimated aggregate worth can be broken down to a cost-per-acre unit of value. This should be looked at as negotiable capital with which to buy or trade for other services or goods. What, for example, is the true value of an intact forest ecosystem? How much carbon-drenched air does an acre of old growth timber filter? How much wind and water soil erosion is prevented by this same acre of timber or undisturbed grasslands? Until very recently, very few economists would have thought that an acre of timber standing would be worth more than an acre of timber cut, but when all the costs are tallied, not just corporate profit, this is oftentimes the case.

The filtering and purifying effects that an intact watershed has upstream of a city can be assigned a real-world dollar value, which can be compared against an increase in property taxes and land values and all the supposedly other expensive amenities that the real estate developer that wants to build on it says the city will receive. Which one makes the most economic sense? From which one will the community at large receive the most benefit? Again, it's the classic confrontation: what are the true costs of development when the lost value of a removed ecosystem is added to the equation? Only by knowing and weighing all the facts and looking at all the angles can a course of action (or inaction) that makes the most sense be determined.

Assuming for the moment that marijuana were to be legalized on the federal level and that revenue derived from it did indeed stream into federal coffers, what new green industries could it help to fund?

- Wind and solar power research and development
- Mass transit
- Water purification and recycling
- Air purification
- Soil restoration
- Forest and grassland reclamation.
- Ocean fishery reclamation

And what services could be funded because of it?

- Reestablishing the Civilian Conservation Corps (CCC)
- Free college at least at the state educational system level
- Realistic addiction awareness programs and prevention
- Free birth control
- Income assisted housing based on economic need
- Actual product donations to hospice facilities

The current environmental mantra of reduce, reuse, and recycle could certainly use a few more "r" words: restore, renovate, and revitalize.

Here's a conundrum of catastrophic proportions: While 70% of the world's population lives within 100 miles of an ocean coastline, these are the exact same areas destined to be impacted first by rising sea levels due to climate change. What's worse, they aren't likely to relocate unless absolutely forced to. Further exacerbating this threat is the current world-wide mass migration from the rural areas back to the cities. One thing that could stem the tide of this massive flow of humanity would be a shift in mankind's current thinking that dictates that humans must live in cities to be near goods and services and to eliminate the high transportation costs associated with acquiring them. A shift to regional economies where goods are produced and services are offered closer to home would make rural living more attractive. Two centuries removed from when Thomas Jefferson first envisioned an American agrarian society, due to population growth and joblessness and out of sheer necessity, it may well materialize.

The time has come to reexamine the concept of a corporation. Initially it was created to spread risk across an entity rather than onto an individual human being(s). The primary thought was that corporate officers may lose their positions, or even their business, but not their personal assets. Therefore, poor business decisions, poor managerial practices, and unforeseen circumstances beyond their control wouldn't cause well-meaning people to lose everything. That's the only element of compassion within the formation of a corporation, and those incorporating soon learned to turn this anonymity of responsibility to their advantage. No individual corporate officer is ever held accountable, either economically or morally. This is way corporations get away with the things they do - polluting the environment, ripping off the public, continuing to send cars with known defects, some of them potentially lethal, out into the public. They do it because they can, because they are a corporation, because nothing bad is likely to happen to any of them individually. When people start turning up dead, the corporation may take a financial hit or even be disbanded, but no officers ever see any jail time. Because of this dynamic, those who set up corporations and those who run them see behavior and practices that are potentially damaging to the public at large as nothing more than calculated risks, their very worst fear being that the corporation may lose some money. Where's the personal accountability? There isn't any, because the corporation isn't a person per se; it's an entity that will behave this way over and over again. It's certainly time to do away with that! If individuals doing bad things can hide behind a corporate veil, then the only rational thing to do is remove that veil by eliminating corporations. Impossible, you say? No, not at all. The United States government, while oftentimes behaving in much the same manner as corporations behave, is in fact not a corporation, and yet it conducts business and continues to endure. But when an individual within government does something really egregious to the populace, they can be removed by losing in the next election, impeachments, dismissals, and/or being coerced to resign due to public opinion. Some can even be held accountable and receive jail time. If this is a good enough policing strategy for those responsible for running the country, why isn't it good enough policing strategy for those running businesses under the umbrella of the country which allows the corporate veil to exist? Death to the corporate business model, because there are plenty of other ones that place accountability more squarely on the shoulders of those conducting its business. If they are able to enjoy insane profit, why then aren't they able to accept appropriate responsibility? Why do they get to have their cake and get to eat it too, and never have to worry about washing the dishes?

What does it matter? Everybody knows that our government isn't run by politicians but by lobbyists contributing to the campaign chests of politicians. We don't even bother to put up a smoke screen of fairness anymore because with the striking down of the Citizen's United Movement in 2010, and the Supreme Court's most recent ruling on April 2nd, 2014 to still allow unlimited campaign contributions by anyone so as not to violate the contributor's First Amendment right to free speech, it's obvious to anyone who isn't brain dead that political offices can now be bought in the United States of America. Shame on a citizenry that allows it to happen, because we the people could make the effort to be better informed, not to follow the dictates of conservative or liberal media, and to make up our own minds based on facts that we ourselves verify, and then vote accordingly. It must always be remembered that it doesn't matter how much money the fat cats contribute to their shill politicians if the population rises up en masse and defeats them on election day.

The environment gets a lot of talk and a lot of coverage, but not a lot of contributions - either politically or by way of grants from American Foundations. In 2006, when I brought out *Econation: America in Environmental Perspective*, I lamented the fact that out of 50,000 foundations only 213 funded proposals having to do with environmental issues. Bringing out *Mobilizing the Green Revolution: Money and Manpower to Save the Planet* later that same year, I provided these statistics concerning where foundations spent their grant money:

- Education   14%
- Health   17%
- Food   15%
- Energy   14%
- Art   12%
- Science   5%
- Environment   1%
- Others   12%

Sixteen years later, those numbers are almost identical, and the "environment" percentage has remained the same. This suggests that the tactic for receiving any environmental grant should be to mask it behind the veil of education or health or food or energy, and it just might stand a chance of getting funded. Foundation Boards are notoriously conservative, and environmentalists, by their very nature, are anything but conservative. Squares view many environmentalists as controversial, which is about the same as how they look at pot advocates when they're being kind. In truth, they just hope the whole ugly unpleasant issue(s) goes away, and they do their part at accomplishing that end by refusing to give them any credence at all. Starve them through lack of funding and attention, in other words. Enviros and pot enthusiasts can't defeat the lack of financing, but they can get attention, which in drama-starved America means creating controversy. Controversy used to sell newspapers, and now sells media attendance numbers, but it doesn't necessarily pay the bills for the enviros. It's extremely discouraging, but the worst thing we can do is give up, even when the odds appear overwhelming. Some chance is better than no chance, and not fighting equates to no chance at all. One thing that cannabis supporters have in common with environmentalists is that they have ample experience in being underdogs. In fact, these people are often one and the same, which can be expected in light of America's national denial, which still believes that pot isn't good for anyone, and that there's nothing to worry about concerning the environment. Enviros and pro-pot supporters can accomplish more on less, because they have been surviving on a shoestring for decades.

The 80/20 rule applies to momentum also. 80% of the effort is expended by 20% of the people, and additionally the first 80% of the task at hand is relatively easy to accomplish, while the last 20% can be extraordinarily difficult. Because of this, many quit within sight of the finish line. It just got more difficult than they could have ever imagined. What's needed is a killer instinct. See the job through. Never assume that to have accomplished 80% is to have done enough. That may be good enough in academia, but it will never be good enough in the real world. It's upsetting to me that so many of the pro-pot supporters assume that federal legalization is simply a matter of time, especially when they know of so many federal betrayals in the past. Anslinger's great lie continues to fuel the feds, even though it's just as stupid as clinging to the word of of the world's scientists who claim climate change is a hoax. They don't need to see a burning bush; they need to be incinerated by the burning bush.

We of the "baby boomer" generation were fortunate to grow up in a time of unprecedented prosperity in America. In our middle years we witnessed something going horribly amiss economically and came to learn that we would not live as well as our parents did. Now, in the year 2019, we are well aware that our children and grandchildren are not going to live as well as we did. Is there anything we can do to stop this deleterious downward spiral? Unfortunately, probably not, except to teach them that which most of us have recently learned as a result of this heinous economic downturn: *There is more to life than money*. This often said, yet not often believed phrase's time has come. With less affluence with which to vacation and visit the rapidly dwindling faraway and exotic places on our planet, perhaps it is time to start caring about and putting a restorative effort towards those places where we live and work each and every day. The "environment" is in our homes, in our yards, in our schools, and in our communities. It and we are one. Yet this seems a mystery to the vast majority of us. Clueless adults raise clueless children, the old adage of, "The apple doesn't fall very far from the tree" put into practice. The time has come for the baby boomers to get a clue and pass it along to Generation Me and the Millennials, and their most recent progeny, Generation Me Me Me. In short, it is time to clean up our own mess which was created on our watch.

Human beings are animals. We *Homo sapiens* are scientifically classified by genus and species, just like all the other known plants and creatures of this earth. Yet we truly believe that we are above it all. This arrogance could well be the undoing of man's reign on planet earth. As animals, we have some instinctive programming that proves meddlesome to our well-being in modern times. Our fight or flee mechanism does not dovetail well with the concept of civilized behavior. That, or those who we cannot pommel or avoid, seem to get the best of us in the form of high blood pressure, hypertension, ulcers, high anxiety, alcohol and drug abuse, or lashing out with overt acts of violence. All are a very high price to pay for our ignorance of the obvious. Either remove the concept of civilization, or let it run its course to completion and become even more civilized. In this context, more civilized means well-informed, well-intentioned, and ready, willing, and able to leave well-enough alone. "Live and let live" is the only belief system that is going to allow us, as a species, to live. An understanding of the natural world that surrounds us can only lead to an understanding of us. How little we truly know of our animal selves. And how much we need to learn *now*, if we are to survive as animals. The key to our survival is to realistically devise methods to mitigate the fight or flee mechanism so as not to feel compelled to do either. An appreciation and empathetic understanding of all life on earth is the only thing that will allow us to feel comfortable in our own skins. This is the thrust of Dr. Edward O. Wilson's biophilia concept, and running concurrently with it, this is the greatest gift we can give to future generations.

Not understanding each other, or worse, not wanting to, is what causes bigotry, exceptionalism, self-absorption, and unconcern for the well-being of others, all of which has led to this near-equal divide in opinion amongst our population concerning federal marijuana legalization, and the derailing of the great economic and environmental good this legalization could bring. If we as a people don't care about each other, what chance does the flora and fauna we share the earth with have?

Post-9/11 overreaction to the threat of similar terrorist acts has caused the populace to lose a great many civil liberties. Bush Second, Cheney, et al were quick to push their elitist and militaristic agendas before the shock wore off on the populace. I hear it time and time again - for the good of national security, for the good of freedom, for the good of the children - and I ask you, who are they to decide what's good for you and I when the basis of our democracy is that everyone should get to vote on that? Now, in America, and even more so throughout the world, there are two classes: the super-rich, and everyone else. Of everyone else there are those getting by, those barely getting by, and those unable to get by. What chance is there of saving the environment when we aren't even able to save ourselves? The odd irony being that if we don't save the environment, then saving ourselves is a moot point.

Marijuana smokers have been looked upon as outcasts for their entire lives, or at least from that point in time when they started smoking until the present. It's been a long, wearisome battle just to get to where we are today, and many, such as myself, fear that a wrong new president in the White House could cause us to very easily lose the ground that's been gained—and if he thought it would garner any more support amongst his base, the Mad King is the wrong president right now who could loose a conservative vengeance upon the unsuspecting stoner population right now.

Favoring marijuana over alcohol is viewed by some squares as anti-American and punishable by prison sentences that they feel are well-deserved. When you think about it, there's little difference between how marijuana smokers and environmentalists are frequently viewed and treated. Few are open to their message, most "normal" citizens are uncomfortable around them, and in their heart of hearts most wish that they and their message, Al Gore's "Inconvenient Truth," so to speak, would just go away and leave them alone. The environmental movement peaked in the seventies and has been losing ground ever since, and outrage over the persecution of personal rights due to marijuana prohibition has followed the same downward spiral from the passion of the seventies to apathy of the second decade of the new millennium. Back then, it was all summed up in Quicksilver Messenger Service's "What About Me?" the title song of their *What About Me* album (1970):

You poisoned my sweet water / You cut down my green trees / The food you fed my children / Was the cause of their disease / My world is slowly falling down / And the air's not good to breathe / And those of us who care enough / We have to do something

Oh, oh, what you gonna' do about me? / Oh, oh, what you gonna' do about me?...And I feel like a stranger / In the land where I was born / And I live like an outlaw / And I'm always on the run...

I smoke marijuana / But I can't get behind your wars / And most of what I do believe / Is against most of your laws...Oh, oh, what you gonna' do about me? / Oh, oh, what you gonna' do about me?

Environmentalism is lost in the wilderness of apathy and greed and needs someone to lead it out. I said as much in 2005 in *Environmental Cognizance: Towards the Year 2020*:

But in order to inherit the Earth, change is inevitable. There are so many of us that you would think that one new leader, one new free thinker, one new child of God might be able to rise up and show us all a solution to the global environmental problems. Yes, it's a big world out there and no one knows when or from where the next prophet will come, yet we all hope she/he will come soon. It's such a big world (p.102).

Unbeknownst to me, that prophet had already been born fourteen years earlier and had turned 30 years old on October 13th, 2019. She is Congresswoman Alexandria Ocasio-Cortez (AOC) from New York State's 14th Congressional District. She rose to power by defeating incumbent Democratic Congressman Joe Crawley in the June 2018 primary election. Crawley's campaign war chest exceeded Ocasio-Cortez's by a ratio of 10 to 1 and he was the fourth most powerful Democrat in The House of Representatives at the time of his defeat. Ocasio-Cortez went on to defeat Republican Anthony Pappas in the November 2018 midterm election. An underdog if there ever was one, her Socialist Democratic platform mirrored that of Vermont Senator Bernie Sanders's, which was put forth in the run-up to the 2016 presidential election. She served on the Sanders campaign and became indoctrinated with the concepts of free college, universal healthcare, abolishing Immigration and Customs Enforcement (ICE), and dismantling the richest one percent through fair and just taxation. None of that, however, makes her a prophet. That was revealed in February of 2019, when she and Democratic Senator Ed Markey of Massachusetts introduced their "Green New Deal."

Adopting the "New Deal" title in similar fashion to FDR of yesteryear, this bold sweeping proposal takes as a given that changes of gargantuan proportions are needed to lift America out of the doldrums of economic stagnation and to make the changes necessary for us to compete technologically in the future on the world stage in the future. In addition to incorporating the initial planks of the Sanders' campaign (free college, universal healthcare, livable wage, federal legalization of pot, power to the people, etcetera), this resolution also proposed that the entire country switch to 100% renewable energy sources and achieve net-zero greenhouse gas emissions by the year 2030, and make major investments in the research and development of clean energy. Inherent in the intent of the proposal is the necessity to revitalize and/or rebuild our nation's crumbling infrastructure.

Republicans instantaneously stripped a gear and *Hannity* went over the deep end. They called her brash. They called her irreverent. They called her cheeky as a thinly veiled slur towards her Puerto Rican descent. What they couldn't call her was wrong. In short, she is an old white man's worst nightmare come to life; unless, of course, some of them care about the fate of their children and grandchildren. Even the Mad King has noticed and readily states that Alexandria Ocasio-Cortez has "it," and thank God she does. I say, like it or not, the prophet has arrived, so deal with it. The Mad King also says, "She doesn't know anything." She knows enough to know that the old paradigm simply isn't working for her and her generation and is certainly smart enough to quickly learn what she needs to know on the job. She has thoroughly absorbed the lyrics of Jonathan Edwards's 1971 hippie classic resistance song titled: "Sunshine Go Away Today."

Sunshine go away today I don't feel much like dancing / Some man's come he's trying to run my life / Don't know what he's asking… He can't even run his own life / I'll be damned if he'll run mine…

Back in 2005 when I decided to add the subtitle to *Environmental Cognizance: Towards the Year 2020,* even I felt that there was enough time to right our listing environmental ship. Boy was I ever wrong. Al Gore had already been robbed of the 2000 presidential election, Bush Two significantly weakened The Department of the Interior and The Environmental Protection Agency (EPA), Obama did very little to re-strengthen them as he talked the talk but failed to walk the walk, and then the Mad King appointed dolts determined to eliminate them all together. Those 15 years slipped by in the proverbial blink of an eye, and now things are so much worse than I originally thought. 2030 is just eight years off, and if the world's environmental collapse holds true to recent form, we may not even have that long; yet the naysayers, the climate deniers, the rich and powerful who want to remain that way, and the entrenched old white men running our country all say that the Green New Deal is a rash overreaction. Well, that's what they have always said while failing to notice (or care) that we are plummeting off an environmental cliff. The conservatives also accuse AOC and her ilk of not caring about an ever-widening generational divide. I say, why should they? The earth is theirs to inherit. I apologize to Generation Me and the Millennials for the mess that we have made of things and are now too old to repair. Most of the boomers will be dead before things get really bad, but these young people will be entering the prime of their lives. *Now* is the time for their voices to be heard. I'm against violence of any sort, which is the telling grace of the vast majority of marijuana advocates, but I'm not against taking it to the streets in peaceful protest. If it comes to that, I hope to see you there.

There is a presidential election coming up in 2024, and the youth that do care are going to have to get out the vote. Remember Einstein's statement that, "No problem can ever be resolved by the same consciousness that created it." Remember that well. Call the ruling generation out on its self-absorption and self-righteousness. We had our shot, and now our time has come and gone. No, we aren't right just because we rolled around in the mud at Woodstock 50 years ago. We didn't change things like we said we would, so the burden now falls to you. Elect someone of your generation who gets it or be disappointed by the ineptitude of those who don't. And if that someone does prevail, I encourage her/him to appoint AOC as head of The Department of the Interior, or as head of a reestablished Civilian Conservation Corps, and then step back, light up a doobie, and watch in glee as the prophet leads us all to the dawn of a bold new day.

The Outdoor Marijuana Grower's Guide

Let's clear the air right from the get-go. Anyone who smokes or otherwise ingests cannabis should be able to grow their own. Self-sufficiency contributes mightily to respectability, in that the public perception of stoners as lazy nonconformists definitely does not apply to home growers. In addition, this helps to take the profit out of a product that originally stood for peace, love, and above all else, generosity, but is now being corporatized, whored out, and sacrificed on the altar of greed. Any state medical marijuana program that does not allow patients to grow their own (i.e. New Jersey when Cristie implemented road blocks, New York, and Ohio) is delusional when it comes to the subject of compassion, because patients are not going to find very much of it at the dispensaries. They simply can't afford the high price of medical marijuana where the patient's "donation" to a dispensary was typically $80.00 for 1/8th of an ounce in 2006, and then it dropped to $50.00 or $40.00 for the same 1/8th of an ounce following the financial meltdown of 2008; it has now leveled off at that price. It was originally $640.00, and still is $320.00, for an ounce of weed, a plant which, pardon the pun, grows like a weed! Greed reigns supreme in the world of medical marijuana, which is the primary reason why the squares are so skeptical of its validity. Ditto for recent gains in the arena of recreational marijuana. We are not talking about the selfishness of cocaine, the sleaziness of heroin, or the insanity of crystal meth. We are talking about marijuana here, which has traditionally been the most affordable of all the stimulants, and could continue to be, because if small growers were left to their own devices, $125.00 per ounce would be more than enough to get by and pay their fair share of taxes, providing that most state tax rates remain at 8%. If this price is still too steep, I would advise: patient, heal thyself and grow your own.

Until marijuana is legalized on the federal level, growing outdoors exists in the gray hinterlands of legality, and any misstep, any miscalculation, any misinterpretation of the law could land the grower in prison. It's a tenuous existence fraught with ample doses of peril and paranoia. So, watch your step, and try to stay abreast of anything that applies yet another protective layer to the thin patina of legality that hopefully covers you. In conversation with others, especially law enforcement and those attached to it, nomenclature is especially important. When conducting growing operations don't call marijuana, "marijuana." In fact, don't call it by any of its street names; it's always referred to as "medicine," because that's what most state laws allow. And there's a labyrinth of laws to negotiate federal, state, county, city, and God's. Federal laws always supersede state laws, and while you may converse with a state, county, or local official, you would never say a word to a DEA agent without an attorney present. I personally beseech God all the time, but it's hard telling if I'm getting through with all the invocations from all the other growers clogging the airwaves. You see, medical marijuana is a relatively new (1996) phenomenon, and recreational marijuana is even newer still, and nobody knows for sure if they are doing everything right. One law rules above all others: *Never grow more than 99 plants.* If things go south, one thing has been proven, time and time again - the difference between 99 and 100 plants equates to the difference between one and five years in the federal pen. It is certainly better to err on the side of caution.

There are other things you pick up, either by word-of-mouth, observation, or incarceration. Fly below the radar, live a simple existence, don't piss off your neighbors, never call 911, don't open a dispensary, and don't grow pot indoors for any extended period of time. Given these loosely organized parameters, common sense and a little horticultural knowledge can go a long way. Extravagance always creates a certain amount of jealousy; your neighbors can always complain and/or turn you in, and it's patently stupid to invite potential trouble to your doorstep. The DEA hates dispensaries because a physical storefront reeks of respectability to them. It's okay to sneak around in back alleys or make discrete home deliveries so long as they're of insignificant weight, but anything out in the open is just too much for them to bear.

All forms of law enforcement, do-gooders, bible thumpers, and fake neighborhood watch sleuths hate indoor marijuana growing because it suggests that someone is getting away with something behind their backs, or worse yet, under their very noses. I'm not too particularly fond of indoor growers myself, but for different reasons. Growing marijuana indoors leaves a multibillion-dollar environmental footprint in electrical usage, to say nothing of the chelated chemicals the plants are pumped up with. And besides, most indoor growers are egomaniacal asses convinced that they grow the best pot, and anything that they can't completely control must be of inferior quality. They never miss an opportunity to berate outdoor grown marijuana as second rate. This, quite simply, is not true. If marijuana is to indeed become the flagship of America's new green industry, it's far better to employ the use of free natural sunlight for efficient and cost-effective production.

The first thing to consider when growing marijuana outdoors is security. Children and teenagers should never be allowed access to a garden, and it's common courtesy to screen your garden from your neighbors' view as well - as being a small price to pay for their silence. Frequently, a grower has more to fear from rippers than from the police, so a secure garden usually ensures a secure harvest. After that, it's a simple matter of adequate sunlight, fertile soil, sufficient water, wind protection, and genetics.

Genetics pertains to the plant's biologically programmed capacity to produce a plant that has a given level of tetrahydrocannabinol (THC), the active ingredient in marijuana that gets users high, or cannabinoids (CBD's), the molecular compounds that are credited with providing the many therapeutic effects medical marijuana delivers. How the plant is handled, and how the floral clusters known as "colas" are harvested, manicured, and stored, are determining factors in whether the end product achieves its genetic proclivity or not. A grower can match it, but never exceed it, because that's all there is, and there isn't any more. This isn't plastic surgery, after all, and it would be good to remember that nature is in charge here.

As THC percentage in a strain goes up, its cannabinoid percentage goes down. North American breeders, in their relentless quest to increase THC, have driven it into the twentieth and even thirtieth percentile, and in so doing have all but bred cannabinoids out of some strains. High-cannabinoid strains, currently most definitely numbering in the minority, have far less THC. A strain delivering 4% CBD is considered quite high, but alas, most at this level contain only 4% or less THC, which should quell the concerns of squares that suffering patients not be allowed the joy of getting too high while convalescing. As in all things natural, *diversity* guarantees the health of the organism and the ultimate health of the ecosystem that the organism exists within. The greater variety of marijuana strains available to any individual human body, the higher the possibility exists that, through experimentation, any given individual can find the strain best suited to their body chemistry, best suited to combat their particular malady, and best suited to give them the high (or lack thereof) that they personally desire. This kind of individualism drives Big Pharma absolutely crazy.

An unsuspected problem exists with such concentrated breeding efforts for high-THC and high-CBD strains because several naturally occurring landraces are being ignored and could conceivably become extinct through neglect without mankind first knowing what beneficial cocktail of chemicals they could provide. Maintaining the diversity of individual strains maintains hope among those seeking a cure, or the hope of simply finding some relief from a malady, that they could well discover a naturally occurring ally. This particularly applies to those strains rating moderate in both THC and CBD. If cannabis were compared to a member of the animal kingdom, it could most fittingly be compared to the lowly coyote. The more you try to eradicate them, the more prevalent they become. Fear not for the extinction of marijuana, but for the extinction of some strains that have not yet fully been tested and tried for their usefulness in the higher court of hippiedom.

Marijuana is scientifically classified within the genus named *Cannabis*, and that genus splits into four distinct species: *sativa*, *indica*, *afghani*, and *ruderalis*. *Cannabis sativa* varieties produce a mind-expanding cerebral high, and *Cannabis indica* varieties produce a body high that is often useful in painkilling. *Sativa* gets you high and *indica* gets you stoned, while crossbreeds of the two provide varying degrees of both. *Afghani* strains are quite similar to *indica* strains while preferring higher elevations and cooler climates than *indica*. *Ruderalis* strains were heretofore very small-growing and low in THC content and were therefore largely ignored. But when growers discovered that they were auto-flowering and could grow under lower light conditions than their cousins, intensive crossbreeding efforts were enacted. Hybrids with *ruderalis*'s auto-flowering characteristics demand less light and mature much more quickly, a definite advantage in northern latitudes. *Sativa*s are generally much taller and have wider-spreading thinner leaves that are spaced further apart on the stems as opposed to the other species. *Indica*s are shorter, stouter, and have wider and thicker appearing leaves that occur closer together on the stems as opposed to *sativa*s.

There are literally hundreds of strains available within these species and crossbreeds between them. The selection of the strain is everything in terms of assuring a desired THC or CBD level, and in accommodating the plant's predisposition to withstand or accept environmental factors such as water demand, temperature tolerance, altitude and atmospheric conditions, and soil preference. Soil and water can be altered and supplied, respectively, to ensure the best crop possible given the conditions. Wind protection through wind foils and proper staking can also assure the health of the crop.

As a registered landscape architect, licensed landscape contractor, certified arborist, and bona fide landscape nut for over 40 years, I've always had my hands in soil, and firmly believe that there is a botanophilic connection between mankind and the surface of the earth that yields the bounty of the land. Coining the term "botanophilic" is a spinoff of renowned biologist Dr. Edward O. Wilson's biophilia theory, which he explains in *The Diversity of Life* (1999):

But consider: human advance is not determined by reason alone but by emotions peculiar to our species, aided and tempered by reason. What makes us people and not computers is emotion. We have little grasp of our true nature, of what it is to be human and therefore where our descendants may someday wish we had directed Spaceship Earth. Our troubles, as Vercors said in You Shall Know Them, arise from the fact that we do not know what we are and cannot agree on what we want to be. The primary cause of this intellectual failure is ignorance of our origins. We did not arrive on this planet as aliens. Humanity is part of nature, a species that evolved among other species. The more closely we identify ourselves with the rest of life, the more quickly we will be able to discover the sources of human sensibility and acquire the knowledge on which an enduring ethic, a sense of preferred direction, can be built.

These are examples of what I call biophilia, the connections that human beings subconsciously seek with the rest of life...(p. 350).

Our botanophilic connection to the plants of this world might be more easily understood if only there were more individuals available to push the research forward. But alas, they're busy elsewhere. Michael Pollen postulates in *The Botany of Desire: A Plant's View of the World* (2001) that horticultural advances amongst the mainstream population have been slow in coming because the best young horticultural minds of our times are underground raising indoor pot. He has a point, because currently there is no agricultural pursuit as immediately profitable as raising and selling marijuana. Aboveground botanists are reluctant to research cannabis because its ranking as a Schedule 1 narcotic precludes it, and likewise precludes any available research funding.

The technology goes where the money is. But technology always comes at a price, and according to Evan Mills, an energy analyst at the U.S. Department of Energy's Lawrence Berkeley National Lab, indoor-grown marijuana in the United States alone accounts for *five billion* dollars in electricity expenditures. Considering the carbon footprint necessary to produce that electricity, it's safe to say that outdoor growing is far more environmentally friendly.

Ironically, even outdoor marijuana benefits mightily if it starts its life cycle indoors, but it is usually for no more than eight weeks under the weakest wattage of fluorescent lights that can be utilized to give seedlings and clones a jump-start in life. Be meticulous about keeping clone rooms clean, as decaying leaves and any other vegetative matter provide the perfect environment for fungi and insects, in particular the dreaded spider mite.

With my four decades of horticultural background, and with extensive experience in detailing and specifying planting operations for a vast array of plant material types, two things immediately stand out as important rules for growers. First, select known varieties, and second, start with well-formed, healthy, and well-rooted stock before transplanting individual plants to their permanent locations from which to witness marijuana's rapid and insatiable march towards full maturity before ultimately succumbing to the forces of entropy (death), and the awesome cycle of life to be renewed again next season, and the season after that, ad infinitum. Providing an adequate amount of light is paramount to the entire process.

Fertile soil and adequate irrigation rank next in importance for growing medical-quality marijuana. To be sure, frequent and well-balanced fertilization plays a large part in healthy plant growth, but we will consider and discuss only organic fertilizers here. For all the issues I personally have with indoor hydroponic growers, a few have turned organically formulated liquid fertilizers into an art form, and they are so well-formulated that it is difficult to burn plants when utilizing them outdoors. Used as directed, most perform admirably.

Irrigation is an issue of observation and common sense. A soil tensiometer can go a long way in providing accurate soil moisture content information. With experience, your index finger works nearly as well. In all cases, it is always better to slightly underwater, than to overwater. Low water usage drip emitter irrigation systems work fantastically well for soil-grown marijuana.

With outdoor growing, there is little to worry about by way of pests and diseases, as outdoor conditions and an abundance of natural predators usually preclude them to the point where they are most often a nonfactor. Indoor gardens furnish a perfect environment for spider mites, which are the number one natural destroyer of pot. Once established, they are neigh on impossible to eradicate, and although most say they don't, indoor growers almost always have to resort to harmful pesticides to get rid of them, or at the very least keep their populations in check.

Spider mites do occur outside, but natural predators, most notably the thoroughly cute but lethal ladybug descend upon them with an almost Old Testament-like vengeance. Juice-sucking aphids and thrips can pose meddlesome, but lacewing wasps consider both a delicacy. Grasshoppers can be flicked off of plants, and snails and slugs can be easily removed or drowned in a shallow saucer of beer. Scale and other forms of fungus can be washed away with diluted dish soap, which degenerates rapidly and is little threat to human consumption. Again, pests and diseases are almost never a problem outdoors, which is as good a reason as any to limit larger scale growing aspirations to outside gardens. Healthy plants shun predators and disease in much the same manner as healthy strong humans do. In all things biological and botanical, a healthy lifestyle promotes longevity.

A brief discussion of *Cannabis*'s history and morphology can enrich and broaden our conversation. Cannabis is most typically an annual, that is, a plant that completes its entire lifecycle in one growing season. Yes, there are examples of keeping mother plants, to be utilized for cloning, alive for a year or two beyond that, but such is atypical and out of character to the plant's natural preferences. *Cannabis* belongs to the botanical order of Angiosperms, meaning that their strategy for reproduction is to produce flowers that ultimately produce seeds, which contain the genetic code that assures what all species great and small strive for: that being the perpetuation of the species. In an odd quirk of nature most specific to agricultural crops, marijuana is dioecious (di equaling two), meaning that it has male and female flowers on separate plants. *Cannabis* is photo/geo/hydro/*and* thermotropic, meaning that it reacts differently to varying degrees of light, gravity, water, and temperature. The fastest way to kill marijuana is to ignore its range of tolerance to temperature, especially its hardiness to resist cold or freezing temperatures. Marijuana functions best between 60 and 90 degrees, with 85 degrees being optimal. The plant can tolerate brief periods below freezing (32 degrees), but it will perish if exposed to 25 degrees or below for even an evening.

The United States Department of Agriculture (USDA) produces plant-hardiness zone maps of the entire United States which are readily procurable, but beware, they are highly general in nature. If you were to examine a colored temperature-range map on any given day in *USA Today* the boundaries of temperature differences would roughly follow the USDA hardiness zones. *Sunset's Western Garden Book* (2012) has been in continuous publication since 1930 and is considered the Bible in my area of expertise. Its planting zone maps are highly specific, and in 1997 Sunset produced a national tomb with maps that are almost as reliable as its predecessor's. The thing to always remember is that hardiness (life and death) is always dependent on temperature, and lifespans, or periods of productivity and dormancy - the growing seasons, if you will, are always dependent on non-freezing days. Latitude (distance from the equator) and altitude (elevation above sea level) are the most determining factors of climate, and a grower would do well to know and heed the restrictions of both. Nothing lives without water, which should be enough said about that, except to note that there is always an optimal amount. Too little, especially in conjunction with hot temperatures, promotes stunted growth, while too much, especially in the presence of cooler temperatures, promotes weak, leggy growth. Assuming adequate irrigation, dry arid climates invariably produce the best pot, while humid climates produce less potent crops, and in humid areas there is always the risk of mildew or mold, which are notorious crop killers.

Light is what allows plants to conduct the process of photosynthesis which in turn produces chlorophyll, the initiating agent in all forms of cellular growth in plants. Rarely can marijuana be exposed to too much of it, and frequently do they receive too little, especially with "guerilla growing" operations that strive to plant crops under foliar tree and brush cover in order to avoid detection. A standing crop of marijuana has two very distinct growing/life periods: vegetative and flowering. Two optimum ratios, in regard to hours of light versus hours of darkness, are 16/8 for the vegetative period and 12/12 for the flowering period. Photoperiodism, a specific organism's reaction to varying durations of light, plays mightily in the natural world. The ratio of daytime to nighttime hours triggers breeding seasons, migrations, and hibernations in the animal kingdom and germination, budding, flowering, and fruit formation in the plant kingdom. The summer solstice of June 21st indicates the greatest duration of daylight hours, while the winter solstice of December 21st indicates the shortest duration of daylight hours, although admittedly, most outdoor marijuana plants won't make it until then.

On the surface, it may seem that there is little to say regarding geotropism, except to mention that it is a really bad idea to plant marijuana upside down in "Topsy-Turvy" and other such nature-defying devices. Gravity does play a part in outdoor growing, however, especially if a grower is to consider positive water drainage away from the plant's root system. Like the vast majority of plants, marijuana does not like "wet feet," that is, to have its roots submerged for too long in standing water. I plant my crop in 18" high raised rows to guarantee positive drainage and to assure that it is virtually impossible to overwater the crop. In the unfortunate event of over-fertilization, I have the option of flushing chemicals out of the raised root system with pure water. As with planting in pots and containers, raised roots can be exposed to hot, drying air temperatures. Thoroughly mulching all surface soil is a good preventative measure, while painting pots white or inserting them in white heat-reflective sleeves usually provides enough heat protection.

Soils exist in a varying range of acidity and alkalinity, which is most frequently referred to as the pH scale. This is a linear scale ranging from 0 on the left to 14 on the right. 7 is neutral, and anything lower in descending order towards 0 on the left becomes more acidic, while anything higher in ascending order towards 14 on the right becomes more alkaline. Marijuana grown outdoors thrives best in a pH range of 6.3 to 6.8, and there are a variety of soil additives and amendments on the market that can be utilized to achieve it. As a rule of thumb, forested environments tend to lean to the acidic, while plains and desert areas lean toward the alkaline. A hand-held soil pH tester can be an invaluable tool in reading and altering pH.

Once a proper pH is achieved, the next consideration is the soil's texture, or its friability. This is oftentimes referred to as a soil's "tightness" or "looseness," and loose soils are always better for growing than tight ones. This is because there are more pockets for air and water penetration, which subsequently fosters root growth. Soil is composed of varying degrees of sand, silt, and stone (parent material). Silt or clay soils are the tightest of the tight. Sandy soils are in the middle of the range, and stony or gravelly soils are the loosest of the loose. As with most things in life, a happy medium is the best way to go, and equal amounts of sand, silt, and stone, in conjunction with organic matter, produces what is known as loam soil. Soil quality can be rudimentarily verified by simply picking up a handful and firmly squeezing it. If it stays together and is difficult to break apart, it leans towards silt. If it stays in a ball but readily crumbles when poked with a fingertip, it is loamy, or optimal. If it almost instantaneously falls apart by itself, it is sandy or stony-type soil, and will be in much need of amending. Here again, raised rows or pots can come to the rescue, because they can be completely comprised of imported potting soil or potting soil in conjunction with varying amounts of other soil amendments. As a general rule of thumb, any soil friable and fertile enough to grow tomatoes is fine for marijuana. Native soil between the rows can be improved as time allows, and eventually the entire garden can be upgraded to a fertile paradise over the span of just a few short years.

Assuming that you have diligently prepared your soil, have a reliable source of water, and can expose your plants to a minimum of 14 hours of sunlight a day at the onset of their lives, the next logical step is to procure plants and sock them into the ground. These plants are referred to as stock, and there are two ways to procure stock: either by seeds or by clones. A seed contains the genetic code of its male and female parents and is therefore less reliable than a clone would be in knowing, for a fact, what the resulting seedling's physical characteristics will be. A clone is an exact genetic copy of one parent plant, either male or female, because it is cut directly from that plant. Clones are therefore more reliable in determining what the characteristics of the mature plant will be. Some determining considerations in the clones versus seeds debate is the subsequent growth rate and ultimate mature size of the plant produced. Because of a botanical phenomenon known as "hybrid vigor," plants germinated from seeds can grow to be as much as 40% larger than plants of the same species grown from clones. The genetic code housed within a seed's outer casing is referred to as that strain's genotype, while the resulting physical plant itself is referred to as the phenotype. In an odd quirk of nature, many different phenotypes can result from a group of seeds all garnered from the same parent plant. This isn't all that unusual in the field of genetics when you consider that brothers and sisters from the same human family of the animal kingdom rarely look exactly alike. The same can be said of individuals within the same species in the plant kingdom. In short, some will be superior to others and will advance the plant's cause in the realm of natural selection.

When time, space, and temperament allow, it is always more advantageous to "step up" the pot sizes of seedlings and clones - from cubes or pot packs to 4" pots, and then to 1 gallon containers before final planting in the ground or in very large pots or containers. This "stepping up" process encourages a well-formed, vigorous, and extremely fibrous root system to form at the edge of the container. As goes the root system, so goes the plant. Like anything else, a good start in life betters the chance of survival to maturity.

When the last frost is behind us - which means it's early June in the North and in the higher elevations of the mountains, early May in the South, and mid-April in the very Deep South, the time is at hand for planting. The first axiom of planting is that the bigger the hole, the better it is for the plant. Disturbed soil is looser and thus easier for young roots to penetrate. The second rule of thumb is to disturb the existing root system as little as possible. Patience is a virtue here as you gently slide the young plant from its container. Check for circling roots that could literally enclose upon the root ball and choke the life out of the plant. These are usually rare in number and are easily cut away with *very sharp* pruning shears. Install the plant at a height where the crown flare, the bulge where the stem and the root system converge, is level with the final grade (soil line). Hand tamp the soil for appropriate compaction, and slowly water the plant in. Some B1 rooting solution mixed with the water works wonders here. The planting operation complete, it is now time to determine an ongoing watering and fertilizing schedule. Don't ignore or pooh-pooh this critically important regime. The bounty of the final crop relies on diligence and attention to detail moving forward.

A plant needs micro and macronutrients to grow and look its best. Vigorous and healthy vegetative growth is necessary to assure the same at the flowering stage. There are three macronutrients: nitrogen (N), phosphorus (P), and potassium (K). Old-school thinking usually went along the lines that nitrogen was for foliar (leaf) growth, phosphorous promoted floral growth, and potassium aided root and some stem growth. For the most part, that's true, but everything in the natural world is interrelated, and hard-and-fast rules pale with the knowledge that everything is a matter of degree. These macronutrients combine, break apart, and recombine with themselves and attendant micronutrients: Magnesium (Mg), Calcium (Ca), Manganese (Mn), Iron (Fe), Boron (B), Copper (Cu), and Molybdenum (Mb) to aid photosynthesis, tissue formation, pest and disease resistance, and finally, flower and seed formation.

Again, all life on earth strives to perpetuate its own species. The angiosperms of the plant kingdom have devised the formation of seeds as their survival strategy. All angiosperms have flowers that form seeds within their structure that guarantee their survival. No matter how small and insignificant the flowers and seeds may seem to clueless human observers, to the plant itself, they are monumentally important. Cannabis is tenacious about seed production, which puts it at odds with mankind, the relentless seeker of tetrahydrocannabinol (THC). It requires vast amounts of energy to produce THC, and a marijuana plant will dutifully expend it, unless female flowers become pollinated by male flowers. In this event, a far greater effort is expended in seed formation, and THC manufacturing efforts are greatly reduced. Pollinated pot flowers yield inferior-quality pot. The object of the whole endeavor, from the grower's point of view, is to bring flowers to the peak of maturity without allowing them to form seeds. Sinsemilla, said to yield the highest quality pot, has the root word (*sins*) meaning without, and then (*semilla*) meaning seeds. Thus, growing pot without seeds is the first objective of any grower. For this reason, male plants are ruthlessly culled from the general garden population the moment they are discovered. The only time plants with seeds are valuable to growers is when they can produce enough seed stock to guarantee the following year's planting or to produce hybrid stock from two genetically desirable parents. Hybrids can yield many favorable characteristics that neither of the parents may individually exhibit; size, floral characteristics, bud potency, and/or taste can be better in the hybrid than with the parent female plant, otherwise no one would waste their time in creating hybrids, and any genetic differences would be left up to either an accident or the wiles of nature.

High nitrogen fertilizers are used during the vegetative stage to spur on foliar growth that will, in turn, encourage flower growth. Marijuana flowers grow in tightly compacted vertical clusters called "colas," which in Spanish means "little tails." This is the most exciting time of the planting season. When the colas come on, the heartbeat of the grower quickens. The taller and thicker the colas, the more resin they contain, with its more potent THC contained within. Fat colas are what the grower is after. I like to think of tall ridged colas as erect middle fingers being directed at the establishment that has continued to believe the many lies about marijuana and has insisted on keeping this 84-year prohibition going.

Those glorious colas form at the periphery of the plant, and the spindly leggy growth that occurs under the outer crown is best pruned away so that more of the plant's energy can be devoted to floral production. Unless you need to reduce the size of the plant for security reasons, such as hiding them from public view behind a screen or wall, it's best to never reduce the height of the colas. This is because THC levels are always higher in untrimmed colas. If you have to cut them, it's recommended that it not be done more than two times per growing season. Unfortunately, a large and damaging misnomer has arisen from this selective pruning practice. The rumor has been widely circulated that removing mature fan leaves will subsequently force the plant to devote more of its energy to cola formation. The fan leaves are the power plant of the marijuana plant. Chlorophyll found in these leaves can and does make its way to floral formation. A good rule to remember concerning growth is: no leaves = no growth = no flowers. The plant basically sets in place if its healthy leaves are removed until new chlorophyll producers (leaves) are developed. In short, it is very counterproductive to trim the healthy leaves from plants. Once leaves turn yellow and can no longer produce chlorophyll, it's okay to pick them off so no more of the plant's energy is devoted to the process of dying, and so that dead leaves do not block the path of precious sunlight to the healthy ones. Arguments that leaf removal allows more light penetration into the center of the plant are true, but with fewer interior leaves to utilize that light and convert it into energy, it's wasted. The last thing a grower should want in a marijuana garden is wasted light. Not allowing photosynthesis to occur because there are no leaves in which it can occur is patently stupid.

Occasionally plants are "limbed up" for better ground-level air circulation within a tightly planted garden, and to keep lower foliage from becoming "mealy" due to water splashed during irrigation or water-soluble fertilization operations. Limbed up shorter plants makes them easier to observe and work with. Lower foliage is of little economic value, so the advantages of "limbing up" plants may be well worth the effort, but be advised, it is far easier to do earlier in the season. Note that all foliage, smaller stems, smaller branches, and anything else to be removed should be crisply cut and *not stripped* from the main plant branches. Stripping rips away the cambium layer and compromises stem strength, as well as leaving a readymade pathway for pests and diseases to become prevalent. Being lazy here can cost the grower a lot later. Patience is the lot of the marijuana grower when shaping the plants in her/his garden.

As the growing season marches on and the day length shortens, to 12 weeks into the season, the plants start setting off flowers, much to the delight of the grower. So far, so good. The halfway mark has been rounded. This is what all the previous effort has been about, and it's an exciting time. However, this is also the time when the most egregious mistakes can be made.

As many growers switch from the high-nitrogen fertilizers of the vegetative phase to the high-phosphorus fertilizers of the flowering stage, the tendency can be to get in a rush and over-fertilize, thus doing more harm than good. In any form of fertilization, always err on the side of caution and use smaller amounts at the lower end of the recommended spectrum. Remember that you can always apply more fertilizer, but it is extremely difficult to flush out or otherwise remove too much fertilizer.

At the onset of flowering most *indica* varieties will mature in six to eight weeks, while *sativa* varieties can take up to twelve weeks. At the onset of flowering most strains enter into what is called "the stretch," where some *indica*s can double in size and most *sativa*s can literally triple in size during a three or six-week period, respectively. The stretch is the best time to be generous with high-phosphorus fertilizers. Shorter day length and cooler nighttime temperatures alert the plants to hurry it up a bit, but nature refuses to be rushed, a hard lesson learned by some *sativa* growers in mountainous locales that who lost out to freezing nighttime temperatures in their race against time and thus lose the entirety of their crop. It is always a wise practice to plant several varieties, as you might lose one or two strains, but it is highly unlikely that you will lose them all.

These plants get in your blood, and the tendency is to worry and fret over them as if they were your children. It's an easy mistake to try to do too much, especially in the area of pruning. A good practice is not to do any form of pruning after Labor Day (around September 3rd). The die is cast within the plant's genetic code. The rush to finish and the insatiable desire to pollinate will push the plants forward to full maturity. Consider the plants to be on automatic pilot. Continue to water and fertilize. Don't change anything in the routine but do proceed gently and with the utmost patience. Now is the time to remember that marijuana cultivation is a marathon, not a sprint. Now is the time to utilize a 30x handheld magnifier to examine the colas for the amount, size, and color of the trichomes on the individual buds. Trichomes are microscopic clear, milky, or amber specialized hairs that develop a mushroom-like ball at their apex. These top bulbs contain the heaviest concentrations of THC, although the stalks are also potent. The more "crystally" the buds and attendant bracts and small leaves appear to the naked eye, the more powerful the pot, if it is harvested at peak potency and handled correctly. The trichomes go from clear, to milky, to amber as they mature. *Sativa*'s are best when the trichomes are half clear and half milky, while the *indica*'s are best when the trichomes are half milky and half amber. Let the trichomes be your guide, not paranoia or impatience in general. Many stellar crops have been downgraded and/or ruined by harvesting too early, rough handling, and improper trimming and manicuring operations. With all the work and worry that went into arriving at this point in time, now is no time to get in a hurry.

Six to four weeks prior to anticipated harvesting, many growers apply a bud hardening and sweetening agent. Arguments abound as to the effectiveness of these, but I can assure you that many of the formulated hardeners from reputable companies can work wonders. In their absence, apply a mild solution of 1 cup of sugar per every 10 gallons of water, or one cup of unstrapped molasses per 20 gallons of water, once every three days. It will dramatically improve the smoothness and taste of the smoke as well as increase bud weight. Try to flush the plants with pure water during the last two weeks prior to harvesting in order to remove any lingering systemic contaminants.

Then comes the harvest, that period of time when the real work begins. No matter what others may claim, trimming and manicuring dispensary-quality cannabis takes an hour per ounce, so it's conceivable that an average of a pound a day can be harvested, if you're willing to work 16 hours a day. Most growers bring in trimmers to help out and accept the risk factor it entail because loose lips can sink ships. Harvest time is rife with treachery, paranoia, and greed, but it also brings profit to defray living expenses and the funding for preparations to grow the next season when the whole laborious struggle starts up anew. Make no mistake about it, marijuana growing is hard work, and trimming time is the hardest and most tedious work of all.

Some growers hang cut colas to dry for a week to ten days and then trim the leaves, separate and manicure the buds, and package the weed. This is a dirty, sticky process best suited to the sadistic. More modern trimming practices include pre-trimming the leaves from the cut colas while they are still green and therefore much more supple. Then the colas are hung for three to five days before "breaking down" the buds and finely manicuring them. The pre-trimming regimen also has the added advantage of cutting just those colas needed for that specific trimming session. Move around the garden from plant to plant, taking a few top and outer colas, and the remaining smaller side colas get a little more time to fatten and ripen their trichomes. Again, fat colas are what the grower most desires. This is biting off only as much as you can chew, and ultimately leads to a more productive harvest yielding better quality bud.

Some growers collect all excess trimmings for the making of hashish, so they are of value, too. An old wives' tale states that hanging the colas upside down causes resin to run into the buds. This simply isn't true; colas are hung upside down because that's the easiest way to dry them uniformly. Further drying, the process known as curing, only occurs if the buds aren't sold immediately, an occurrence that rarely happens if the grower has primo weed. Curing buds in closed glass jars that are "burped" twice daily to release moisture condensation can produce some very smooth-tasting stellar pot. Long-term curing, however, is an endeavor usually reserved for private stock.

This is a business unlike any other business because a grower feels safer when nobody knows they're in business, but in order to conduct business, *somebody* has to know they're in business. It's all a matter of how much time a grower has, and what their tolerance to risk is, and most growers, due to a host of things that can go wrong, want to move their product as quickly as possible. When they're out, they're out, and there's little to do but look forward to next season. However, due to a glut of available weed, prices in "Croptober" can fall dramatically, and some growers will decide to wait it out, knowing that June, July, and August will come, and the laws of supply and demand will smile more favorably upon them. Any grower who doesn't move their product is soon sitting on top of a mound of weed. If rippers failed to steal the crop green, there is a better chance that they will try to steal it processed after the heavy work is done. There's always something. Working, waiting, and worrying define the life of a grower, and the outlaw's life is never as glamorous as it seems.

There are other rewards, however, most relating to the aforementioned botanophilic theory. For many growers, nothing gives them more of a sense of peace and serenity than being in their marijuana gardens on a midsummer's day, worrying over and tending their plants. Prior to state legalization of medical marijuana, very few men knew that joy, although admittedly, fewer men would have wanted to.

In Defense of Outdoor-Grown Marijuana

In their ongoing campaign to smear sun-grown marijuana produced under the great blue sky, as nature and evolution truly intended, the indoor and greenhouse growers have now taken to calling it "dirty pot." I can see why they do it; they have to. Their cost per unit to produce their final end product is so much higher that they want to eliminate any competition, real or imagined. And do they ever apply their imaginations in discrediting outdoor weed. Where the "dirty pot" rap comes from is anybody's guess, but I imagine that there are two main schools of thought. In hot arid areas, there is bound to be a lot of windblown dust, which will stick to the trichomes of unprotected outdoor marijuana. Not that dust in and of itself is unhealthful, and given the standards applied to "bag appeal" in today's market, most of it will be trimmed away from the pretty but definitely overworked buds. Secondly, the indoor growers in particularly don't have as many options in their selection of organic fertilizers, especially fish emulsion and a variety of manures. Dried and pulverized bat guano is popular everywhere, being championed the most by Soma. But greener manures used in compost teas reek to high heaven, while fish emulsion will send applicators scurrying out of the greenhouse or the grow room holding their noses and vowing to never use it again. Outdoors the smell is tolerable, and all but gone in an hour. Also, there is the phobia associated with what, after all, is shit, and if its shit, it must be dirty.

The truth is that most mankind-controlled grows use industrial fertilizers and non-natural pesticides. Neem oil, which is pressed from the seeds of the Indian Neem tree, is deemed organic, and is fine but not particularly effective in large indoor grows, while anything else that's a chemical is just plain bad. Rarely are natural pest control measures applied indoors. The lab coat crowd just can't warm up to anything living doing a better job than they can. They might tolerate cute little ladybugs, but lacewing wasps and menacing-looking praying mantises are just too much for them to bear. So, consumers can rest assured that somewhere in the preponderance of the time necessary to bring a mankind controlled grow to fruition, some unnatural fertilizers and pesticides have been used. The buds, due to aging and flushing techniques, may not test positive for them, but they were used just the same.

The indoor growers love to boast that they are in control of everything and therefore are capable of producing better pot than Mother Nature, but I feel this instinctively, I feel it deep in my bones, that every time mankind tries to improve upon or tweak Mother Nature, the more she comes right back around to prove that she had a better plan all along. Its what mankind isn't aware of that frightens me the most. Just as Big Pharma has to isolate every component of a naturally occurring drug or it's worthless to them, the cannabis control freaks have to isolate every factor of growth, and in so doing promote strains that bend to their will. Other strains with other attributes that could potentially avail themselves in the future are ignored, forgotten about, and eventually culled out of existence. This is natural selection in reverse, and a price will be paid if mankind continues to insist upon these enforced extinctions.

The mankind-controlled growers have short-circuited the evolutionary processes that are evidenced in the fast-disappearing landrace strains of cannabis. Any garden-variety biologist or naturalist will tell you that ecosystems are the healthiest when they display the greatest amount of *diversity*, and because of space limitations and a very controlled maturation timing regimen, most man-controlled grows are a monoculture. One unforeseen pest or disease will wipe the entire population out. Indoor growers almost always opt for indica strains that are shorter and mature more quickly than sativa strains. Crosses between the two strains do produce more hybrid strains, but they are limited in their ability to withstand the elements outdoors so their chances of escaping into the wild and positively contributing to the gene pool are slim indeed. The primary goal of the indoor grower is fast crop rotation. The more harvests per year, the more profitable the entire operation is. They are constantly culling slow-growing stock and cloning the (pardon the pun) early bloomers in an endless quest for rapid growth, but any decent botanist knows that fast growth equates to weak stem tissue, and weak stem tissue, due to the ease of penetration, is far more prone to attack.

When left to her own devices, somewhere, somehow Mama Nature has natural processes at work forming a superior product. It usually takes longer because the evolutionary processes are more complex than ruthless culling, but in the end, she will produce a far more superior climate and soil adapted strain. About the only advantage I can definitely see to growing in enclosed environments comes with the ease with which carbon dioxide can be introduced, because it certainly spurs plant growth. But too much of anything can be a bad thing, and I firmly believe that it will eventually come out that there is some negative consequence associated with this form of environmental enrichment.

The "control everything" crowd likes to say that outdoor marijuana has a heavier smoke, as if that's a bad thing. They like their weed smooth and light, and if that's their preference, they're certainly entitled to it. But to say their type of smoke is automatically better is like saying that Coors beer is better than Heineken. It's all in the taste buds of the beholder. They like to argue that the buds of outdoor weed look rougher which, again, only matters to the worshipers of bag appeal, and again, I personally doubt the potency of pretty over-manicured bud. Smoke it and get high like a real stoner; don't get all jiggy looking at and ogling it like a rank amateur.

The enclosed-environment growers point out that the outdoor grower is at the mercy of the elements. For those in less than perfect environments this is most assuredly true and let me add that there is no such thing as a perfect environment. There's always something, but I'll take my chances, because I'm located one degree in latitude south of and 200 feet lower than Kabul, Afghanistan with infinitely better soil. They have been making it happen for centuries, so I can endure whatever years I have left. Note to readers: if you want me, I'll be in my garden tending my weed. You should be so lucky.

Many advocates for indoor weed claim that indoor growers cure their marijuana better than outdoor growers, simply because it's assumed that nothing ever goes outside. Oh really? It's never transported to a separate trim house? With the space limitations indoor growers have, a lot of the pre-trimming, manicuring, drying, and final cure are done elsewhere. I have a great trim house with three exceptional hang rooms. My office is set up for long sessions, as I become a cola pre-trimming machine during football season. Every experienced trimmer has to have their spot that is specific to their body type and general demeanor. I go in there, shut the door, crank up the game on the television, and everyone knows to leave me the hell alone. Every few hours or so, I call for an associate to come in and get another bucket of trimmed colas to hang while I march out to the garden to collect fresh ones. I have to be driven to stay ahead of four manicurists and single-minded in letting them know that the entire operation is more productive if they can do whatever they can to keep me in that chair.

Some of the pot brokers are the worst of the worst and criticize me for refusing to further break down my beer-can-size buds. They'll say my bags look "stemmy" because every large bud has to be held together by a larger section of base stem. Bullshit. They want those little teeny-weenie buds because that is most typically all an indoor grower can produce, and I know for a fact that my weed is just as good, if not better than theirs, and what the brokers are really trying to do is pass it off as indoor bud based on a misguided and entirely misinformed bag-appeal standard alone.

And the turkey bags some of the brokers insist on; don't get me started. They are no more moisture-proof than high quality Ziplock bags, but they are clearer and shine up the bud better. The Ziplock's are easier to use, stack better, and are much easier to access when it becomes inevitable that the weed needs to be rehydrated. Some of the brokers would use smoke and mirrors if they thought it would make them another nickel. And then there are the bottom feeders who want to buy your trim for next to nothing and reap huge profits with extracts. They always make the point that it has no value to the grower, who simply doesn't have the time or financial wherewithal to mess with such a complicated process. There's bubble-bag hash and heat-pressed rosin, that are natural processes that are about as simple as it gets. What they are referring to is wax and shatter processed with butane, and here again, I would like to see the governor of California outlaw any chemically manufactured extracts. In my humble opinion, they need to be prepared naturally and organically or not at all. When you think about it, the processed ganja movement is defined by two groups: the baby boomers who are returning to weed in droves and the kids who keep pushing the potency envelope to the breaking point. This pretty much mimics the division between outdoor and indoor growers, or the old school versus the new school. The youth are comfortable with unnatural processes, and the old wouldn't dream of using any of them. Know that I hate to be seen as a stubborn old geezer too stuck in his ways to get out of theirs, which will be a moot point soon enough because we boomers will shortly die off, but my biggest fear is that so too will the "better living through chemistry" loving kids if they don't cool it. That would be a real tragedy for the movement because the "No one has ever overdosed on marijuana," argument would go the way of the dinosaur.

    I'm a realist, however. I know that perceptions pervade reality. I know many good marijuana brokers who believe in their hearts that indoor grown is better. The opinion of the marketplace always sets the price, so I don't argue with being paid less for something that is just as good, because I'm not going to lie and pass my bud off as indoor, even though I know I could. For the record, I won't back down from my stance. I'll put my weed up against anyone else's anywhere, anytime and let the chips fall where they may. I'm not infallible or undefeated. I have been beaten on occasion, but always by an outdoor grower.

There is something primal about outdoor growing that goes straight back to that time in history when the majority of mankind opted to go from a hunting/gathering existence to a farming paradigm. The value of the land rose dramatically then, and a man's attachment to it became almost paternal. Take any man or take me for instance; I love the cycle of the seasons, the burst of spring growth, the dog days of summer, the work of the harvest, the rest of the winter. I love the sun biting at my bare back, the smell of the soil, the soft summer breeze. I love the challenge of bucking up in late winter and accepting the challenge of taking on the elements for another year. But most of all, I love the sense of satisfaction of bringing it in, of surviving, and being rewarded for it. The life of the indoor grower seems boring to me. He/she probably works harder than I on balance, and I commend them for doing it, but once they get it down, it's all pretty much the same. One crop rotation spills into another, any lines demarcating the seasons blur; same shit, different day, which day is it, anyway? Outdoors, every season is different, and you remember them all for their distinct characteristics. Diversity, remember? Diversity is what makes the cycle of life go round. The diversity of the seasons makes my heart beat harder for each and every one. I couldn't stand to be cooped up indoors. That would drive me insane, and I can only imagine that it's worse for the plants.

The carbon footprint of indoor marijuana is astronomical in comparison to sun-grown, and the strain it puts on California's third-world electrical grid is becoming enormous. All growers need fluorescent lighting to establish clones or seed stock to get their season or grow rotation kicked off, but that's as much that artificial lighting should stress the electrical grid. I would've liked to have seen Governor Moonbeam, or to now see recently elected Governor McDreamy, step in and decree that all indoor and greenhouse light-deprivation marijuana cultivated for the purposes of harvesting for eventual sale can only be grown using lighting sources strictly dependent upon *solar energy* to power them. That would be a game changer, and I would revel in seeing just how fast the smear campaign against outdoor weed would come to an abrupt end, not to mention the stabilizing effect it would have on dispensary price structures. The carbon footprint would virtually disappear, except that energy which is used to produce the solar panels and operating equipment. All manufacturing produces some carbon as a byproduct; that's unavoidable.

Consider that the sun's natural light spectrum produces more cannabinoids and terpenes, which concurrently increases the plant's potency and taste. All other factors being equal, outdoor weed has tested at least one percentage point higher in THC than its indoor-grown counterpart.

While reading the blogs of indoor growers, an old-school hardhead such as myself must feel like he's been dropped into the midst of a gaggle of mad scientists. It's all about the nutrients, adjust this, tweak that, better living through chemistry. It's like Jefferson Airplane's "White Rabbit" from *Go Ask Alice,* for Christ's sake - how to escape an emergency situation that maybe they shouldn't have ever gotten themselves into in the first place. They all present themselves as experts who don't agree on anything, yet they're all convinced that they're right. That's the meat of it. That's the point I've been floundering to make all along. Successful outdoor growing, above all else, requires preparation, not panicked reaction. The soil is everything; turn it, amend it, worship it, and know that it's the base upon which the entire crop depends. Nutrients are an additional enhancement, nice to have but not essential, and certainly not the be-all and end-all of everything ganja.

I love to allow my plants to achieve their God-given full genetic potential and cheer them on during "the stretch." This is that period of time that ensues after the first flowers appear, usually in early to mid-August when the indicas bolt skyward for four weeks while the sativas do likewise for six or even more. A plant can literally double and occasionally triple in size during the stretch, which I find awe-inspiring, while the indoor and greenhouse growers are shitting their pants for fear of running out of room. Their blogs are rife with desperate cries for someone to tell them how to defeat the cursed stretch as if it is as dangerous as a plague of locusts. It all seems so counterproductive, in a business hysterically driven by the weight of the final end product, to take every measure to slow down the development of that weight due to the lack of room. But that is exactly what they do. They top them, they contort and bend them, they pray fervently to the cannabis gods for the dreaded stretch to come to an end. The sins of the grower's choice of environment are visited upon the plants, and it isn't good. Outdoors, the mantra of growers during the dog days of summer is loud and clear: "Let them grow, let them grow, let them grow!"

The worst of outdoor growing lies in the lack of seclusion. Sure, I feel comfortable in the midst of my crop. I can't see ten feet ahead of me, and because of my enclosure, no one can see in, or so I foolishly allow myself to believe. Then here comes the helicopter. That fucking helicopter! Jesus-God-almighty, I hate that miserable fucking helicopter, and don't they know it. Google Earth can easily reveal what they want to know at far less expense, but the bullies just have to intimidate me and my ilk. Hovering around, making lots of noise, shaking the plants with the wind turbulence from their whirring rotating blades, making the earth beneath my feet tremble almost as much as I do. Go away, helicopter. Leave me alone. The indoor grower has none of that if he can stop the light leaks and filter the smell.

Mankind's relationship with cannabis dates back centuries. Michael Pollen wrote an entire chapter about it in *The Botany of Desire: A Plant's View of the World* (2001). Not only does mankind like cannabis, but cannabis also likes mankind. Greg Green in the foreword to the second edition of his *The Cannabis Grow Bible* (2003) takes the same stance. There are many others who feel the same way; it's not a new point of view. This is figuratively and literally a symbiotic relationship. Each benefit from the existence of the other. Cannabis soothes and delights mankind, while mankind contributes mightily to the perpetuation of the species, which is the primary goal of all life on earth. So, in that sense, all growers are the friend of cannabis, but I like to believe that some growers are even better friends, specifically the outdoor growers.

I will give credit where credit is due and say that all growers owe a debt of gratitude to the indoor cultivators of yore. They kept the movement alive during the dark ages of the Reagan/Bush I reign of terror. Even the great D. J. Short, in his marvelous book *Cultivating Exceptional Cannabis* (2003), and an individual who advocates growing outdoors whenever possible, has a section entitled "The Humble Indoors," because it's what kept him and others going until the laws and the social stigma of being a marijuana smoker changed.

Anyone growing marijuana, either in a hall closet or out in the open on 20 acres, is a member of a select fraternity of mankind. All are trying to somehow, someway improve this plant into whatever their image of botanical perfection is, so let's at least give them all a hand for that. If you love cannabis, you must grow it as the ultimate expression of that love. We are really splitting hairs here in trying to argue which method is the best, because anyone who spends any significant amount of time around this marvelous natural creation comes to deeply revere it. This plant has drawn them in and now has them firmly within its clutches. Who's using who, in the final analysis?

Honesty being the best policy, why do I say that outdoor-grown is better than indoor-grown? Because, just like the indoor grower, I have to.

The Lull

It happens every year when August descends upon me. Approximately two months shy of even beginning the harvest, and six months past when this horticultural journey began, the lull hits. A dictionary definition of this period would suggest a time of calm and repose, a soothing, restful, quiet interval splitting the bustling planting season from the humdrum monotony of the impending harvest. In other words, a time to take it easy, recharge my batteries, and enjoy life in general. It's anything but that for me. The lull is merely a waiting period rife with apprehension which quickly gives way to numbing paranoia. And then the depression sets in. It's hard to get out of bed in the mornings. It's even harder to concentrate on anything. I find myself out in the garden standing among the plants, imploring them to hurry things up a bit. Most of the strains are only in preflower, meaning there's a minimum of ten weeks to go. But the plants appear healthy, which is a testament to all the hard soil-preparation work done in the spring, a successful cloning effort, and the reward for diligent irrigation and fertilization programs. In other words - so far, so good. What could go wrong? *Plenty*.

The work may have abated, but the worry has just begun. The lull is like white noise, like eye floaters. You only notice either when time practically stands still, and during the lull, you have nothing but time.

I can't write. Henry Miller once said, "The surest way to kill an artist is to give him everything he needs." All writers feel that they never have enough time, but the truth is that too much time kills inspiration. It has for me. I am most prolific when I'm under the gun and firmly believe that without stress, nothing gets done. But the stress of the lull is very nuanced. It begets inaction and inactivity. Usually I combat these periods by reading, but the only thing that currently interests me is my stable of books on marijuana growing. I'm perusing them in hopes of unearthing some helpful hints, of being reminded of something I've forgotten that might prove useful. Here is my top baker's dozen:

Cultivating Exceptional Cannabis: An Expert Breeder Shares His Secrets (2003) by D. J. Short. There is no doubt that D. J. Short is an expert breeder of marijuana who has paid mightily for his career aspirations by being forced to live a simple life underground. In a recent interview, he stated that marijuana has always survived underground through decades of vilification and persecution and could easily do so again. Short's book is practical, no nonsense, and above all else, old-school. He possesses exceptional senses of taste and smell, being the creator of his famous "Flavor & Olfaction Chart," which most of the old pros recognize as the gold standard in determining the quality of any given strain. The father of the strain "Blueberry," Short is considered by many to be one of the top, if not the top, marijuana breeders in the world. He advocates a drama-free non-flashy lifestyle as a means of avoiding incarceration for merely doing what we love.

Marijuana Botany: An Advanced Study: The Propagation and Breeding of Distinctive Cannabis (1981) by Robert Connell Clarke. Note the copyright date and know that Clarke was a pioneer, and the consummate botanical professional. It is utterly astounding just how completely he pegged it, even way back then. All the information an outdoor grower would ever need is contained between these covers. A true classic that presents the nomenclature in a scientific manner. Again, science is science, and never the twain shall meet. Clarke's *Hashish* (1998) is also well worth purchasing.

Ed Rosenthal's Marijuana Grower's Handbook (2010) by (you guessed it) Ed Rosenthal. Touted as the, "Official Course Book of Oaksterdam University," this is the book for anyone more prone to reading the captions under the pictures before delving into the actual text. It is beautifully photographed. Similar to D. J. Short and Soma (to be mentioned later), Ed tugs at my heartstrings by recommending growing in soil under natural sunlight as the very best way to realize all the chemical subtleties that marijuana has to offer. He is exhaustive in explaining the importance of light, especially light from manmade sources for indoor growers. I very much admire Ed Rosenthal, who has been around for years, but he lost me with *Beyond Buds: Marijuana Extracts: Hash, Vaping, Dabbing, Edibles, & Medicines* (2014), because if you need butane, or any other chemical to make it, I'm not interested. Organic bud, water-bag hash, and heat-pressed rosin is as far as I'll personally take it. More on the true meaning of "organic" later.

Marijuana Horticulture: The Indoor/Outdoor Medical Grower's Bible (2006) by George Cervantes (aka George Van Patten). It's very complete, well photographed, has helpful diagrams and is logically compiled. By the time he published *The Cannabis Encyclopedia* (2015), Van Patten had apparently come out of hiding by losing that ridiculous black beret and looking his age by letting his white freak flag fly. This book also contains complete information, but the fatal flaw of encyclopedias is that they don't contain a glossary. I'm big on conducting a quick nomenclature review as a way to cram study, and to me, any instructive manual that doesn't contain at least a rudimentary glossary is incomplete.

Organic Marijuana, Soma Style: The Pleasures of Cultivating Connoisseur Cannabis (2005) by Soma (aka [he's apparently not telling]). Soma is a throwback to the peace and love era when heads said it and truly meant it. Weary of ongoing harassment from misguided U.S. law enforcement, he moved to Amsterdam in 1996, where he operates Soma Sacred Seeds. His strain "Lavender" is one of my favorite purples, a very pretty plant. This book is loaded with useful advice, the best of which is probably: "May this book help to make you and our planet greener." Right on, brother.

Marijuana Grower's Insider's Guide (1993) by Mel Frank (aka James J. Goodwin). An expansion upon *Marijuana Grower's Guide* (1978), which was written in conjunction with Ed Rosenthal, this effort was brought out under the masthead of Goodwin's own Red Eye Press. Goodwin also supports outdoor growing and takes exception to the ongoing smear campaign of the indoor growers and their ilk who have now taken to referring to outdoor-grown as "dirty pot." Dirty tricks is more like it.

Marijuana Horticulture Fundamentals: A Comprehensive Guide to Cannabis Cultivation and Hashish Production (2016) by K (aka Kenneth Morrow) of Trichome Technologies. K is another underground cat who has recently surfaced with the relaxation of draconian marijuana laws in what is now the predominance of American states. His lifelong relationship with growing marijuana bore fruit in a three-year period between 1997 and 2000 when K won *nine* California Cannabis Cups. This is a feat that has never been duplicated which has elevated him to legendary status in Northern California growing circles. A thick book of 425 pages, it is a deceptively easy read being broken into several logically organized short sections. The author presents a mighty interesting argument for chopping plants or cutting colas for harvesting at daybreak. Although the author very adequately explains the nomenclature of the trade, a glossary would have put this work up higher on the list.

The Cannabis Bible: The Definitive Guide to Growing Marijuana for Recreational and Medical Use (2010 2nd edition) by Greg Green. Well photographed, good diagrams, good advice, decent glossary, but leans a little too heavily towards indoor growing for my taste. Also, a bible? It's as thick as the Bible, but all these books can't be the definite work, the be-all and end-all of pot growing, and least of all the bible.

Primo Plant: Growing Marijuana Outdoors (1998) by Mountain Girl (aka Carolyn Elizabeth Garcia). She's lived the life. Author Tom Wolfe wrote of her as a teenager as, "a tall girl, big and beautiful with dark brown hair falling down to her shoulders...". Such attributes were sure to open doors in the budding hippie culture. One of Ken Kesey's Merry Pranksters, she became romantically involved with him and bore their child Sunshine in

1966. After a decade-long relationship, she became married to the Grateful Dead's Jerry Garcia in 1981 and divorced from him in 1994. Colorful would hardly describe her journey on planet earth. She now sits on the board of the Marijuana Policy Project. I love the old-school books, and a version of this one first came out in 1976. The 1998 version is simply worded and phobic about composting and organic soil-preparation. The words on the back cover are an affirmation to live by: "Home Grown Is the Best."

Marijuana: Outdoor Grower's Guide (2007) by S.T. Oner. With an emphasis on guerilla growing, this book contains solid advice and foregoes genuflecting at the altar of indoor growing, save for addressing cloning under fluorescent lights, which is far as I go with it. It has a troubleshooting section that has proven useful through the years.

Growing Medical Marijuana: Securely and Legally (2013) by Dave DeWitt. Definitely a beginner's guide, as the wording is exhaustively simple with a layman's approach. Securely and legally? Thank God for the passage of Cali's Proposition 64, and the recent efforts of Senator Cory Booker in proposing the Marijuana Justice Act. But not all states are legal, and not all governing entities in legal states are fair. Nevertheless, it is a helpful work that barely made the list because it lacks a glossary. Shame, shame.

Dank 2.0: The Quest for the Very Best Marijuana Continues: A Breeder's Tale (2001) by Subcool (aka Mobius Dank [yeah, sure]). How cool is the name Subcool? This book is beautifully and lovingly photographed by the author. I generally don't like bud picture books because, honestly, I oftentimes can't tell one strain's buds from another's and seriously doubt most of those who claim to be experts at this form of identification know either. But Subcool is different, with occasional pictures of entire plants and an emphasis on showing enough of some very stellar colas that an experienced grower gets the drift. And besides, I have four of his strains growing in my garden right now. Three are featured in this book. It's the text that I'm enamored with. This man is passionate about his craft and it shows in his attention to detail as he explains the trials and errors it took to bring some excellent strains into the world of high grade cannabis. I also admire the man's honesty when he states that most of the purple strains, on balance, are no more potent than the less colorful ones. Yeah, but they sure are more gorgeous to look at. Subcool readily admits that his "Black Cherry Soda" isn't all that powerful, but it is so beautiful to observe that I want to grow a few next season. Know that for the outdoor grower, next season represents all of life's hopes and aspirations almost within reach. You can garner some solid growing advice from the text, especially concerning the cloning/seedling growing room. Best of all, the glossary provides a very clear view into the breeders' nomenclature.

True Living Organics: The Ultimate Guide to Growing All-Natural Marijuana Indoors (2012) by The Rev (aka [he isn't saying]). You have to have something exceptional to offer to make my list with the word "Indoor" in your book's title, and the Rev does. This book represents a moral and dedicated effort to bring clean, safe pot to the cannabis world. It is also one of the few titles that delves into the subject in any kind of depth. In all fairness, this title could have occurred further up the list save for my bias, but know that most indoor growers have been relentless in disrespecting my outdoor weed, which I would put up against theirs anywhere, any time. If you're serious about growing organically, buy this book and forget about the USDA government website and its definitions, which are less than useless.

All hail the underground breeders who have kept the dream alive for their and my entire lifetimes. Six of these 13 titles are by breeders, most of whom have paid dearly for doing what they believe in. They, more than anyone else, are the true heroes of this movement. Give them their due. Men like D. J. Short, Subcool, Soma, (and probably many of the others) appear to have very evolved senses of taste and smell, which is an attribute that I quite simply do not possess. Besides this obvious shortcoming, I see no advantage in trying to breed marijuana strains because I am now too old, very poor at genetics, too impatient and greedy, and just don't have the space. As I walk my rows, however, I do keep a keen eye out for any mutations that may look like hell but smoke like heaven. That would be the only way that I could ever leave an imprint on the craft of strain creation - clone only, of course.

There's lots of things to mull during the lull. The lull is like *Waiting for Godot,* only it's worse because he will actually show up at the worst possible moment. The lull is the reincarnation of the movie *Groundhog Day,* where everything stays the same no matter what you do to break out of the routine. I have my very worst nightmares during the lull: home invasions, hordes of rabid police descending from helicopters, being held up at gunpoint, having my throat slit in my sleep. Idle time only strengthens the gripping fear that's inherent in a business rampant with paranoia. And, as is often said, just because you're paranoid, doesn't mean that they aren't out to get you.

When the governing entity outlaws the sale of weed under any circumstances, life becomes an iffy proposition for the local grower, for it becomes in no way unclear that what he is doing is deemed illegal on his property, even though everyone else in the state seems to get a hall pass. Local law enforcement knows full well that if you're growing, you're selling, because no one could personally smoke that much marijuana. When imbued with the knowledge that today could well be the last day of your freedom, that you could easily be cuffed and carted away on the whim of a nosey and/or vengeful complaining neighbor, it's hard to stay on an even keel. Sleep is kind, sleep is your friend. You wish you could sleep straight through the harvest, but you know that you can't. So, you try to tune it out. You rationalize that others in your neck of the woods are growing far larger quantities than you are, that you're not connected to any criminal element, that law enforcement really doesn't want small potatoes such as yourself. Knowing that they have bigger fish to fry is comforting. Everybody you know in this business tells you that they are not afraid, but these are the same people who scatter like cockroaches when a helicopter hovers overhead.

The outdoor grower dedicated to his craft intimately understands the rhythm of life; the ebb and flow, the yin and the yang of it all. Every season is different, with some being most definitely better than others. When you grow outdoors, nature will remind you that she has the upper hand. She does nothing for your convenience. Some seasons are abysmal when everything seems to go wrong, and what's worse is that half the time you don't even know why. Panic can set in with every unexplainable yellow leaf that seemingly appears overnight, and it's disquieting to know that you're just as likely to misdiagnose a suspected nutrient deficiency as to get it right. When your entire livelihood depends on your decision making, the last thing you want to do is overreact to problems, but conversely, no reaction can easily spell disaster. Bad seasons are often a balancing act between bad and worse. Other seasons, the plants take off as if exploding from the sound of a starting gun, and they seem to have a mind of their own as they aggressively bolt skyward. You never know how a season is actually going to go until you are in the midst of it, and with outdoor growing, there are no do-overs. You deal with events as they present themselves, and are forced to live with every bad move and bad decision you make, and you must endure any stroke of bad luck that befalls you.

So, with time on your hands during the lull, you turn to the plants themselves to reveal the answers. They are not mean-spirited, and they have never knowingly let you down. But you know in your heart that being nice to the plants by talking sweetly to them or playing soothing music for them only amounts to so much bullshit. With animals, the term is anthropomorphism, which is the belief that they can think and talk like humans. This accounts for all the baby talk we humans direct towards our pets. If only they actually could speak, I can only imagine that they would tell us to shut the fuck up and give them some peace and quiet. There's no term (yet) for the application of human traits to plants, but most assuredly most growers do. Let me propose to coin the term botanomorphism, logic be damned. In reality, the only legitimate explanation is that such behavior positively affects the mindset of the humans in such a way that they become more attentive to the needs of the plants. Science is science, and old wives' tales such as "plant on a waxing moon and harvest on a waning moon" hold little water in the grand horticultural scheme of things. Either the trichomes plump up and turn color under the microscope, or they don't, and that's that. Acceptance of the vagaries of nature can be an outdoor grower's biggest virtue. At least it keeps you from going insane.

But the boredom of the lull also causes you to analyze those hard years of the past, those years when worry accompanied you right out of the gate, and each plant lost or otherwise compromised portended a diminished harvest. Every mistake made in the spring would exact its revenge in the fall by adding time to the harvest window; so much time, in fact, that an early freeze sometimes made harvesting a moot point. Those were the years of no sweet anticipation. Those were the years heavy with anticipatory anxiety, which quickly transformed into a self-fulfilling prophecy of hardship and ongoing suffering. So, if it makes you feel better to talk to your plants, if it eases your troubled mind, by all means, have at it brothers and sisters, and Godspeed.

The lull is a barely audible annoying hum that you just can't ignore, much like low-grade tinnitus. Chinese water torture is less persistent. You finally give in to it by questioning everything you've done so far and everything you're about to do. Nowhere is this more evident than in second-guessing your fertilization schedule. The only antidote to this lack of sureness and confidence is the value of experience, and experience in this business teaches you that there is no substitute for patience. Think of safe fertilization as akin to safe driving, where nothing is abrupt, every motion and reaction is smooth and steady, and attention is paid to the subtle nuances that surround you - traffic signs for drivers and the plant's general disposition for growers. Gradually up the nutrient dosage to these botanical junkies over time and they will reach higher and higher.

I'm no rocket scientist, but there is some basic math that occurs with fertilization. Maintain the soil pH at between 6.3 and 6.8. There are 3 teaspoons to a tablespoon and 39 teaspoons or

13 tablespoons to a cup, so call it 40 teaspoons when mixing into 20-gallon containers, and each quarter dose equates to 5 gallons. If an additive says to use a half teaspoon per gallon, that's .5 times 20 or 10 teaspoons - a quarter cup. When in doubt, err towards a lower dosage. You can always up it later, but you can never get it out once it's in the soil.

Other helpful math for later in the season is that 20 $50.00's = $1,000.00, 50 $20,00's = $1,000.00, 100 $10.00's = $1,000.00, 200 5.00's = $1,000.00, and if you don't know how many hundreds equal a thousand, I can't help you.

While we're at it, know that one of the most common misnomers in this trade is that an ounce weighs 28 grams. Not so. An ounce weighs 28.5 grams, which means the magic number for a pound (28.5 x 16) is 456 grams. If this seems like splitting hairs, consider that the difference in an overall pound is 8 grams, or slightly over a quarter ounce, which is something that matters to me.

The lull causes you to doubt yourself. I fret over whether I am absolutely, without a doubt, growing 100% organic. Am I unknowingly lying to my customers? I certainly don't want to, but Jesus-God-almighty - am I? I don't trust any fertilizer manufacturer who claims to be organic, and most, like Springsteen's poets down in "Jungle Land," say nothing at all. But I have to know. It would be hard to live with myself if I caused someone harm by putting something I grew in their body. I don't want that rap, that reputation, or that karma. So, I've used the time that the lull provides to do the research, and I can tell you this: it's spotty at best. When in doubt, let nature make the call by utilizing one of the humblest of all her creatures - the common earthworm. Like frogs, earthworms are a key indicator species because the outer skin that encases their organs is poikilothermic, which means their body temperatures fluctuate with the rising or falling temperatures of their surrounding environment. These skins are also quite sensitive to toxins, which explains why the earth has lost half or 2,000 of its 4,000 known amphibian species in just the last 50 years. Ditto for earthworms, who also respire through their skins. If their immediate environment is not conducive to their well-being, they die off quickly. I actually take a handful from my earthworm bin and put them in soil prepared with a fertilizer I'm considering using. If they die, I know all I need to know about just how "organic" their fertilizer really is, despite what the manufacturer says on their label. So, what is truly organic? A grower can feel relatively comfortable if a product displays the OMRI (Organic Materials Review Institute) label. To be 100% sure, you have to limit products to those exclusively being made from either plant or animal parts. This is a short list, I know, but there's solace in knowing that it's a safe one.

Organic growing doesn't just apply to the soil; there's also the above-ground foliage to consider. Avoid chemical pest control like the plague. Instead turn to the living animals themselves. Lady Bugs and Lace Wing Wasps are beneficial and industrious little creatures with which to thwart infestations of annoying thrips and/or the dreaded spider mite. Always remember that the highest mammal (or so we like to think), man, can utilize his opposable thumb and index finger on either hand to crush grasshoppers and caterpillars.

Much like football in the NFL, there is no off season for the serious outdoor grower anymore. Players stay in shape pretty much the year round, and likewise, there is always something that needs the grower's attention: the mother plants in the clone room, the ever-expanding compost pile, the readying of the hang rooms, and the search for trustworthy clients for the impending harvest to replace those who ripped you off last season. But the lull causes you to be lazy. I try not to be drawn into the false sense of security that it instills. Some growers get complacent, and complacency always kills passion. It's easy to fall into the trap because the plants appear healthy and there's at least two months' time before starting the finish and the critical flush. But problems can and do rear their ugly heads in the form of branch-breaking late summer hailstorms, dust devils that spiral directly into your garden as if they had it out for you, and, worst of all, the dreaded *botrytis* or evil gray mold. This fungus is a true masochist that prefers to show up two weeks before harvest, and if not detected and physically cut away from the plants, it can wreak devastation in a matter of days. Wildfire has nothing on botrytis, and even that has happened up here on the high chaparral, as some unattended guerrilla grows have been destroyed by them. So, despite the apparent calm of the lull, I worry. *I worry a lot!*

And then there's the fear of the rippers. Those loathsome motherfuckers who are only too willing to take from the sweat of another man's brow. You can hire security, but you have to pay them, and with the ever-increasing numbers of amateur rippers, you have to bring them in by early September at the first sign of tightening colas, to guard against the thieves don't know that the plants aren't yet ready. All they know is that it is better to strike early rather than late because this is the time when their marks are least expecting it. Bud quality matters not a whit to them, or any other kind of quality for that matter. Honor amongst thieves? Give me a break. If they had any honor, or decency whatsoever, they wouldn't be in the line of work they're in.

This year is the hottest year on record. It's hotter than last year, which was hotter than the year before, which was then the hottest year on record. It's been a long hot summer with no end in sight. The plants are sucking up more liquid than a fraternity beer bash. A few years back, the well's pump went out, and I really had to scramble, hauling in water procured from other generous growers to keep the plants marginally going until I could afford to get it fixed. My biggest worry? What if the well went dry? No pump in the world could save me then. I march about the property looking for hose leaks, dripping faucets, and waterline breaks like one of the Royal Canadian Mounties determined to get their man. It's just plain immoral to waste water in an arid region, yet I fear that I could be. The steaming hot days of the lull are no time to take minutes off the irrigation controller. In raised rows, composed of well-drained soil, it is almost impossible to overwater marijuana. The plants seem to be saying, "Bring it on!" Botanomorphism, remember? Why tempt fate? They seem to be liking their environment, and until the daytime temperatures start to routinely settle into the mid-eighties, I'm afraid to do anything that might upset them. There's no doubt about I; the plants are in charge, the plants rule my life. They dictate to me, and not the other way around. Good thing I like plants better than people.

On those nights when I don't have nightmares, the plants are forefront in my dream state. I walk the rows, trying to mentally calculate when they will be ready for the harvest and just what the all-important harvest weight will be. But they can be sneaky. Some are in no hurry to leave the comfortable confines of preflower mode. Others seem to have figured out how to grow even slower than last season. Poetic justice, I suppose. I won't let them breed and fulfill their true purpose in life, so why should they make any effort to accommodate me? With me waiting with bated breath to chop them down and grind their woody carcasses to sawdust, why would they be in any hurry to meet their fate? That's the worst of the lull - the plants take their sweet time in leaving it behind. Their halcyon days truly are the summer, and it seems that they are well-aware of it. But gradually, the days will shorten and photoperiodism will rule over them. As August dwindles, the hint of fall wafts on the early morning breeze, telling me that, come the harvest, I'll be busier than a one-legged man in an ass-kicking contest. A genuine sadness begins to hang over the garden that even seems to affect the plants themselves, because the cycle of their lives will soon come to an end. This is only to be followed by a new cycle of life next season, which will only bring another depressing lull for me to have to deal with.

The Last Harvest

In the event that I am fortunate enough to see my follow-up marijuana book, entitled: *California Crazies: The Former Lives and Deaths of Outlaw Pot Farmers (2022)* make it to publication, and assuming that the federal laws do not significantly change in my favor, then the 2014 growing season will be my last. I do not wish to receive the same treatment as Tommy Chong did in 2003 when his home was raided as part of "Operation Pipe Dreams" and "Operation Head Hunter," which was overseen by then U.S. Attorney for the Western District of Pennsylvania, Mary Beth Buchanan. The rap against Chong was that he was an accessory to illegal activities by financially backing his son's marijuana paraphernalia business, which primarily sold bongs over the internet under the company masthead of "Nice Dreams," which was a takeoff on comedy team Cheech and Chong's third feature-length movie, released in 1981. Chong's involvement in "Nice Dreams" quickly turned into a hellish nightmare when he was forced to plea-bargain and plead guilty to one count of conspiracy and accept a sentence of 9 months in Federal Prison, as well as being fined $20,000.00 and losing another $103,500.00 in forfeitures, in lieu of seeing his son and his wife stand trial with the certitude of prison sentencing. The autobiographical and surprisingly well-written *The I Chong: Meditations from the Joint* (2006) put the extreme pettiness of this witch hunt, which cost $12,000,000.00 and involved 2,000 officers, into perspective when Chong wrote:

Cheech knew, as I knew, that this was the government's payback for all the Cheech and Chong movies that ridiculed the hypocrisy of the government's War on Drugs (p. 102).

That Chong was the target and sacrificial lamb of this dragnet is hard to deny, considering that none of the other 55 people indicted received any significant jail time (more than 30 days). Glory-mongering Bush Two Administration Republication appointee Mary Beth Buchanan made national news once again on December 6th, 2008 by announcing her refusal to step down, which was a common courtesy that all of the other 92 Republican U.S. Attorneys extended the incoming Democratic Obama Administration. The gall and abuse of power of law enforcement directed towards the laws and the political entities they are supposed to represent knows no bounds, and any marijuana grower who isn't perpetually high knows with a finality that if they really want to get you, *they will get you*. And those they want to get the most are those with the audacity to question their omnipotent power. Enough said, and my last harvest looms with the paradoxical emotions of excitement and foreboding.

An example of this type of foreboding was amply displayed in the early spring of 2014 when I penned this lament, entitled:

The Accused:

On a high plateau nestled within Southern California's interior foothills, a beleaguered old man goes about tending his marijuana garden. At 9:00 a.m., the late May sun has already got some bite, and even at 4,000 feet in elevation, it tells him that it is going to be a long hot summer. There is much to worry about - the law, the rippers, the elements, and the Puritanical views of society in general. Twelve days ago, California Child Protective Services (CPS) took three of his lover's grandchildren away. Her oldest daughter, age 34, an avowed crystal meth addict, had run her mouth, and now he's being accused of child endangerment by virtue of the fact that he smokes and grows marijuana, and domestic abuse by virtue of the fact that such seems likely in the eyes of his accusers. He admits to the former, and vehemently rejects the latter. The fact that he can become vehement about anything, as old as he is, must be a sure sign of instability, because all the fight should have been kicked out of him a long time ago. His lover advises him not to worry because nothing bad is likely to happen; or so says she, the one who seems not to notice that bad things are happening to them all the time. They got two of the three children back within a week at a placement hearing, but that's not the end of it, not by a long shot. There's a custody hearing in three weeks, and the biological parents (two fathers and one mother) could well lose their children, and thus his lover lose her grandchildren, one of whom she's cared for his entire seventeen years upon this earth. It's just not fair, he knows, but latent resentments have boiled over into daily arguments, the upshot of which is that they may forever separate, after 21 years, for the good of the grandchildren, to say nothing of the good of Puritanical society. He had worked his fingers to the bone to provide for her, her three daughters, and three of her eight grandchildren, but all for naught. Current events have dictated that he's a bad influence, a bad person, and just bad in general.

As this bad guy weeds the rows and fastens rapidly growing root stock to lodge-pole pine stakes, he wonders how he has arrived at this sorry state of affairs. He kicked the mother of the children out last July, having had enough of her hard drug abuse, laziness, child neglect, and belligerent attitude. In rage, she did what all drug addicts do: claiming righteous indignation and questioning who was he to judge her, for he was a "pothead," a lowly low-life pothead who was no better than her. He didn't see it that way, for he was supporting the lot of them, worked sunup to sundown, had never used cannabis in the presence of the children, and at that time hadn't smoked any pot for well over three months. She stated she would turn him in, which seemed rather odd, for without him her children would be homeless. The incident took place on July 3rd, and the next day, the Fourth of July, a *national holiday, the County police helicopter that had flown over his garden at least three times during each of the previous four growing seasons flew into the valley from the southwest, came to and then hovered directly over his garden, and then left the way it came without stopping to observe any of the dozen other marijuana gardens in the area. It was obvious to him that she had turned him in, although all involved denied it; but just his specific garden? On the Fourth of July, no less? No arrests were made.*

The old man liked to assume that law enforcement had deemed his medical marijuana collective state-legal because he had jumped through all the hoops, dotted all the i's, and crossed all the t's, gotten a state seller's permit, gotten a business permit, paid taxes, suffered through County environmental compliance inspections, and prayed to Jesus of Nazareth for clemency. He knew that California's medical marijuana laws, and the growing of source material, were an iffy proposition, more or less leaving anyone accused at the mercy of the arresting officer, and thereafter, dependent upon the beneficence of the presiding judge - if worse ever came to worst. Normally it didn't, unless someone lodged a complaint, and he knew who that someone was. Now, less than a year later, she was at it again, trying to get the only man within her immediate family who could support her kids arrested for being a pothead. Hatred runs rampant in the world of the chagrined drug addict, and logic has no boundaries.

He had already been at this for four months: prepping the soil, setting the gopher cages, pounding the stakes, spreading the mulch, acquiring the clones, fixing the enclosure, planting, irrigating, fertilizing, weeding, ad infinitum. And the real work hadn't even begun. At last year's harvest time he had sat in a trimming chair for fourteen hours a day, seven days a week, for three straight months. He pulled them out of their most pressing debt, yet here it was again, pressing in upon him again. He wouldn't sue over the character assassination that had befallen him. He didn't have the money, the heart, or the vindictiveness to pursue it. Vengeance is a young man's game, survival an old man's. He stopped often, the cold numbness of the reality rapidly closing in upon him in sharp contrast to the warming sun. The early summer breeze promised forgiveness of a sort, but he suspected that such wasn't going to come. Not now. Not this time. Domestic abuse? *He had never lifted a hand to anyone. He shouted when angry, pouted when ignored, but domestic abuse? That was like saying he was a bully, a thug, an asshole to be sure. In his mind, he kept saying over and over -* it's over. *His 63rd birthday was tomorrow, June first.*

He worries constantly; the alopecia areata was back, and hair was falling out in a concentric circle halfway down the back of his head. His normally long hair, his "freak flag," couldn't hide the bald spot because he had cut it to curry the favor of the court before the last hearing. His stomach hurt constantly. He had written in a recent poem that when you're old you piss thumbtacks and shit battery acid, and he was doing that at all hours of the night. Sleep was elusive. A pounding headache was commonplace, and he simply couldn't stop the constant playing and rewinding and replaying of the negative tapes inside his head. Everything that was bad in his life, every mistake he had ever made, every stupid embarrassing thing he had ever done played out in his mind, over and over again. The depression was stifling. When they take the kids out of your home, that's like saying, "You're the worst parent ever." And of all the "parents" involved, he wasn't even a parent, but of all the responsible adults, as has previously been determined he was the bad guy - the worst of the worst. Domestic abuse? He couldn't abuse anyone anymore if they weren't here, and soon, he suspected, they wouldn't be. Everything he had worked for over the last two decades was all for naught. Picking up and staring over at 63. Happy birthday to me, *he thought,* happy birthday to me.

The old man wondered if he would be forced to tear out his crop, go to jail, leave his property, and suffer even more humiliation simply because he was attempting to support those who apparently resented him for doing it. A conviction would mean losing his social security and the revocation of his landscape architectural registrations and seven state contracting licenses. Aside from a meager income from this nonprofit collective, they were his only avenues to income post-2008's financial meltdown. Every year it got a little worse until he could no longer accept the colloquial term "economic recession," and called it what it was to him: This Next Great Depression. He looked for other work, quickly discovering that nobody wants to hire an old guy. He determined to stick to his guns. If this crop wasn't going to make it to harvest, it wasn't going to be because of him. Let them *cut it down, and tack on even more jail time in punishment for his defiance, if that's what his accusers chose to do.*

He was sick and tired of these self-appointed moral compasses that have surrounded him and levied their accusations at every turn. He had heard their accusations his entire life, most of them starting with, "You don't know," escalating to, "You don't know shit." Shit being the pinnacle one could hope to achieve in the pursuit of knowledge and the enactment of career aspirations. "You don't know how to behave." "You don't know how to write." "You don't know how to draw." "You don't know shit about being a landscape architect." "You don't know shit about being a husband." "You don't know shit about being a parent." "You don't know shit about building swimming pools." "You don't know shit about growing weed." His true character flaw was that he didn't know shit about not listening to their shit. No matter, he had wanted out for some time now.

The America that he thought he knew something about in his younger years, because he at least knew how to read, and was able to comprehend what he read, no longer seemed to be the America defined by its own Constitution and Bill of Rights. *The First, Fourth, and Fourteenth Amendments seemed to be violated by government and law enforcement with impunity. The Fifth Amendment received a lot of media play, but accusers in general seemed to give it only token credence. It was in these words, "presumed innocent until proven guilty," where most of the old man's confusion lie. He knows that those exact words never appear in the* Constitution, *but rather occurred as part of a Supreme Court decision (Coffin v. United*

States) in 1895. The premise of the "presumption of innocence" concept is generally attributed to be an unwritten tenant of English Common Law, and to its credit, the court traced it all the way back to Ancient Rome and Greece. The old man felt he was innocent of what most of his accusers levied upon him, but he also knew that while the burden of proof rested with them, they couldn't care less.

He also now knows that CPS lies, cheats, and switches facts and testimony around to the area where it will do the accused the most harm. They are sneaky, underhanded, and willing to do anything to win, and it's all about winning to them, despite what they mouth about, "For the good of the child." It's a game to them, and the money and the power lies with them. Rich parents rarely lose their kids, but poor parents frequently do. Victory is achieved when they take children out of their parents' or grandparents' home. The old man knows that he is caught up in yet another war on the poor. They have to somehow defend themselves, or anything goes.

The old man is well aware that the legitimacy of the marijuana garden he so diligently tends is based on a "states' rights" argument that has always crumbled everywhere else every time the DEA struts in. His saving grace to date has been that he is small potatoes, has tried to keep his nose clean, and has tried to abide by the "rules," however vaguely defined they seem, and such as they are. Now, he knows that someone is always opposed to what he does, and he has been stupid to raise his voice in his own home. His accusers have won, not so much because they are right, but because he is simply too worn out and tired to fight. If family history, and genetic proclivity hold true, he has ten years left to live and would prefer not to spend any inside a jail cell. But that isn't up to him - the accused.

Shortly after writing this, on June 5th, 2014, I watched the *CMT Country Music Awards* marveling at the glorification of alcohol. It seemed that about half of the performances featured songs about free and breezy recreational drinking, getting drunk on airplanes, or "boys from around here" guzzling cold beer, driving four wheelers about and tearing up the environment, and raising hell just for the hell of it. The crossover into rock is now over two decades old, and country music no longer remotely resembles anything having to with the great George Jones. It got me to thinking about what the performances would have looked like, and what the songs would have been about, if pot were legal, in the event that Carter wouldn't have tucked in his balls and spooked back in '78. The gag order on marijuana promulgated by Anslinger, Nixon, Reagan, Bush One, and his dim-witted kid has done weed and our society a complete disservice. I like to think the musical message wouldn't have been so, "Aw, fuck it, let's drown our misery in booze, and who gives a damn anyway? We're good ole' socially irresponsible redneck boys, ready to fight at the drop of a hat, quit our jobs, and call up our ex-old-ladies and tell them to go to hell to boot." With all the pissing, and bitching, and moaning I hear from fine upstanding whiskey pounding conservatives about protecting "the children" from the evils of marijuana, there doesn't appear to be much thought given to these hell-raising alcohol fueled social vignettes of men acting like boys and women acting like that's perfectly acceptable and highly sexy virile behavior. Pot smokers at least like to tell other pot smokers to take it easy, watch out for the law, take into account the feelings of others, and be cognizant of their surroundings because there just might be something wrong:

It's nature's way of telling you something's wrong / It's nature's way of telling you in a song / It's nature's way of receiving you / It's nature's way of retrieving you / It's nature's way of telling you / Something's wrong / It's nature's way of telling you in a breeze / It's nature's way of telling you, dying trees / It's nature's way of receiving you / It's nature's way of retrieving you / It's nature's way of telling you / Something's wrong

Spirit: "It's Nature's Way" *The Twelve Dreams of Doctor Sardonicus* (1970).

In a nutshell, what's wrong for me are these feelings of extreme envy, bordering on contempt, that I feel towards alcohol and those who so blatantly get to attach its effects to "what partying is really all about." That's not my idea of a good time. I often privately go off and get high at square parties just so I can feel like I fit in, or not to feel so grotesquely out of place; but inevitably the evening wears on, and the worshippers of alcohol get sloppier by the minute, and I have to wonder why I'm even there. I make every attempt not to look down on them, knowing that I wish I could hold my liquor, as if they would ever be willing to extend me the same courtesy. At my own previous parties, before I basically went underground, I provided some alcohol or made it BYOB (bring your own booze) and I always provided primo weed. Still, I was not immune to the disparaging glances I would receive from many of the drinkers, aghast at my openly doing something illegal. I'm jealous alright. Jealous that they get to look down upon me for making far less of an ass of myself than they are making of themselves, and yet the law dictates that I'm the one who's in the wrong. It's enough to make me a loner, and good riddance to them, say I.

    I upped the garden's nitrogen intake through the month of June and the marijuana plants shot up like the weeds they are. The separate vegetable garden was progressing so that, if nothing else, I knew we would eat through the last quarter of 2014. The parental custody hearing in late June wasn't good for the parents (it was continued), but the grandmother kept the kids, and kept her resolve to nurture them here with me. I admired that, stayed in the background, and helped out where I could.

    I let the garden rest for two weeks after the summer solstice (June 21) and in early July started to hammer it with high-phosphorus organic fertilizer. For the plants, that is the time when the real work begins, and they certainly appeared to be up for it. The dog days of summer had Stella, my constant canine companion, and Max, the garden guard dog, lying in the shade of an old Elm tree inside the garden enclosure. They whimpered for me to get out of the hot sun and come rub their bellies. At least somebody had some common sense around here. I'd been taking in the Showtime Network's environmental series *Years of Living Dangerously* and it was scaring the bejesus out of me. Primarily about climate change, the series content didn't bode well for the grandchildren. But again, I'd be dead before it got really bad. Better to concentrate on that which I could control, as if I was really in control of anything at all - these plants ruled my life; they did the dictating, and I catered to their every whim - which was the ultimate manifestation of botanophilic feelings playing out on a daily basis.

After the morning garden work, I'd go into my studio to write, and despite what is said about marijuana and creativity, I must admit that it has never worked that way for me - Sly Stone's "different strokes for different folks," I suppose. I never smoked while I was writing, because I presume a minimum level of dedication to my craft. In the early days of my landscape architectural career (I still couldn't believe it was over) I would smoke during marathon late-night to all-night drafting sessions, but that was when I was doing drone-like repetitive work, and it relieved the oppressive boredom. I never smoked when I was designing, not wanting to in any way impede the flow of creative juices. So, I was pretty square in some regards, and even I could see that I was controlling. The last thing I would ever want to be out of control would be myself. In recent years, when I smoked weed, I smoked *hard*, the origins of the nickname "Old Leather Lungs." But I did it in private, and I *never* drove. During the harvest, it was different; it was a lot like my early drafting days, doing lots of tedious repetitive work while sitting in a drafting chair hunched under a drafting lamp. The more things changed, the more they stayed the same. Then I got stoned all day long at two-hour intervals and let the television play in the background. NFL football is a perfect spectator sport while trimming; all you have to do is look up every forty seconds; the crowd noise tells you when to do it. Trimming is a penance.; there's just no other way to look at it. It's never fun, but it can be made tolerable. I deal with it the way marijuana deals with my pain. I just get my mind off of how long the ordeal is going to last, and I'm off and running. I try to tail off smoking by the Super Bowl and stop entirely by April in preparation for the next planting season. The next crop is always looked upon with anticipation, bordering on joy. I wrote about this sensation in another recent poem: *Summer will come / And things will be better, you'll see / The soft gentle kisses of life / Will waft upon the evening breeze.*

Mid-August arrived, apparently determined to punish me with impunity. Then came the colas, fatter with each passing day. The excitement built; so, did the paranoia. The plants needed to be wired up higher on the lodge-pole pine stakes, as an unexpected blast from an errant wind, or worse yet, a violent late summer hailstorm, could've wrought havoc. That's happened before, and stems have split, while their top-heavy colas drooped to the ground. The will of this plant to live is utterly amazing, and so long as the stems didn't break entirely, I was able to rejoin them and wrap them in duct tape, and then with proper staking and wiring they would make it to season's end. I learned my lesson, however, and the old idiom, "A ounce of prevention is worth a pound of cure," rules in the garden now. Some growers don't bother to stake plants at all, feeling that they get enough product off the plants that muddle their way through. These, "plant 'em, forget 'em, and take whatever happens" guys are usually the ones doing the least amount of work and are the ones willing to accept the most amount of dumb luck if it smiles upon them. Sometimes their entire crop makes it to harvest unimpeded; most times it doesn't. With all the preparatory work I do, however, I'm unwilling to leave the final outcome to chance. If I lose just one plant, usually to determined gophers, despite my best efforts to repel them, it literally makes me sick. All of my "girls" deserve the right to shine, and when they don't, I take it personally. It has never been any different in any of my other professional endeavors, and what outdoor growers need most in order to quell the constant criticism of indoor growers is a heightened level of professionalism.

During the last two weeks of September, I stopped all fertilization, trying to flush the plants of that which had already been applied. Twice-weekly applications of black strap molasses dramatically improves the taste of the buds and increases bud weight as well. The sugar literally bleeds out onto the leaves, giving them a characteristic shine. We were getting close, very,

very close. There were more yellow leaves to pick off because the plants were starting to slow down their vegetative growth process. Some helpers have called it "de-yellowing" the garden. No helpers this year. The de-yellowing was tedious, and I had ample time to daydream while conducting it. As I sat there sweating in the hot sun, worrying about last-ditch gopher attacks and the such, I asked myself how a man of my credentials had allowed himself to apparently gravitate to a career that would not have required even just one of these said credentials? In truth, I didn't gravitate I ascended to an intellectual place in which I accepted the fact that I am who I am, and anything done to suppress that fact would indeed shorten my lifespan through the internal stress of knowing I was being a phony, a shill, a pawn, and a pretender. What's more, I lived that life for years, and now regret that I wasn't more of an individual rather than less. Underneath it all, I was always a rebel, if not vocally, at least by some actions that, even if no one else noticed or cared about them, had some meaning to me.

At Washington State University it was immediately impressed upon me that the only people who mattered were the Greeks. They hoarded the foxiest girls on campus and had rules in place whereby any one of them that strayed an independent's way would be ostracized, and worse yet, burdened with a reputation. So, like Morrison's "back door man," I had some precursors to what is now referred to as a "booty call," swearing secrecy and to never talk to said objects of said booty calls in public. The whole thing seemed stupid and ridiculous, which pretty much explains what I mostly feel about most rules. During the age of disco, which characteristically arrived three years late in Phoenix, I refused to pay the $250.00 bi-annual club membership fee to instantaneously be let in the side door of the hottest club in town, opting instead to wait two hours in line in the sweltering heat of a midsummer's evening before getting in through the front door with the rest of the regular (that is to say not special) people. I have always instinctively railed against any form of exclusivity, and that trait has cost me mightily, especially among the golf/country club set that I eventually wound up catering to. I just couldn't seem to hide my disdain for their haughty exceptionalism, primarily because, in most of them, I couldn't see anything exceptional at all. Now I know, in the upper crust of society, that those who go along to get along usually do very well, but I hate that rule almost as much as I hate those who enforce it.

The biggest portion of my contempt is reserved for design review committees peopled by individuals who typically use them for their own personal gain. I understand the concept behind country club guidelines, design standards, et al, and I accept that there has to be some format in place to assure a minimum level of quality and establish a desired look and feel for any given community. Typically, what results, however, is that everything winds up being just like everything else. The fear that someone will stray too far from the herd leaves nothing distinctive within the herd. What I can never accept are the opinions of those who feel that if I don't do something exactly like they would do something, then what I do has no merit. Design review committees are set up to enforce standards for a reason, but they quickly turn into a good old boys network run by the buddy system and fueled by favors. Much of what I felt was my best work was watered down or eliminated due to fears that someone was going against the grain. I didn't violate any expressed standard, but someone in the herd just didn't like that what I was doing was different, and so they reeled the design in to their realm of conformity, and in so doing virtually assured that no greatness would be given a chance to manifest itself under their watch. The membership of these committees reminds me very much of academia in that they hold as a primary objective the desire to protect their own. I hated it so much that I wanted out by my forty-fifth birthday but couldn't afford to leave. The financial meltdown of 2008, which occurred when I was 57, finally gave me an out. I surrendered 75% of my business to a younger associate willing to put up with this constant castration of individuality, and I now sit in this garden, sweating and happy to have gotten out before the nuanced conformity of these glorified boy's clubs finally killed me.

I laugh at the square research, which is about as unscientific as it comes, and always attempts to discredit marijuana. Most of these "professionals" have never smoked a joint in their lives, although they are quick to claim that marijuana smoke is roughly three times as carcinogenic as cigarette smoke. I'll grant them two times as bad, knowing that *all smoke* is carcinogenic and that cigarette smokers are still behind the eight ball because the majority of them smoke a pack of 20 cigarettes a day while a heavy cannabis user rarely would smoke more than four joints a day. Anyone seriously worried about this could always opt for a vaporizer that heats marijuana to the point where its fumes can be inhaled without any smoke. The true marvel of marijuana lies in its synergistic cocktail of chemicals, some of which act as a system of checks and balances to others. People want to smoke THC to get high, and that smoke admittedly contains at least as many carcinogens as tobacco smoke. However, that smoke also delivers CBD's which counteracts the damage done by the smoked THC. In other words, marijuana has a propensity to be self-correcting. One thing is bad, but another thing counteracts it. There is also the issue of what happens when marijuana smoke versus tobacco smoke reaches the lungs. Mitch Earleywine, Ph.D. contributes a chapter entitled *Pulmonary Harm and Vaporizers* to Julie Holland, M.D.'s marvelous book entitled *The Pot Book: Its Role in Medicine, Politics, Science, and Culture* (2010). States Dr. Earleywine:

Those unaltered rates of lung cancer in marijuana smokers seem odd given the parallels between marijuana smoke and tobacco smoke. Recent theorizing suggests the key differences between the two plants might account for the absence of marijuana induced lung cancer (Melamede 2005). Cannabis smoke contains cannabinoids but no nicotine, tobacco smoke contains nicotine but no cannabinoids. Nicotine's activity in lung cells actually increases the chances of cancer, while the cannabinoids might decrease these chances.

The processes involved are complicated, but they essentially arise because respiratory tissue has many nicotine receptors but no cannabinoid receptors. Damaged cells in the respiratory system often die off. New cells replace the damaged ones, keeping the respiratory system functioning. In the presence of nicotine, however, cells become less likely to die. Although keeping cells alive certainly sounds like a good thing, nicotine can prevent damaged cells from dying. This increased presence of damaged cells makes cancer more likely.

In contrast, cannabinoids do not preserve damaged lung cells, permitting the natural replacement of these cells with new, functional ones. In addition, cannabinoids can decrease inflammation and tumor growth in ways that nicotine cannot. Thus, despite many similarities between cannabis and tobacco smoke, key differences in their components make tobacco smoke potentially more carcinogenic (p. 155).

In the real world, most arguments about marijuana leading to lung cancer are quelled by the question, "Where are the bodies?" Amazingly, there aren't any.

I also detest negative "scientific" findings concerning marijuana coming from pre-compromised test groups. Consider that a lot of times the results of this research only come from those who make themselves available to it. The findings are tainted by the examples taken. Sociologists and psychologists are reporting the statements of people who had problems to begin with and sought their services out. The police's take on things is derived from people they pressured to talk to them. Always remember, when cornered, that they only know what you tell them.

And suppression of the facts, in the Anslinger mode, simply to protect the population from the truth and themselves, is unconscionable because a liar who lies to benefit what they personally feel is a "higher purpose" is the worst liar of all, for the exposure of those lies they've told oftentimes damages the credibility of that purpose, sometimes beyond repair.

As late September rolled in the *indica*s were ready for harvest. Sitting at the trimming table for the first time that season, I thought of Anslinger; what a piece of work that racist bastard was, and why was he so vindictive in the extreme? He continues to strike at hippiedom from the grave. He obviously hated marijuana, but early on he was a realist and instructed his agents not to concentrate their efforts on pot busts. He needed exposure to keep his reign of terror going, and heroin busts were what brought that. In the beginning his tactic was to rile up state and local law enforcement, always in a lather to appear as important and powerful as the feds, to do his dirty work for him.

Typical of bureaucrats and the turf wars their overinflated egos oftentimes engender between them, FBN chief Harry Anslinger was jealous of and hated FBI chief J. Edgar Hoover, and vice versa. Because of much higher profile arrests, the FBI usually hogged all the camera time, media soundbites, and national adulation for doing such a good job, and this drove Anslinger to distraction. Every dog does indeed have its day, however, and six years after his enforced retirement at the age of 70, Anslinger wielded the death blow to reefer by copying the same tactic used to protect, of all things, migratory birds. America's ratification of the Single Treaty in 1968 was Harry's hole card that took the jackpot. By constitutional mandate, treaties are in essence contracts with other nations that then become the supreme law of our land and can even overrule Supreme Court decisions. The only way to get around that is to withdraw from the Single Treaty, and the feds claim that would bring the scorn of those nations that we originally pressured and/or bribed to enact tougher drug laws right along with us. So be it. But historical precedent has been set because the U.S. has withdrawn from other treaties that were detrimental to our national interests. This is a bad contract doing bad things to good Americans, and it needs to go. No president wants to deal with withdrawal from an international treaty, and the decriminalization of marijuana is simply a half measure, so what do they do? Nothing. And what do we do? We wait for the right president to come along in hopes that she or he will break this never-ending cycle of cowardice, ineptitude, and denial.

This national dysfunction was put on display again in 1961 when J. Edgar Hoover in a speech he delivered in Salt Lake City, Utah was quoted in the *New York Daily News* as saying, "The biggest threats to America are the Communists, the beatniks, and the eggheads." In other words, he considered as threats anyone outside his perceived norm, especially anyone intellectual enough to question unbridled authority, or anyone with enough cognizance of what free speech really meant to actually utilize it to criticize government. Nowhere housed in the narrative of our Constitution is there a description of what a deserving citizen should look like, only descriptions of what all citizens should deserve as a member of the United States of America.

Nothing rational actually explains our nation's obsession with drug addicts, or its contempt for those who succumb to drug addiction. The populace fails to understand the true nature of drug addiction due to an apparent fixation on the "chicken or the egg" syndrome. Did drugs turn frequent users into addicts, or did an addictive compulsive personality cause those so predisposed to turn to drugs, and thus become addicts? Drug and alcohol abuse are symptomatic, not causative.

October 7th, 2014. The harvest moon was here! That big orange orb slung low in the sky would act as a beacon for guerilla growers Cali-wide. The most elusive of the elusive, who had slunk about in the shadows all spring and all summer, would be out tonight bringing their crops in without the attention-attracting glares of lanterns or flashlights. The crop was coming in tonight from Eureka, to Fresno, to Bakersfield, to Riverside, to San Diego, and innumerable points in between. The harvest moon, the guerilla grower's annual symbol of defiance, success, and most of all, impending profit that the feds would never see, shone brightly down upon the denizens of the world of weed. The harvest moon is a glowing symbol of the feds' ongoing prohibition of marijuana, not to mention their ongoing stupidity. The harvest moon cast warm welcoming light down upon growers on the down low, on the lam, off the grid and living by sleight-of-hand. Some deep in the forests. Some were strewn across the chaparral. Some were hiding in plain sight. All rejoiced at the illuminating arrival of the harvest moon tonight, for this was an invincible signal of civil disobedience. The harvest moon was here, bringing with it a massive sigh of relief, and for growers Cali-wide, the paranoia, the fear, and the relentless worry ended tonight. All hail the harvest moon, while the outlaws work feverishly under its guiding light. Another growing season reluctantly drew to a close, signaled by its presence tonight.

The *sativa*s go late into the season, which typically runs its course by late October, but because of warmer weather than usual (climate change/global warming?), they were hanging in until Thanksgiving weekend. This greatly aided my one-man trimming operation as I cut colas only as needed and reduced the plants to their rootstalk slowly. Soon there would be nothing left in the garden but these dismal cut-down stumps.

The insatiable push to get the crop in is one step removed from a psychosis. Eventually, I get cabin fever and start to feel like a caged animal. The only thing I can compare it to is the History Channel's *Gold Rush*. Bubble-bag hash production is exactly like it, only the sieving equipment is much smaller and far less sophisticated. The trimmings are the pay-dirt, while running water through the bubble bags equate to the wash plant. The hash garnered is similar to the clean-out of gold. Nothing is more important than keeping the process going. Pre-trimming 140 pounds of sticky resinous colas requires dogged determination. I always know I'm going to be in that chair with my fingers stuck together for 12 to 16 hours each day, and those days will string together for three straight months. Like the motto of Alcoholics Anonymous, I have to take it "one day at a time," or I will implode or explode from within. The weed stinks, I stink, the processing facility stinks. I became nose blind to it after a while, but I know from experience that others don't. I limit my time around the family and basically go underground for a quarter of my calendar year. I don't go into town, and I receive precious few visitors. Stella and the boob tube are my only companions. It's just me and the colas, and I can't let up until they are no more. Two large rooms of string lines must be constantly filled with upside down hanging and drying colas. An empty string line is an affront which I react to much like a beaver reacts to running water. It must be stopped and there will be no rest until it is stopped. I call it "charging the lines," and an uncharged line is similar to a disrupted electrical flow. It must be restored, and the sooner the better. Like salmon swimming upstream to mate, like lemmings approaching a seaside cliff, like birds migrating south for the winter, the lines must be filled, for without that nothing makes any sense and life is thrown hopelessly out of whack. A quarter of my year is taken, and the only way to limit its effect is to get the crop in. Above all else, get the crop in. For three straight months, it's all that matters. Get the crop in. For Christ's sake, get the crop in.

The dreary darkened skies of December make the scene all the more depressing. These noble plants that gave their all have been ungraciously reduced to this. But with death comes the regenerating and renewal of life, the natural cycle starting up anew. I let the rootstalks dry out in the soil until February and then pulled them out, gopher cages and all. Then I'll hang them on the lodge-pole pine stakes to further dry before breaking them out of the cages.

Decision time was fast approaching. Do I stay or do I go? The eternal question of all growers after a heavy harvest. I couldn't go very far, as all this harvest had done was clear debt that had rapidly amassed shortly after the last harvest.

The small "conventional" and guerilla growers have been underground for so long that they don't recognize real change, even when it's staring them directly in the face, and they certainly are not about to trust those who have pursued and persecuted them for decades. Many come from economically depressed and socially backward areas. Although they had nothing to do with the economic meltdown of 2008, it had everything to do with them. Economic crashes last longer in the backward and poorer areas. Hovering just above sustenance level to begin with, a crash hits hard, digs deep, and leaves misery, broken families, and heartache in its wake. What may last four, five, six years in "normal" areas can last decades for hillbillies, rednecks, and the rural poor. To cultures where change comes slow, rapid change, like the aforementioned crash, leaves slowly too. There's economic wallowing in mud too thick and too slick to allow much purchase. Once you're in it, it's difficult to get out. Not getting sucked under it is a more realistic goal than trying to rise above it.

We had been hanging on by our fingernails for the last six years, and I expected that it would be like this until the end of this decade (12 years total). We wouldn't have made it this far if I didn't grow, and I know if I get sent up that the family, such as it is, will disintegrate. It's hard to get out of bed in the morning imbued with the feeling that this may be your last day of freedom. Again, back in 2014 I liked to think that I operated within the dictates of state law, but other horror stories from other growers now give me pause. When I started up, I enlisted the services of four different attorneys and got four very different interpretations of what "state legal" really meant. And they're *supposed* to know the law(s). If the DEA descends upon me - I'm screwed. I try to take solace in the fact that I'm too small to present much of a headline-grabbing target, but given the extreme pettiness of other DEA busts, I know in my heart that they are capable of anything.

In addition, research for this book has led to many sleepless nights, moments of sheer terror, and bouts of the aforementioned acute depression. Still, I have to go on. I have to put fears aside and attend to these plants that grow like weeds for some, but not for me. If I want stellar marijuana, I have to acknowledge that these plants have transcended demanding and have become the bosses of my life. It won't be that way for me anymore, should I choose to go. Wouldn't it be nice to take a year, or two, or five off? Should I stay, or should I go? As of that particular moment in 2014, logic dictated that it was to be my last harvest, and if I were to leave, I wouldn't plan on coming back any time soon, at least not until Cali or the U.S. legalized weed. At least, that's how I felt at the end of 2014.

So…You Think Federal Marijuana Prohibition is Over?

Think again my friend. As alluded to in the preface, following are three articles I sent to various renegade online magazines apprising them of California's war on "black market" marijuana growers. If things are this bad in the state that is the epicenter of marijuana cultivation and is supposedly the last bastion of the peace and love revolution, just think how bad it is on the federal level. Law enforcement is in no hurry to lose their cash cow, and concerning outlaw growers, know this: they can do anything they want.

Prescript: Dateline April 20th, 2020

The underground Southern California marijuana scene remains a reign of terror conducted by El Choppo. During the pleasant sunny midmorning hours of April 20th, the famed 4/20 date celebrated by stoners nationwide, a caravan of police cruisers, and the reviled "chop wagon" descended upon my peaceful neighbor's grow. It looks like not even the Conoravirus Pandemic can keep these oppressors from their appointed rounds. The Anza Valley now appears destined to have another tumultuous summer. Well…this has certainly rekindled some very bad memories in me. Read all about them below:

El Choppo on the Right Side of the Law: Or so He Claims

Riverside County Sheriff Chad "El Choppo" Bianco loves to chop marijuana plants. It must make him absolutely giddy to partake of the lowest of the low-hanging fruit. Not that he won't create fruit of his own through preposterous claims as to the size, scope, and dollar value of his busts while taking every opportunity to claim cartel involvement and wildly exaggerated seizures of lethal weapons.

El Choppo rose to power by prevailing over his archrival, incumbent Sheriff Stan Sniff, by just over 13 points in the November 2018 runoff election. Sniff did not go quietly into that good night and claims that his successor is delusional concerning his operational budget, which lies somewhere between fabrication and fantasy land. Concerning whatever amount of money that is still on the table, El Choppo is spending it faster than a Mega Millions winner with terminal cancer. He's ramping up hires of new law enforcement officers to beef up his fear campaign and to staff the new 4,000 bed prison expansion in Indio. So far, so good for El Choppo, because the well as of yet has not run dry, and besides, just like any other glory-mongering politician, it's nothing more than Monopoly money to him.

El Choppo managed to enlist the services of the National Guard because 40th U.S. President Ronald Ray Gun, known for infamously announcing that drugs would be nonexistent in America by 1995, acted on this edict by amending the Posse Comitatus Act of 1878, which was designed to limit federal military intervention in local law enforcement issues, in order to allow the Guard to assist in state-run marijuana eradication efforts. Overkill perhaps, but there was just too much marijuana for El Choppo to chop all by himself. And the ineptitude of the state's ever-evolving marijuana policy in general was on high display during this modern-day police riot that occurred in the Anza Valley on Wednesday, June 5th, 2019.

Local growers who took the time to read the State's initial *Adult Use of Marijuana Act* (2014) and fast follow-up *Cannabis*

Cultivation License Application Overview (2017) took heart when the claim was made that the corporations would be held at bay for a period of five years, thus allowing small businesses to gain a foothold before being swallowed up, strangled, and/or otherwise left as roadkill in the ever-popular "green rush." Greed Rush would be a more appropriate term, and it is now raging. The truth be told, it's all about the corporations, and they are worming their way in everywhere.

With the passage of California's Proposition 64 in the fall of 2016 calling for complete statewide legalization of marijuana, it appeared that the insanity of the aforementioned and now-burgeoning "green rush" would finally be put to rest. Nothing could be further from the truth, however. Government overreach has turned what the squares and bible thumpers have always referred to as the "black market" even blacker. The small growers, too poor and too independent to toe the regulatory line, are doing what they always have done. They grow marijuana illegally.

California's state government is to blame for this most recent muscle flexing, chest pounding fandango of absolute power gone awry. First, because they actually thought that they would get rich in just their second year of operation. Profit projections in excess of $100,000,000.00 or the first quarter of 2018 fell abysmally short by a whopping 66% when a mere $34,000,000.00 was actually collected. Apparently, the exchange rate for their Monopoly money doesn't convert to actual cash. Nobody knows for sure what the county's final price tag will be, but the state fees already in place represent a chokehold on the small grower. Under Prop 64, there's a 15 percent statewide excise tax on all cannabis product retail sales. This is in addition to an existing general sale (bud, paraphernalia, tee shirts, posters, et cetera) and use tax of 8.5 percent, as well as a $9.25 per ounce cultivation tax for cannabis flowers that growers are supposed to pay. Most dispensaries charge $40.00 per 1/8th ounce, which would make the final cost $49.40, or a 29.5% markup. This all equates to a total price of $395.00 per ounce, and even when discounted for a volume purchase to $300.00 an ounce it still pales in comparison to $60.00 per ounce for "street pot." Everyone wants their cut in the legal market, which is contributing to the blackening of the so-called "black market." The State and County can get real about their profit projections, or failing that, they can turn their henchmen like El Choppo loose to exact their pound of flesh. No mention has been made as to what he's already costing the County, but that pigeon will be coming home to roost sure and soon enough, and those now siccing him on the ganja populace will soon be complaining about the price tag that this grass inquisition really entails. What sweet poetic justice it would be if El Choppo simply spent himself into extinction. Local vendors will suffer in the long run, many families are already suffering, and all Anza is really good for in the eyes of this county is property taxes and functioning as a way station upon which to dump released convicts, including child molesters.

Secondly, by allowing local jurisdictions such as Unincorporated Riverside County to determine their own fate, they loosed a peckerwood vengeance upon the former drug of peace and love known as County Ordinance 925, enacted in July 2015. Now that the County has finally devised a way to get its hand firmly planted in the till, by purposing permitting that's anticipated to start at $10,000.00 for a typical R1-5 (5-acre) lot, it's time to find some clients willing to line their coffers. This fee is on top of State fees, which combined would total $20,000.00 for a 10,000 square foot outdoor grow operation. To date, no permits have been issued. The problem for the small growers is that they quite simply can't afford the price tag. The death knell is that the County's proposal will only allow 50 total grow operations. Who do you think will be first in line, and who do you think will be left out in the cold? With El Choppo acting as judge, jury, and executioner, to say nothing of his role as government/corporate errand boy, it's readily apparent what this bloodletting of misery is all about - money. In the immortal words of The Who, "Meet the new boss, same as the old boss." The fact remains that in the final analysis, it's just marijuana, and there are no recorded cases in the history of the entire world of anyone ever dying from using it. To its detractors, I ask: Where are the bodies? Anza and Aguanga frequently make the national news due to deadly explosions of crystal meth labs, and it is a drug, to be sure, that is rotting these communities at their core. But they're more well-hidden, populated by criminals who actually are dangerous, and don't make for nearly as splashy a news story as El Choppo's scorched-earth raids.

Given what's happening to personal rights on the national level, and the Jeff Sessions scare when he went on record to say "Good people don't smoke marijuana," the question must be raised: What would happen if the feds overturned state's rights marijuana legalization and sent marijuana back to the dark ages of national prohibition now in effect since 1937? This is why every user should still support California's Medical Marijuana Program (MMP) that hardly anyone ever talks about anymore. It's a good program, their fees have actually been cut in half since 64 passed, and the State does deserve something for supporting compassionate use by waiving its taxation for anyone in possession of a medical marijuana card. Between the doctor's recommendation and MMP's fees, the out-of-pocket expense is usually less than $150.00. The feds might get recreational users, but it's doubtful that they would be heartless enough to outlaw compassionate use; so there's a level of protection for those who seriously need the pain-killing and/or epilepsy-negating effects of *Cannabis sativa*, or *indica*.

Considering how badly California has botched the rollout of legalization, perhaps it would be better if the federal government did take over and right this listing ship. The federal government could legalize marijuana and charge every individual user an annual use fee of $100.00 to acquire a federal marijuana card. Conservative estimates count frequent marijuana users at over 30,000,000, which when multiplied by $100,00 equals 30 billion dollars right out of the gate. One hundred bucks is a small price to pay to assure your freedom from police harassment and incarceration. This could be as easy as checking a box on your federal income tax return. This initial economic shot in the arm could fund other green and/

or restorative industries such as the "Infrastructure Package" the politicians keep dancing around.

If you don't like what's happen before your disbelieving eyes, there is something you can do about it. Ban the dispensaries with their overpriced shiny-object packaging because their ownership is populated by corporate douchebags who never knew the first thing about weed. Ignore the statements of Harborside Health Center's (a dispensary) owner Steve DeAngelo claiming all kinds of concern for his dispensary's medical marijuana patients because he is a long-haired, pigtailed corporate shill. He, more than anyone else, has raked in the ill-gotten profits of the green rush. And no, despite what DeAngelo claims, no one ever had the stones to tell Quanah Parker to cut his pigtails. Next, contribute to LEAP (formerly Law Enforcement Against Prohibition that has morphed into Law Enforcement Action Partnership) because they speak the truth concerning America's War on Drugs and because a cheap publicity-seeking cat like El Choppo literally turns their stomachs. Finally, *grow your own*, because you're allowed six mature plants that any local California jurisdiction can't overturn. Forget Riverside County Ordinance 925's Trojan Horse offering that allows up to 24 plants per legally permitted property, because it will be overturned just as soon as the corporations take over, and El Choppo will come a' chopping'. Chop, chop, chop; apparently, that's what really gets him off.

Hard-ass (10/7/2019)

Amongst any team of arresting officers, there is always one hard-ass who plays a little fast and loose with their legal firearm and assumes omnipotent power in barking out commands, even those that are completely opposite to one another. This hard-ass had his pistol pointed directly at my heart as he commanded me to walk towards him, stop, turn, no turn back, no turn around again, get on my knees, and then put my hands on my head. He made sure to grab ample amounts of my hair as he put my hands behind my back and then handcuffed me, *hard*. As the cuffs bit into my wrists, he pulled me to my feet and dragged me towards this car and then that car, apparently deciding upon the one he eventually stuffed me into. I knew not to complain about the cuffs because that was exactly what he wanted, and I had no doubt that to do so would only result in him clamping down even harder. I was determined not to be a fool and give him the satisfaction.

These were all local yokels from Riverside County, and thankfully, no federal agencies were represented. There were 14 of them; 10 men and four women, and most seemed mechanical and completely disinterested. Next to be stuffed into the back seat of the cruiser, was my wife, who was visibly upset and scared, but fortunately, not handcuffed. The lead investigator took me from the car, lead me into a shaded area, and then read me my Miranda Rights before embarking on his questions that seemed casually conversational but were definitely intended to entrap me. To all except two I stated that I did not wish to speak unless there was an attorney present. The two I answered were that my wife had nothing to do with the marijuana grow, and that I was formally a landscape architect in another life. "How did you go from that to this?" he inquired, seeming genuinely bewildered. "I just got old," I replied and then added, "I just couldn't compete anymore." That was the truth. He was professional and perhaps just a tad bit too kind in stating that I wasn't going to go to jail today, nor would be my wife. He then took her for separate questioning as I was put back in the cruiser to watch them descend upon my home, and then the inevitable chopping of the crop commenced. It sickened me to my core to see an entire season doomed and know of the hardship that would soon follow.

The lead investigator had me taken from the car and had the hard-ass uncuff me. The hard-ass said, "Don't do anything stupid," which was advice that apparently pleased him very much. I replied, "You got my attention, when you cuffed me. I'm completely nonviolent. I have no intention of doing anything at all." My submissiveness seemed to relax him as he basked in the warmth of complete control. Again, the others seemed like they could care less. They stopped to have lunch and throw their papers and wrappers and bottles about my property. Finally, off they went like a conquering Roman army, leaving as much scorched earth as legally possible behind. In truth, they could have behaved much worse. They really could have tossed the place, but it took less than fifteen minutes to put everything back in order. It was obvious that they were hunting for cash, but none was present, and after this, it would be in short supply in the ensuing months as we tried to survive and put this ordeal behind us.

At times like this, I would always try mightily to remember that these are human beings: sons and daughters, fathers and mothers, brothers and sisters who have a network of other human beings who care about them and would be heartbroken if anything bad were to happen to them. The political and cultural divisions in America are now stark and frightening. These were, after all, people who simply held an opinion opposite of my own. That didn't make them bad people; it only made them people who disagreed with me. The only problem was that their opinion was the one that counted, and they had the power to jail me because of it. One thing was certain: I was now officially drummed into retirement. At 68, my will to fight on was gone. We would await the charges from the District Attorney, and sleep was elusive as I stressed nightly over just how bad things could get.

Considering that the recently past summer had been the hottest one on record, it was surprising just how cold the early October nights had become. Everything seemed out of step, discombobulated, and strangely weird. Nothing would ever be the same again. Troubled times had finally come to our heretofore peaceful life. Aside from the legal worries, the one penetrating question that gnawed at the edges of my psyche was: that once this all shook out, what was I going to do with the rest of my life? A week later, the harvest moon glowed brightly high in the sky, reminding me that it was time to conduct the harvest; only there was nothing left to harvest.

Everything was gone, all gone, and would never be coming back again. Each evening, as the harvest moon seemed to radiate even brighter, the stark reminder was thrust upon me that it was finally over. There would be no coming back from this. I was done and would not try again. This enforced retirement brought the numbing reality that, like it or not, resist it or not, my life was winding down. Life now dictated to me. I was not in control of my own destiny, which would be revealed to me soon and sure enough. Depression set in, hard and heavy. I was able to conduct basic chores, but my will to do anything beyond the bare minimum was in shambles. I sat dazed in front of the television, watching the Mad King make a mockery of our great nation on the world stage. The speed at which I and my homeland were declining was shocking, sickening, and beyond belief. The harvest moon finally began to wane, the unmistakable symbol that it was all over, the end.

The Tank
(10/6/2020)

The first thing you notice is the gleaming stainless-steel toilet that no one wants to take a dump in. It is the only thing that gleams, or even looks remotely clean in this holding cell at the Riverside County Jailhouse. It might gleam, but it is far from sanitary, being covered with urine while toilet paper hangs at various angles and in various states of decomposition from its sides. As for the toilet paper, there's none available as any rolls are in use as pillows for detainees trying to sleep off or sleep through their misery. In this small fifteen-foot square room affectionately known as "the tank" the newly incarcerated await their fate. Once fingerprinted and otherwise "booked" the slow arriving bail amount is revealed as well as the date of arraignment in the event that bail cannot be arranged. It used to be that law enforcement couldn't hold you for more than three days before you would have to be brought before a judge, but now, due to Covid 19, Riverside County has finagled the requirement to ten days. Why? Because they can – that's why.

The tank will receive up to 12 prisoners at a time, and when it does, there is no such thing as social distancing, especially at feeding time when all who want to eat have to drop their masks to do so. The jail did provide masks at induction, but it was little solace after being transported 30 miles in the prison wagon with five other unmasked violators of the law. At 69 with preexisting conditions, if any of them had Covid symptoms, I would be as good as dead. So, law enforcement, all who were wearing their masks, apparently wasn't too concerned with playing Russian Roulette with our lives. I was scooped up in the mid-morning on the strength of a "Failure to Appear (FTA) Warrant." Ditto for the five other wagon riders. None of us had received any notice to appear.

As the oldest prisoner, and one with prostrate problems, I hung next to the toilet to urinate whenever I could, and when the tank held 12 people, this was difficult as someone always used the toilet to sit on as a chair. I adopted a Casper Milk Toast persona, only talked when spoken to, and gave up my seat on the wooden bench in favor of the concrete floor when it was obvious that anyone wanted it. If I could have become invisible, I would have done it. Survive, just survive the ordeal, that's all that mattered. At induction, a women officer asked me for permission for them to medically treat me, which I quickly refused feeling that they were capable of doing anything to me. Then she said, "What if you get in a fight? We couldn't treat you." So, I accepted the medical care feeling that they would never be too quick to break up a fight. What did it matter to them, who got hurt? Their general demeanor rightly suggested that they viewed us all as scum. Better to patch someone up after the fact than to take any preventative measures.

I suppose I should mention my crime. I got popped in October of 2019 for growing marijuana. I have written numerous other pieces about this dolorous experience, so I won't belabor the point here. I wasn't taken to jail that day and was informed by the arresting officer that I would be hearing from the District Attorney as to what would happen next. Let me reiterate, I *never* heard from anyone. The FTA is one of law enforcement's favorite tricks. With that warrant they get to come on your property and catch you off guard; nose around, so to speak, to see if they can find anything else to charge you with because they witnessed it with their own eyes, and as such, now have "probable cause." I will say this: when they resort to lying and cheating to achieve their objectives, I see no separation between them and the criminals. It's no longer about right versus wrong, but it is now all about winning. Winning at all costs is all that matters to them.

There's a phone in the tank with a speaker so loud that few can sleep when it's in use, and it's in use 24/7. This phone operates on a collect call basis, and I was to learn that most personal cell phones are programmed not to receive collect calls. This leaves the bail companies who have their business cards plastered to the walls. You call them. They query as to your ability to pay, and if interested, they will call who you want to reach for help. The calls are monitored and recorded so it's important not to incriminate yourself. Bail companies require you to pay 10% of the total amount and they guarantee the rest. You lose this 10% as it is what they make in profit for their services. Bail companies are not humanitarian organizations, and to cross them is worse than to cross the police. This is literally a dog-eat-dog business. My bail payment was $1,000.00, which I was able to pay after 24 hours, but I was far from free and clear due to necessary "paperwork," and know that they move as slowly as humanly possible because the entire aim of this whole experience is to make it as unpleasant and time consuming as possible. I posted bail at 11:30 a.m. and was finally cut loose at 4:00 a.m. the next morning. My initial arraignment was set for 8:00 a.m. that day but the last thing I wanted to do was to appear before a judge disheveled in an orange jumpsuit, totally disoriented, and unprepared. I was also aware that said judge could decide at that time to *raise* my bail amount. Better to get out while the getting was good, regroup, find a creditable attorney, and formulate a plausible plan of attack. Besides, if Biden was elected and were to make good on his promise to federally decriminalize pot, this whole thing could simply fade away and become much to do about nothing. Buy time, if time can prove to be your friend.

Law enforcement wasn't going to make it easy. I was comfortable in the tank. I actually felt protected by many of the Mexicans, who I can assure you, respect the elderly far more than the gringos. This old gringo knew that if he could stay as close to invisible as possible that the coast would probably be clear. That's when my jailers decided to "house" me, and more experienced inmates informed me that when they sent you to the cellblock it took longer for them to complete the bail out paperwork. My cellmate was a 55-year old homeless man who had been there for 17 days and was recently returned from his hearing where all his charges were dropped. He was obviously mentally compromised making me wonder how he passed his mental evaluation. I had mine conducted at 4:00 a.m. on my first day and it was an absolute joke. I answered "no" to all questions except this demeaning one: "How do you feel about your current situation?" "It is what it is," I answered. My cellmate loudly flushed the toilet nonstop as he yelled at his enemies in the next cell, until he used the toilet to wash his feet which he referred to as a "biker bath." He referred to me as, "A man of few words." What could anyone say? We were taken to another holding cell containing nine other individuals at 2:00 a.m. I was happy that I was not released with him because he now considered me his friend and wanted to stay in touch.

A cab dropped me at the bail company at the end of the street and my wife arrived two hours later. The nightman at the bail company informed me that the vast majority of their business came from FTA's and that it was his considered opinion that law enforcement never actually sent any notices to appear. It was just a game to them. "They shouldn't be allowed to do that," he said. I replied, "They're the police; they can do whatever they want."

Resolution
(8/25/2021)

My arraignment date was set for early February in 2021. It was continued as were three successive court dates. They kept me twisting in the wind as I had to appear at the county courthouse on five separate occasions. As I frequented the courthouse I couldn't help but notice that the cops working there were respectful and polite to all unlike the swinging dicks that were terrorizing my hometown. They probably had some form of sensitivity training because they were able to maintain their command presence without being intimidating. So I knew that cops could behave like human beings, and I rationalized that a person's being poor must be what brings out the worst in cops. I got a court appointed public defender who was distracted and overworked, but I sincerely doubted that I would fare any better with an expensive private attorney. Law enforcement was processing marijuana growing busts as if they were on an assembly line – they were going to do what they were going to do no matter how good or poor the representation was. I saw it as pretty much a rubber stamp operation and I was simply caught up in the grinding gears of the machine. Finally, in late August, the matter was settled when I pleaded guilty to growing more than six marijuana plants and my felony charge was dropped to a misdemeanor and a years' conditional probation under my own recognizance with the annoying exceptions that *any* probation officer or cop could shake me down whenever they wanted to with no requirement for probable cause. They wouldn't need a warrant to enter my home, they could just do it for the duration of the probation period. I had always believed that the police are in actuality a superior society. Once they get you down, they step on you. Their first objective is to disarm you and render you helpless, after that they just strive to harass you whenever they feel like it for as long as the courts allow. This is just too much power in the hands of the insatiably power hungry. All this over a drug that has never killed anyone. I knew that my growing days were over. The cops could do a conga line through my house for all I cared. They had gutted me, and rubbed my nose in it to boot, but that's all they can legally do. I am finally done with all of it. The only question that remains is: are El Choppo and his henchmen really done with me?

Timeline of Events Relating to Marijuana

6000 BC Cannabis seeds used as a food source in mainland China.

2500 BC Aryans from Central Asia and Eastern Europe invade Persia and India. It's believed that they brought landraces of cannabis with them as seed stock. The Indians would elevate cannabis cultivation to an art form. Soon its products are utilized in religious ceremonies.

1500 BC Cannabis is more extensively cultivated in China for food and fiber. It's believed that the Chinese are not yet utilizing the whole plant or making hashish for the purposes of intoxication.

1400 BC References to cannabis appear in the *Atharvaveda*, the Hindu holy book, as a "sacred grass" giving rise to the modern-day slang expression of marijuana as "grass." There is also mention of Shiva the Lord of Bhang. Bhang is a liquid concoction comprised of whole marijuana parts, frequently mixed with tea.

700 BC Scythian tribes now rule in Central Asia. They often leave cannabis seeds as offerings in their royal tombs.

221 BC China embarks on constructing the Great Wall in order to keep barbarian Mongol tribes out. The spread of cannabis to neighboring peoples is temporarily stifled.

206 BC Completion of the Great Wall of China. The rise of the Han dynasty. The Chinese are now smoking cannabis.

202 BC Emergence of the Roman Empire with the establishment of trade routes into Eastern Europe and the Mediterranean region. Cannabis travels well.

128 BC The Silk Road becomes an established trade route between Europe and China. More cannabis reaches Europe.

100 BC Greeks discover the Trade Winds and travel to India often. There is an atmosphere of open trade between East and West. Cannabis becomes an item of barter.

90 BC The Chinese medical book, the *Pen Ts'a,* records the uses of cannabis for medicinal purposes.

70 BC A Greek medical manual known as *The Dioscorides* notes that cannabis can be employed as a medicament.

50 BC A Samaritan gold and glass "stash box" found in a Siberian tomb is believed to been used to store and transport cannabis.

1 AD Death of Jesus Christ marking the emergence of the Christian religion and splitting the marking of time between BC (before Christ) and AD (after the death of Christ). All dates presented hereafter are AD.

610 The prophet Mohammed receives his first revelation. He will go on to pen the Koran, the holy book of Islam. Islam forbids the use of alcohol but leaves a loophole for cannabis by not mentioning it at all. This gray area concerning marijuana and hashish will become much debated, and the debate continues to this very day.

950 There is debate amongst scholars of the day as to the merits and drawbacks of eating hashish.

1000 War-interrupted sea trade between Europe and the Orient is restored. Hashish once again arrives back into Europe.

1080 The Christian Crusades begin by the forces of several European nations invading the Middle East. Both sides, Islamic and Christian, claim victory, although the conflict was more or less a standoff, with its most noteworthy accomplishment being the cultural exchange that would benefit both regions.

1206 Genghis Khan unites all the Mongol tribes and sets his sights on world domination, such as the extent of the world was known at that time.

1231 During the reign of Caliph Mustansir, hashish is introduced to Iraq.

1258 Mongol invaders sack Baghdad. Their furthest incursion into the Islamic world will end in 1260.

1260 The rise of "The Assassins," believed to be the first undercover Islamic terrorist group. The rumor was widely spread and used to much advantage that their ruthless behavior was fueled by ceremonies involving the imbibing of cannabis. Later accounts attribute their drug intoxication to opium, not that it mattered to Harry Jacob Anslinger, 677 years later, used stories of the Assassins' ferocity and stealth to assist his cause of fear-mongering purposes to kick off full-fledged cannabis prohibition in America (see 1937).

1271 Italian adventurer and explorer Marco Polo rediscovers the Silk Road, and hashish starts to once again reach all nations of Europe.

1320 The Turkey-based Ottoman Empire is at its peak. Turkish hashish becomes some of the finest in the world.

1378 Ottoman Emir Soudoun issues an edict outlawing the eating of hashish. This is the first recorded example of cannabis prohibition. The edict is largely ignored despite the occasional beheading—the heart wants what the heart wants.

1456 Johan Gutenberg prints the first bible on hempen rag paper.

1533 King Henry VIII, as founder of the British Navy, decrees to fine farmers for not growing fiber hemp for the purposes of making sails. A jib sail thus became the reason working men referred to marijuana aboard their ships as "jib."

1611 The British crown makes hemp growing mandatory in the English colonies of the New World.

1650 Baghdad resident Mohammed Ebn Soleiman pens an epic poem entitled: *Benk u Bode* in which there is an allegorical battle between wine and hashish with hashish the clear winner. Knowing already that the Koran condemns alcohol, this work is taken by some in Islam to mean that hashish is acceptable in their religion. Others disagree.

1682 The Virginia colony makes it legal for a farmer to pay off 1/4 of his total debt in hemp.

1690 In the Virginia colony, every farmer was required to raise a minimum of 100 hemp plants.

1753 Swedish taxonomist Carlos Linnaeus classifies marijuana as belonging to the genus *Cannabis* (fragrant cane) and the species *sativa* (cultivated). *Sativa*s are tall with thin leaves and produce a soaring mental high. When one is "high" it is usually from the effects of a *sativa* variety. Cannabis is in the plant family *Cannabacae*, which has only one other genus, that being, oddly enough, the species *Humulus lupulus*, the hops plant for making beer.

1776 The first draft of The American Declaration of Independence is drawn up on hemp rag paper.

1776 Betsy Ross sews the first American flag, utilizing hemp thread and hemp cloth.

1783 French taxonomist Jean-Baptiste Lamarck classifies *Cannabis indica* for the Indian variety. *Indica*s are shorter with broader leaves and produce a "body high." When one is "stoned" it is usually from the effects of an *indica* variety. The *afghani* strains recently being bandied about by breeders are cultivars of *indica* and grow similarly with broader leaves while producing a similar high.

1790 Hashish has now become a major item of trade between Central and Southern Asia.

1798 Napoleon declares hashish illegal in Egypt. The order is largely ignored by nationals and his own troops. Note that throughout history, whenever an emperor wished to impose absolute power, cannabis is most often the first drug targeted. This is because of its ease of availability among the masses.

1809 Leading Arabist historian Antoine Sylvestre de Sacy reveals the true etymology of the words "assassin" and "hashishin," debunking the violent myth that marijuana usage lies at the heart of the Assassins' treacheries. As is often the case, the public, especially the media, prefer the legend to the truth. (See 1260).

1822 Englishman Thomas Penson De Quincy publishes *Confessions of an English Opium Eater*, which is only mentioned here because subsequent but less well-written "confessions" style books dealing with hash use would be patterned after it. Those books often led to the comingling of cannabis and opium in the general public's mind.

1850 Cannabis is listed in the *United States Pharmacopoeia* and was said to relieve a vast array of ailments.

1857 American Fritz Hugh Ludlow publishes *The Hasheesh Eater, Being Passages from the Life of a Pythagorean*. In comparing hash "addiction" to opium addiction, Ludlow gave the puritanical Christian society dominant in America at that time ample excuses to vilify cannabis in general and hash in particular.

1876 American Centennial Exposition in Philadelphia featured a Turkish hashish stand in which anyone visiting it could try hash out.

1884 *Confessions of an English Hashish Eater* is published anonymously in London to little acclaim.

1894 *Indian Hemp Commission's Report* running to 3,500 pages contained in seven volumes is released to the British government. This report finds that claims that cannabis and hashish are undermining the military rank and file, and causing the lowest manual labor class, the "untouchables," to be lazy are completely unfounded. The Commission recommends taxation as a means to curbing cannabis use, if the British government so chooses to restrict it at all. 125 years later, it still stands as the most comprehensive study done on the societal effects of cannabis.

1906 Pure Food and Drug Act requires labeling of all medicines, of which opiates and cannabis were included. While not specifically outlawing marijuana, this act served to further connect it to opium.

1913 French author Jules Giraud publishes French version "confessions" series entitled *Testament of a Hashish Eater*, in which he laments society's worsening attitude towards cannabis users and all drug users in general. The founder and publisher of *Cannabinologi,* a magazine dedicated to cannabis use, Giraud uses it as a platform to speak out against societal stereotyping and oppression.

1914 Harrison Narcotics Act was passed in the United States to cut into the Asian opium and South American cocaine trade. The act required that all doctors, pharmacists, and drug importers keep detailed records of all transactions and pay for a tax stamp. While marijuana was originally included, it was later removed due to complaints from the medical industry stating that its common uses in corn plasters and veterinary products would make it be too hard to regulate.

1919 The prohibition of alcohol is enacted in the United States through the passage of the Volstead Act inherent in the Eighteenth Amendment. Among poorer peoples, the emphasis chosen for personal intoxication switches from alcohol to less expensive drugs, in particularly, still-legal marijuana. A young German scientist named Albert Einstein, upon visiting the U.S. in 1920 and observing Prohibition in action, is quoted as saying: "The prestige of the government has undoubtedly been lowered considerably by Prohibition. Nothing is more destructive of respect for the government and the law of the land than laws that cannot be enforced." This is equally as true for today's marijuana prohibition.

1923 International Police Commission known as Interpol is formed and headquartered in Paris, France. As part of their directive to investigate international criminal activity, they are to extensively investigate drug trafficking.

1924 Janischewski, a Russian botanist, classified *Cannabis ruderalis*. *Ruderalis* grows very short, rarely exceeding 30" in height, (and frequently being only 18" high). It contains relatively little (2% or less) THC and was widely ignored (perhaps that's why nobody seems to know or care what Janischewski's first name was) up until the new millennium, when it was discovered that, unlike its cousins, *ruderalis* is auto-flowering, meaning that it is time dependent rather than phototropic (growth responding to light levels) as it progresses to maturity. Through interbreeding with *sativa*s and *indica*s, there have been decent TCH level strains that grow in lower light latitudes, and during lower light seasons, and under lower light interior conditions. They mature quickly, sometimes in as little as eight weeks from cradle (seed) to grave (harvest), being a boon for growers forced to operate under less than optimum conditions.

1925 U.S. government commissions a study of U.S. military personnel in the Panama Canal Zone that are smoking marijuana. The study found that marijuana was not a narcotic, and therefore not addictive. Based on this, previous orders prohibiting the possession of cannabis by military personnel are revoked.

1925 Initial work on the United States Narcotic Drugs Act begins and goes through several renditions before being finalized in 1932 (see 1932). The Act goes one step further than the Harrison Narcotics Act of 1914 (see 1914) by allowing states to get in on the action by allowing them to seize illicit drugs and punishing those in possession of them with incarceration.

1929 Congress passes the Narcotic Farms Act (NFA), which misclassifies "Indian Hemp" as a narcotic. (Perhaps the real trouble started here, with a mistake the feds just won't correct.) This act does authorize the establishment of two hospitals within the federal prison system dedicated solely to drug rehabilitation.

1930 Formation of the U.S. Federal Bureau of Narcotics (FBN), with the appointment of Harry Jacob Anslinger as its first Commissioner. He retains the post for an astounding 32 years.

1932 The United States Narcotic Drugs Act begun in 1925 (see 1925) reaches its final version, and by the mid-thirties 31 states subscribed to its dictates.

1933 The Volstead Act for alcohol prohibition is repealed as the Twenty-first Amendment. The emphasis of the criminal element switched from alcohol to drugs. It's a simple equation: illegality increases rarity, and rarity always increases value.

1934 Between 1930 and this date, 33 U.S. states have passed laws restricting or outlawing the use of cannabis.

1936 The Geneva Trafficking Conventions are held with Anslinger advocating criminalization of all facets of opium, coca, and cannabis production. The U.S. refuses to sign the final draft of the treaty, considering it too weak in the areas of extradition and confiscation of any known trafficking profits. Anslinger is already trying to build an agency that could at least partially sustain itself on plunder.

1937 The Marihuana Tax Act is passed by Congress after two days of hearings. The tax of $1.00 per ounce virtually guarantees nonpayment for nonexistent tax stamps because marijuana only cost $2.00 per bulk pound in 1937. Anslinger, never a medical doctor, acts as the government's expert medical witness. The only true quasi-medical expert is pharmacist Dr. James A. Munch, who initially conducted studies on dogs. Making the dog-to-man leap, Munch states under oath that, "Continued use will continue to cause the degeneration of one part of the brain, that part that is useful for higher or psychic reasoning or the memory..." Call Munch the godfather of "amotivational syndrome." Soon, murderers are trying to avoid the death penalty by claiming temporary insanity by using marijuana. Acting as an expert witness at one such trial, Munch testifies that he personally tried marijuana *once*: "I passed into an ink bottle. I peeked over the edge and I wrote a book. I was in the same bottle for 200 years. After that I flew out." He was actually taken seriously. After this performance, Anslinger contacts Munch and directs him to deliver no more testimony, as defendants are indeed spared the death penalty due to their insanity pleas.

1938 The film *Reefer Madness*, originally released by a church group under the title *Tell Your Children*, is loosed upon the nation, most of which had no idea what marijuana was at that time. Through the years, particularly in the sixties and seventies, when the baby boomers turned to marijuana as a recreational drug, stoners kept the film in circulation as a comedic cult classic. It's still good for a laugh today.

1938 La Guardia Report commissioned by New York City Mayor Fiorello La Guardia is completed. The 31 member panel of medical experts from The New York Academy of Medicine studied 77 prisoners detained on Riker's Island. The report speaks the truth, basically stating that there is nothing wrong with marijuana, and the lies promulgated by Anslinger and his ilk are just that - lies. Anslinger dismisses and represses the report at every turn.

1944 La Guardia Report finally released to the general public. Anslinger starts yet another smear campaign, saying that the sampling was too small. He writes articles in various cop journals encouraging that they ignore it and conduct business as usual.

1952 The Boggs Act is passed, instituting mandatory sentences, upping the time of sentences, and making the punishment the same for marijuana and heroin. Two-time drug offenders could never get parole, even though such was possible for murderers and rapists.

1956 U.S. Narcotics Control Act. Now FBN and Customs agents were to be armed.

1961 Single Convention on Narcotic Drugs. The International Treaty is not ratified by the U.S. because Anslinger considered its language too weak. The treaty wallows in obscurity.

1962 Kennedy White House initiates the Conference on Narcotics and Drug Abuse. The subsequent Prettyman Report exonerates marijuana as not being linked to criminality, suggests removing mandatory sentencing, and concerning Anslinger's ongoing oppression of marijuana users, states it to be "in poor social perspective." There are rumors that Kennedy used cannabis for chronic and excruciating back pain.

1964 Israeli scientist Raphael Mechoulam isolates, and later synthesizes, the THC (delta-9-tetrahydrocannabinol) molecule, which was discovered to be the active ingredient in cannabis that gets user's "high." In the early 1990's Mechoulam, along with a support team of other scientists, discovers CBD (endogenous cannabinoids) compounds later proved to be the ingredients that suppresses pain and actually fight some diseases such as glaucoma and epilepsy.

1964 American Alan Ginsberg and fellow poet Ed Sanders found the organization called Legalize Marijuana (LeMar) on December 27th of that year. LeMar is usually considered the precursor to NORML.

1967 Single Convention on Narcotic Drugs is revisited. This International Treaty is now ratified by the U.S. at Anslinger's request because he now states that international marijuana traffic has dramatically increased. Today there are 180 member nations. Patterned after the International Migratory Bird Treaty Act of 1918, it's believed that international law trumps the laws of individual nations. Constitutionally, this is true in the U.S. Since pot is illegal on the international stage, it's felt it can never be federally legal in the U.S.A. unless *all* international laws we are currently engaged in are challenged. This is a ridiculous notion - just ask any number of Native American tribes.

1969 The Wootton Report commissioned by the British government is released in January. A panel of noted doctors, a police chief, a magistrate, and prominent sociologist Baroness Wootton (after whom the report was is named) all agree that marijuana was far less dangerous than any other popular drug, less dangerous than alcohol, and not a gateway drug. The report further went on to state that no one should ever go to prison for possession of moderate amounts of marijuana. Most tellingly, it states: "...*we find ourselves in agreement* *with the conclusion reached by the Indian Hemp Drugs Commission appointed by the Government of India (1893 - 1894) and the New York Mayor's Committee on Marijuana (1944), that the long-term consumption of cannabis in moderate doses has no harmful effects."* The English Press largely discredited it, stating that the committee members had caved to pro-pot lobby demands. Baroness Wootton publicly refuted these accusations in a letter to *The Times*. The British Government reacted by stiffening marijuana penalties in 1971.

1969 Nixon strikes with "Operation Intercept," the first blow being the "sealing" of the U.S./Mexican border and searching *every* vehicle. This was thinly veiled intimidation to force the Mexican government to go along with a Paraquat spraying program on Mexican marijuana fields in the summer of 1970.

1970 The U.S. Federal Narcotics Bureau morphs into the Bureau of Narcotics and Dangerous Drugs (BNDD).

1970 The Controlled Substances Act (CSA) is passed. The Supreme Court rules that The Marijuana Tax Stamp Act of 1937 (see 1937) is unconstitutional, which appeared to be good news for stoners, but it was short-lived as the court concurrently allowed marijuana to land on the Schedule 1 list. The death knell for any potential federal marijuana legalization was officially struck.

1970 Paraquat is sprayed on Mexican marijuana fields. Mexican growers harvested what could be salvaged and shipped it to the U.S., anyway. Poisoning marijuana smokers was now considered fair play by the man to become known as "Tricky Dick."

1970 Staunch marijuana activist Dr. Todd Mikuriya and Michael Aldrich (originally of LeMar) found the pro-pot group Amorphia, which would serve as a bridge organization between LeMar and NORML. Mikuriya advocates for treating alcoholics and morphine addicts with cannabis to lessen withdrawal symptoms, and if need be, as a substitute drug with far less deleterious life effects. Mikuriya believes marijuana is an exit drug, not a gateway drug.

1971 The U.N. sets up the Fund for Drug Control, later to be known as the U.N. International Drug Control Program.

1971 Attorney Keith Stroup founds the Washington D.C. based pro-marijuana-legalization lobbying group called The National Organization for the Reform of Marijuana Laws (NORML). Originally launched by a $5,000.00 grant and refortified a year later by a $100,000.00 grant from Hugh Hefner of *Playboy Magazine*. Today NORML boasts a national total of 65,000 members.

1971 At the King's suggestion, the Nixon White House appoints Elvis Presley BNDD "Federal Agent at Large," in a move quite similar to appointing a fox the main guard of the henhouse. Presley adamantly speaks out across the nation on the evils of marijuana. On August 16th, 1977, the King literally dies on the throne from an overdose of prescription drugs.

1971 John Lennon holds a free benefit concert in Ann Arbor, Michigan to free marijuana activist and founder of the White Panther Party, John Sinclair, from a ten-year prison sentence. It's a smashing success and Sinclair is released the following week. At Nixon's request, Lennon is perpetually harassed under the directive of J. Edgar Hoover, the head of the Federal Bureau of Investigation (FBI). Lennon's death made this ongoing harassment moot. In honor of the concert, and as a tribute to a more liberal cannabis-friendly city charter being adopted three years thereafter, an annual citywide "Hash Bash" is thrown on April 1st.

1972 The Canadian Le Dain Commission issues the results of its study on the *recreational* use of marijuana and urges the national government to legalize it for personal use similar to alcohol. John Lennon and Yoko Ono, no strangers to Canadian media after their 1969 "bed-in" at the Queen Elizabeth Hotel in Montreal, are invited to testify. Stated Lennon, "The one thing that can be said about marijuana is that it's nonviolent. If any government wanted to use it to calm people, they have got the ultimate weapon." Apparently, the Canadian government wasn't just any government, because they chose to ignore the report in its entirety.

1972 California Marijuana Imitative (CMI), the "backyard pot initiative" presented as a decriminalization measure (spearheaded by Amorphia) gets put on the state ballot. The original Proposition 19 goes down to defeat by a 2/3 to 1/3 margin. Undaunted, supporters take heart that the measure did garner 2.7 million support votes and ran 50/50 in Northern California's more liberal enclaves.

1972 Nixon forms the Office of Drug Abuse Law Enforcement (ODALE), operating straight out of the White House. The agency's specific purpose was to fund and spur local law enforcement agencies into a more concerted effort in pursuing drug busts, particularly concentrating on marijuana. Although ODALE was short-lived, it was particularly effective in terrorizing and traumatizing hippies. ODALE operations saw the birth of the "no knock" warrant and between April 1972 and May 1973 ODALE oversaw 1,439 raids. As bad as things were, they were about to get worse when ODALE got rolled into The Drug Enforcement Administration (DEA).

1973 Nixon commissions and handpicks 9 of the 13 members of the National Commission on Marijuana and Drug Abuse, which soon becomes known as the "Shafer Commission." Upon releasing its findings that marijuana is basically benign and recommending decriminalization, Nixon swings into action by ignoring his own requested report and forming the DEA.

1973 Formation of the Drug Enforcement Administration (DEA). Nixon consolidates several disjointed federal narcotics agencies such as the Special Action for Drug Abuse Law Enforcement, Office of Drug Abuse Law Enforcement (ODALE), and the FDA's Bureau of Drug Abuse Control (BDAC) into one super-charged constitution-violating agency. Warrantless searches, asset freezing, wire taps, arrests on mere suspicion, and confiscation of property were to quickly become standard modius-operandi.

1973 The U.S. government pays the Afghanistan government, under the rule of King Zahir Shah, $47 million to repress its in-country hashish and opium trade. Fields and houses were burned, and the occasional farmer shot on the spot. CSNY's, "Tin soldiers and Nixon coming," was now going international.

1974 The BNDD is officially disbanded in favor of the DEA.

1974 John King Forcade launches *High Times Magazine* as a quarterly publication; later to become a monthly. Many "knock-offs" were to follow. Today, *High Times* sells an estimated 10,000 subscriptions, with estimates that each magazine is viewed by over nine readers. A master smuggler, Fourcade's outlaw's life was a perilous one, and succumbing to various legal and personal pressures, the official line is that Forcade commits suicide by shooting himself in the head in October of 1978. Some who knew him personally refute this, stating that the left-handed Forcade was shot in the right temple, and they point to the motives of many who wanted him dead.

1974 Mississippi Senator, Democrat James Eastland, an avowed bigot determined to stop the "mongrelization of the white race," during the civil rights movement a decade ago, is now at it again. He convenes the senate subcommittee "Eastland Hearings" because of his concern over the marijuana and hashish epidemic sweeping America. In his opening statement, Eastland attests that, "If the epidemic is not rolled back our society may be taken over by 'marijuana culture' - a culture motivated by the consuming lust for self-gratification and lacking any higher moral guidance. Such a society could not long endure." Only anti-pot people were invited to testify. "We make no apology for the one-sided nature of our hearings - they were deliberately planned that way," Eastland said. Not-too-surprisingly, this committee did find something wrong with pot. Star witness Gabriel Nahas of Columbia University, an anesthesiology professor, testifies that he has discovered "the first direct evidence of cellular damage...that inevitably weakens the body's immune defenses." NIDA (National Institute on Drug Abuse) was so excited that it poured money into research to back Nahas's claims, all of which faltered or died on the vine of complete inconclusiveness. So disappointed were they in Nahas's credibility that they discontinued his funding. Other witnesses officially coin the term "amotivational syndrome" (see 1979). Nahas went on to pen many (9) books defamatory to drugs in general and two that reviled marijuana entitled: *Marijuana - Deceptive Weed* (1973) and *Marijuana - Keep Off the Grass* (1979). In much the same mold as the movie *Reefer Madness* (see 1938), they are good for a laugh.

1975 Not sharing the opinions of Anslinger or Nixon, President Gerald Ford orders a new marijuana study, which only served to confirm the previous Shafer Commission's findings. Mexican farmers in the rugged Sierra Madre Mountains, however, forced Ford's hand by growing poppies for heroin production alongside marijuana fields. Ford orders a reopening of the Paraquat spraying program. As before, Mexican farmers harvest and ship the severely compromised cannabis to the U.S., anyway.

1975 The Center for Studies of Narcotic and Drug Abuse of the U.S. National Institute of Mental Health release the results of a five-year study of marijuana (locally called ganja) use on the Caribbean island of Jamaica. (It was then estimated that over 70% of the island population used marijuana even though it was, and still is, illegal there.) The study found no links to crime, no links to brain damage, and a significantly lower percentage of alcohol use in comparison to neighboring Caribbean islands. The study went largely ignored in the United States and within the marijuana prohibiting nations of the international community.

1975 University professor Robert Randall is arrested at his home in Sarasota, Florida for growing marijuana in his yard. A glaucoma sufferer destined to go blind, Randall utilizes marijuana to relieve intraocular pressure in his eyes, which enables him to function. Randall claims a "medical necessity" and takes his case all the way to the United States Supreme Court. The court orders the feds to supply Randall with marijuana, and they procure it from the Investigative New Drug Program (IND) at the University of Mississippi. The university grows some incredibly poor pot, ships it to North Carolina to be rolled (ground stems, leaves, and all) into joints that are then sent to a chemist near Randall's home. Others attempting to join the program are harassed and harangued by the feds and very few actually get in. There were less than two dozen members when Bush the First shuts the program down in 1992, claiming that he was going to get even tougher on drugs. The feds allowed the remaining patients to be "grandfathered in." Randall died on June 2nd, 2001, having never gone blind. As of 2011, only four patients remained, and the program will go defunct when the last one finally dies. Although highly unlikely, because the program seemed to go out of its way to grow shit weed, an urban legend exists that the powerhouse marijuana strain "G-13" was developed at the facility in greenhouse number 13.

1975 On November 14th, 1975 at 1:05 p.m., Harry Jacob Anslinger dies.

1978 Upon taking office, President Jimmy Carter recommends full federal legalization of up to one ounce of marijuana and appoints British-born pharmacist Peter G. Bourne to institute a viable program. Bourne immediately comes under fire from conservatives for writing a bogus Quaalude prescription for one of his assistants. Carter backtracks, and the program is abandoned.

1979 "Amotivational syndrome" officially hits, and anti-pot enthusiasts have a new rallying cry. Fast-forming parent groups such as Families in Action, National Federation for Drug-Free Youth, ad infinitum, are birthed at the behest of Robert Dupont, the head of the National Institute on Drug Abuse (NIDA). It said that marijuana caused laziness and a lack of motivation in general, thus the term amotivational syndrome. It gets wheeled out even to this day, even though there is a dearth of evidence to prove it exists. People who were lazy before using marijuana remain lazy because of that predisposition. Amotivational syndrome gets comingled with ever-popular brain damage theories, all of which are unsubstantiated, at least in adults over the age of 21. Head shops are outlawed as part of a building national hysteria, although a few states still allow mail-order businesses to exist.

1980 Alaska declares marijuana possession by adults under their own roof as being protected by constitutional laws of privacy. In 1990, President Herbert Walker Bush strongarms a reversal of this decision by threatening to withhold major federal funding.

1982 President Ronald Reagan's reign of terror sharpens its teeth with the formation of The White House Drug Abuse Policy Office. Reagan reinstitutes mandatory sentencing, allows property seizures on suspicion alone, and swells the federal prison population for marijuana related offenses from 16% in 1970 to 62% in 1994.

1982 Reagan pushes through IRS tax code 280E, which

disallows any deductions for any expenses incurred in growing or researching marijuana. This would have far-reaching effects when medical marijuana made inroads towards national acceptance and respectability. Growers and dispensaries still can't claim any marijuana-related deductions on their federal income tax returns.

1982 Nancy Reagan's *Just Say No* program is unleashed upon the school systems of America and soon births DARE and other such narc-riddled programs. There are documented cases of children turning in their parents for drug use, the parents imprisoned, and their snitch progeny sent into foster care. It was later revealed that Reagan herself, like Elvis before her, was addicted to prescription painkillers.

1982 President Reagan dismisses yet another highly respected scientific report favorable to cannabis, this time from the National Academy of Sciences (NAS).

1984 Employee drug testing hits the American workplace.

1984 The Comprehensive Crime Control Act raises federal marijuana penalties while mandatory sentencing and the "three strikes rule" are enacted.

1988 On a pleasant April day, Debbie Goldsberry, a sophomore student at the University of Illinois in Campaign-Urbana, is on her way with friends to enjoy an annual on-campus outdoor pot smoking celebration. Upon approaching the "Hash Wednesday" festival, she is appalled as police in riot gear start beating students with Billy Clubs without warning, arresting nine people in the process. On the spot, she determines to be a devoted cannabis activist and founds the Cannabis Action Network (CAN). CAN caravans take their show on the road, crisscrossing the nation and getting the word out. CAN is still going strong today.

1988 Alan Howlett, leading a team of U.S. researchers, discovers the cannabinoid receptor system in the human brain. This is a groundbreaking game changer, as no other drug in existence contains compounds that are the exact same chemical composition as compounds found in the brain. Later, in 1992, William Devane, a member of Howlett's original team, discovers anandamine, a chemical that aids cannabis-ingested CBD's to bind with the human brain's CBD receptors. Stoners like to argue that it seems like cannabis and mankind were literally made for each other.

1988 The DEA's chief administrative law judge, Francis L. Young, issues a 69 page opinion on September 6th in response to the agency's long-running battle with NORML. Young stated: "Marijuana in its natural form is one of the safest therapeutically active substances known to man." Typical of their past and future behavior, the DEA ignores its own judge!

1989 President George Herbert Walker Bush declares yet another War on Drugs, this time called: "Operation Just Cause." Its primary target is Panamanian dictator General Manuel Noriega, accused of drug running and money laundering. Seeking asylum at the Vatican, U.S. forces terrorize Catholic opera buff Noriega with extremely loud heart-pounding rock and roll music. After 72 hours, Noriega gives up, is extricated, tried, and sentenced to 40 years in prison, later reduced to ten. Observers were uncertain if the Pope was able to tap his feet to songs by Bob Marley and The Wailers - probably not.

1989 On October 26th, Bush One, with the aid of his secret police, the DEA (no surprise here), unleashes "Black Thursday" by raiding hydroponic supply stores and warehouses in 46 states. This once again proves that no other marijuana growers give law enforcement a bigger hard-on than indoor hydroponic growers.

1990 The Solomon-Lautenberg Amendment became federal law, which allowed the revoking of the driver's license of anyone convicted of a drug offense, including marijuana possession.

1995 Acting as government shills and searching for findings a day late and a dollar short, the Environmental Protection Agency (EPA) issues a statement declaring that, "no lung or other injury in marijuana users has ever been attributed to Paraquat contamination." A bald-faced lie if there ever was one.

1996 California voters pass Proposition 215, the "Compassionate Use Act," allowing for the emergence of medical marijuana and its state legal distribution to patients with a doctor's recommendation. Poorly written, the law was open to broad interpretation and even broader harassment on the part of law enforcement.

1996 Republican Speaker of the House Newt Gingrich introduces before Congress the Drug Importer Death Penalty Act (H.R. 4170). It was passed in 2001 and gives the Attorney General wide latitude in determining if *any* confiscated imported drug exceeds 100 individual doses. If such is determined, the arrested peddler is sentenced to life imprisonment without parole. A two-time loser, by way of an earlier similar offense, can receive the death penalty. Gingrich has admitted to smoking marijuana during his undergraduate days with the gross rationalization that it was merely illegal at the time. Now, Gingrich makes the distinction that using marijuana is not only illegal, but also *immoral*. Immoral by whose standard? Gingrich's - I suppose. This law is still on the books.

1998 In response to the passage of California's Proposition 215, the feds pass (by a vote of 310 to 93) House Joint Resolution 117, which struck down any whiff or remote chance of federal medical marijuana legalization by stating: "[no] medical use without valid scientific evidence and [FDA] approval."

1999 The Center for Medical Cannabis Research (CMCR) opens in San Diego, California.

1999 Acting as shameless shills for Big Pharma, the Institute of Medicine declares, "If there is any future for marijuana as a medicine, it lies in its isolated components, the cannabinoids and their synthetic derivatives." This once again proved modern medicine's dogmatic need to be in complete control. They simply can't accept a synergist paradigm to pain relief and healing. One reason is that if they can't isolate it, then they can't charge for it. Doctors and pharmacists sticking together for the good of the profit motive - who would've thunk it?

2000 Democratic President Slick Willy Clinton, apparently miffed at the success of California's Proposition 215, threatens to revoke the prescription writing privileges of medical marijuana doctors. The doctors sue and prevail in Conant v. MaCaffrey, where the doctors' First Amendment rights are somewhat protected. In splitting the thinnest of hairs, the court rules that the doctors must recommend but not prescribe the use of cannabis.

2001 The country of Portugal, an original signer of the Single Convention in 1961, decides forty years later to try a different approach, and decriminalizes procession of all drugs. Portugal chose instead to concentrate on stopping the spread of HIV virus amongst heroin addicts, and on improving rehabilitation techniques and facilities. It is documented that since decriminalization, drug use has actually *decreased* in Portugal.

2001 In United States v. Oakland Cannabis Buyers' Cooperative, the Supreme Court rules that federal anti-drug laws would not allow an exception for medical use, citing the Controlled Substances Act of 1970, (see 1970) effectively forcing the club to shutter its doors.

2002 Law Enforcement Against Prohibition (LEAP) is formed. The core group of founding members were primarily composed of retired police, DEA agents, and judges who were disgusted with the ongoing hypocrisy rampant in the War on Drugs. Today LEAP boasts 100,000 members, 5,000 of which are active and retired law enforcement officers. If you can only donate to just one pro-legalization group, please make it this one, as they are the ones most supportive of the little guy, and they have their feet most firmly planted on the ground.

2003 The United States National Institute of Health states that cannabinoids are helpful in treating and even preventing diseases relating to the auto-immune system, preventing strokes and seizures, relieving trauma symptoms, and alleviating the symptoms of Parkinson's, Alzheimer's and HIV-induced dementia as their reason for filing patent #6,630,507. That's right, the U.S. government holds the patent for marijuana in order to lock down the lucrative position of being first in line to ride on the legal cannabis gravy train in the event that they are ever forced to legalize it. The patent is assigned to the U.S. Department of Health and Human Services.

2003 On his way out of office, as a parting shot to conservative Republicans who mounted a campaign to make him only the second Governor in U.S. history to be recalled, Democratic California Governor Gray Davis signs Senate Bill 420, commonly known as the Medical Marijuana Program Act. Citing alignment with the Tenth Amendment, the bill clarifies the intent of former Proposition 215 (1996). The "420" numbering is tongue-in-cheek, as every stoner knows that, "it's 4:20 somewhere."

2003 Comedic actor Tommy Chong's home is raided as part of "Operation Pipe Dreams" and "Operation Head Hunter," which was overseen by anti-pot zealot U.S. Attorney for the Western District of Pennsylvania, Mary Beth Buchanan. The whole stupid, sordid affair is covered in Chong's surprisingly well-written memoir entitled *The I Chong: Meditations from the Joint* (2006).

2004 Montana allows medical marijuana, but their program comes under unrelenting attack from the DEA.

2005 In Gonzales v. Raich, the Supreme Court strikes again in a 6 to 3 vote disallowing California's "states' rights" position on medical marijuana by once again citing the Controlled Substances Act of 1970. In effect, this allowed the DEA to continue to operate with impunity within the state and prosecute marijuana violations to the full extent of federal law. This continues to this day. Marijuana has to be removed from Schedule 1, or there is really no hope that federal persecution will ever end.

2006 Star National Football League (NFL) running back Ricky Williams is suspended by the league for the entire 2006 season for violating its substance abuse policy by testing positive for marijuana. Williams, a shy man of good character, is reviled by fans through the ensuing years, made a mockery of in spoofs on *Inside the NFL*, and generally discredited as being of weak moral character. The University of Texas running back won the 1998 Heisman Trophy, and currently ranks 31st among the NFL's all-time leading rushers, with 10,009 yards spread over an 11-year career. Williams was a power back with speed and was no shrinking violet on the field. He played the 2007 season in the Canadian Football League (CFL), receiving criticism from self-righteous stateside analysts such as Joe Theismann for doing so. When it comes to a man's livelihood, let the man decide what's in his best interests, say I. Williams was not alone amongst NFL players in being persecuted for smoking pot, and it should be noted that the NFL's hardcore stance on marijuana use is much stricter than its stance on domestic violence between players and their wives and girlfriends. Double standards abound (see 2013).

2007 Felipe Calderon ascends to the presidency in Mexico and almost immediately declares war on the Mexican drug cartels. Calderon, like so many U.S. presidents before him, actually thinks that this is a winnable war, and favors armed conflict over all other alternatives. As a result of this mentality, which was egged on wholeheartedly by the DEA, there are more cartels, more violence, and even more corruption in Mexico than ever before. Arresting and killing entrenched cartel leaders simply led to more splinter groups with younger, less experienced, but definitely more violent opportunists rushing to fill the voids.

2009 The ill-fated and ill-followed Ogden Memo is issued by the Justice Department, encouraging federal law enforcement (DEA, FBI, ATF) to only go after medical marijuana providers deemed to be in violation of their respective state laws.

2010 As an intimidation tactic designed to diffuse any mounting inertia for California's Proposition 19 (full marijuana legalization) in July, the DEA issues its 54-page booklet entitled: *DEA Position On Marijuana*, as if we didn't already know. It's clear that the DEA is a square jobs program and persecuting marijuana users is nothing more than trafficking in human flesh just to keep it going. It's not about right or wrong anymore, but simply about winning. The game has become more important than the reason why it was invented in the first place.

2010 Medical marijuana dispensaries are allowed to operate in the District of Columbia. Some have excellent views of the Capitol Building. It's a matter of convenience, because now lobbyists for Big Alcohol, Big Agri, Big Pharma, and Big Prison can all stop by and purchase a soothing relaxant after a hard day of lobbying against marijuana on the hill. D.C., where the polar opposites of dreams and reality both come to die.

2010 Former Republican California Governor Arnold

Schwarzenegger, who was caught on film smoking a doobie in his 1977 film *Pumping Iron*, wrote in an op-ed, published in the *Los Angeles Times* in September, arguing in opposition to California's 2010 Proposition 19 that, "We wouldn't want to be a laughing stock." No, no *we* wouldn't, but what about you, Mr. Governator?

2010 Retired Michigan police captain Howard Wooldridge rides again - this time in support of California's Proposition 19 (full pot legalization). He and his faithful horse Misty have already traversed the breadth of America twice, and now they are covering Cali from north to south and east to west. One of the founding members of LEAP (Law Enforcement Against Prohibition), Wooldridge's tee shirt sports the message: "COPS SAY LEGAZE POT. ASK ME WHY." Apparently, not enough people did. The New Right turned out in droves while many apathetic stoners stayed home, and the measure was narrowly defeated.

2010 Arizona allows medical marijuana.

2011 The DEA threatens and intimidates banking institutions in medical marijuana states, in particular California, into not allowing medical marijuana businesses to have bank accounts. Several accounts (including mine) were closed with no explanation given. However, the explanation on the street was that banks feared criminal repercussions on the federal level, including losing their ability to offer their customers FDIC insurance.

2011 Wachovia, once a major U.S. bank, was implicated for laundering money for Mexican drug lords. They surrendered $110,000,000.00 in forfeitures. No arrests were made, and nobody within Wachovia's organization saw jail time.

2012 Rhode Island decriminalizes.

2012 Connecticut allows medical marijuana.

2012 LEGALIZATION AT LAST!!! Voters in Colorado approve Amendment 64, and voters in Washington State pass Initiative 502, allowing for statewide marijuana legalization for adults over 21 years of age. The eyes of the nation, if not the world, are upon these two living laboratories.

2013 NFL Commissioner Rodger Goodell hints that the league may be willing to consider marijuana as a drug safer for player's overall heath than any number of league-approved prescription painkillers they are currently being given in pill form or shot up with. It's ironic that one of the most macho institutions in the U.S. was now considering hippy-dippy pot as a viable alternative medicine. Why? Survival. The average shelf life of an NFL player is three years, or one-year shy of when their league pension merely starts to kick in. But the real reason is to keep star players on the field. Their bodies are their stock in trade, and they know more than most how damaging the side effects of Big Pharma's drugs are. Big Alcohol and Big Pharma have a cow, and internally pressure Goodell to backtrack at a "State of the League" address to team owners prior to the Super Bowl in February 2014. Now, with younger rising stars such as Daryl Washington and Josh Gordon being suspended, the nation sees the need to legalize pot or risk watching inferior Sunday, Monday, and Thursday professional football. In an irony of all ironies, the then 78-year-old marijuana witch hunt could have come to an end, not for the sake of the wrongly incarcerated little guy, but to preserve our national pastime, and its highest paid athletes. Any port in a storm, say I. Of course, this never came to pass.

2013 In December, the South American nation of Uruguay passes full cannabis legalization, taking Portugal's decriminalization model one step further.

2014 In a March 2nd televised interview on *Meet the Press*, Democratic California Governor Jerry Brown shows signs of becoming a crotchety old man by stating, "How many people can get stoned and still have a great state or a great nation? The world's pretty dangerous, very competitive. I think we need to stay alert, if not 24 hours a day, more than some of the potheads might be able to put together." During his first stint as Governor from 1975 to 1983, Brown dated cutie-pie country crooner Linda Ronstadt, who was inducted in 2014 to the Rock and Roll Hall of Fame. At the time, Brown confided to aides and friends that a marriage to Ronstadt would cost him the White House. Star-crossed lovers, Brown was aware that Ronstadt smoked grass and had done so much cocaine that she had to have her nose catheterized. She was so enamored with Brown that she cleaned up her act, to no avail. The attraction may have balanced on Brown's one time liberal politics, which conservatives considered so far out that Chicago news reporter Mike Royko nick-named him "Governor Moonbeam" as a dig at his young, nontraditional, idealistic, and definitely liberal constituency. Years later, Royko recanted and formally apologized. Concerning Brown - how the mighty have fallen.

2014 At an international conference of law enforcement held in Rome, Pope Francis speaks out against drug legalization, stating: "Drug addiction is an evil, and with evil there can be no yielding or compromise." Francis, who by all accounts has been the most moderate and coolest pope ever, up until now, indicated disapproval at Roman Catholic Uruguay's full national cannabis legalization and at other Latin American countries now poised to follow suit.

2014 A day late and many dollars short, Congress passes the Rohrabacher-Farr Amendment, which passes in the House by a 219-189 vote and directs the feds to suspend raids on legitimate state-legal medical marijuana facilities. Yeah, sure.

2014 On July 16th The House of Representatives votes to lift banking restrictions for medical marijuana dispensaries in states where they are legal.

2014 Vermont allows medical marijuana.

2014 Maryland decriminalizes and allows medical marijuana.

2014 Alaska legalizes.

2015 Delaware decriminalizes and allows medical marijuana.

2015 Minnesota allows medical marijuana.

2015 Let freedom ring! Two additional states and the District of Columbia have now legalized marijuana: Alaska on February 24th, D.C, on February 26th, and Oregon on July 1st. Hawaii now appears to be the next logical candidate.

2015 Bad news for stoners reared its ugly head with the April 27th swearing in of our nation's newest Attorney General, Democrat Loretta Lynch. An Obama appointee, and even more of a conservative knucklehead than her predecessor Eric Holder, Lynch was a hardliner with a major jones against reefer. When it comes to the feds and marijuana, the more things change, the more they stay the same.

2016 This was the rumored date for California to once again vote on Proposition 19, calling for full marijuana legalization, which eventually became a reality. Two of the main criticisms of 19's defeat in 2010 was that it was poorly written, and that the timing was all wrong. It's estimated that only 30% of liberals vote in state elections, which was the case in 2010, while 50% of liberals vote in national elections, which was be the case in 2016. Still, there was no guarantee that legalization was a shoo-in. A failure on the part of stoners to vote in 2010 is what really doomed 19 then. Complacency kills passion, and marijuana supporters had to work harder than ever to get out the vote. Proposition 19 morphed into Proposition 64 and did pass in November of that year by a 66% to 34% margin. Note that 34%, in reality, means that almost half the state is still anti-pot.

2016 Florida allows medical marijuana but burdens it with a myriad of convoluted laws. Ditto for the state of Arkansas.

2016 Despite Louisiana's hardcore anti-pot stance, the city of New Orleans decriminalizes marijuana possession.

2016 Rhode Island allows medical marijuana.

2016 Massachusetts and Nevada legalize.

2017 In January, Law Enforcement Against Prohibition (LEAP) morphs into Law Enforcement Action Partnership (still LEAP). They are essentially the same righteous dudes speaking the truth concerning the hypocrisy and stupidity of America's War on Drugs.

2017 Hawaii allows medical marijuana.

2018 Pompous ass supreme, Attorney General Jefferson Beauregard Sessions III rescinds the Cole Memorandum, which was a little known (and little followed) Obama-era policy of encouraging federal law enforcement (DEA, FBI, ATF) and overzealous U.S. Attorneys to look the other way in regard to state-legal cannabis businesses. Thus, Sessions made good on his earlier public comment that "Good people don't smoke marijuana."

2018 On December 18th Republican Senator Charles Grassley, the outgoing chair of the Senate Judiciary Committee and the Senate's second-most senior Republican, effectively blocks the proposal of Republican Senator Cory Gardner of Colorado to obtain unanimous consent in considering amending a recent criminal justice reform bill to add legal protections for people who use and provide cannabis products in compliance with a myriad of state laws. Sounding the same old tired Republican drumbeat, Grassley stated, "This amendment is inconsistent with current federal law and would allow states the right to break existing law."

2018 Indiana, Texas, and Virginia all allow low-THC CBD oil. Indiana, being the land of wild man Mike Pence, and fearing stepping out too far over the line only allows the oil to be extracted from hemp. Really - *hemp?* Big whoop.

2018 Ohio allows medical marijuana but with severe restriction.

2018 Iowa, Missouri, New Hampshire, New Jersey, New Mexico, North Dakota, Oklahoma, Pennsylvania and Utah all allow medical marijuana.

2018 Maine legalizes, but as of 2019, fails to implement a program for sales.

2018 Oregon and Vermont legalize.

2019 Republican President Donald J. Trump (aka The Mad King) nominates William Barr to be our U.S. Attorney General at the tail end of 2018. On January 18th in his Senate confirmation hearing, Barr states that if appointed he would not prioritize going after state-legal marijuana operations. Immediately thereafter he backtracks with this clarification: "I think it's a mistake to back off on marijuana, however, if we want a federal approach, if we want states to have their own laws, then let's get there and let's get there the right way." Here again, whenever the feds say "the right way," what they are really saying is "no way." Barr throws out the usual meatless bone, stating his opinion that Department of Justice policy should align with congressional legislation (if any were to ever get passed). Barr becomes our nation's 85th Attorney General on February 14th when U.S. Supreme Court Chief Justice John Roberts administered the oath of office. Shortly thereafter, in summarizing and fictionalizing the Mueller Report, Barr reveals that he is merely the Mad King's lapdog. Barr's past hardcore stance on all controlled substances (of which marijuana is on Schedule 1) during a one-year stint as Attorney General under Bush One should give stoners pause. Sure, he acted cool during his recent Senate confirmation hearing, but he desperately wanted the job, and if his behavior concerning the Mueller Report is any indication, he was probably willing to say anything to get it. Know that if Trump sets his sights on marijuana, Barr's hands-off stance concerning states' rights cannabis legality will fall faster than dominos succumbing to gravity.

2019 Marijuana and any of its derivatives are still completely illegal in Alabama, Idaho, Kansas, Kentucky, Louisiana, Mississippi, Nebraska, North Carolina, South Carolina, Tennessee, Wisconsin, and Wyoming.

2019 Georgia allows low-THC CBD oil.

2019 Illinois and Michigan legalize.

2020

General Note Concerning the United States of America's Convoluted, Dysfunctional, and Totally Insane Status of States' Rights Marijuana Legality:

The DISA Globe Solutions website's (https://disa.com/map-of-marijuana-legality-by-state) *Map of Marijuana Legality State by State* is by far the best reference resource for trying to decipher to what degree the ground you're standing upon at this very minute is cannabis friendly or averse. DISA teams up with the Medical Marijuana Policy (MMP) to provide a quick, explanatory, at a glance chart of each U.S. state, and then provides a narrative of every state's laws and historic positions on legalization (or not) with a click. In most of the states of the Deep South (or the former Confederacy, if you will), marijuana is still illegal and punishments are very harsh - stay underground and tread lightly, my friends. In the liberal Northeast, medical marijuana has made significant inroads and a smattering of states have legalized entirely. Along the entire free and breezy west coast, recreational use is legal. The Midwest is a mixed bag, with some allowing medical, some still illegal, and some only allowing low-THC CBD oil, which concedes compassionate use but forbids anyone from actually getting high and enjoying themselves. Surprisingly, in Wisconsin, once a bastion of liberalism, marijuana is completely illegal. *Don't* travel through Nebraska when leaving Colorado with *any* cannabis products in your possession, because all are unequivocally illegal there and the Highway Patrol is on a feeding frenzy for out-of-state license plates. Know that in any state where marijuana is still illegal, the police can confiscate any amount of cash over $3,000.00 on mere suspicion that it could be drug money, and being an army that readily sustains itself on plunder, they *will* most certainly suspect you. The solution to ending all of this "some say yes and some say no" madness is to insist on total federal legalization, which will necessitate voting the old white men who still run this country and have a conservative chokehold on cannabis and most every other human right out of office in 2020 or whenever their next reelection comes up. Take recent attacks on Roe v. Wade as an indication that the squares and the bible thumpers will eventually get around to attacking states" rights marijuana legality; it's inevitable if they can keep their Republican politicians in power. Dumping the Mad King and Mitch McConnell (aka the self-described Grim Reaper) has to be priority one. Next to get the axe has to be all of their diehard goober ilk. Accept nothing less than complete federal marijuana legalization, because anything other than that isn't justice, it's mere placation that leaves the door open for any gains to be wiped away and a return to the dark ages of total illegality. Stay strong, unite, and go forth and get this done, and all of your lives' will be immeasurably better.

2021 New Jersey legalizes.

2021 Connecticut legalizes.

2021 On July 14th United States Senators Chuck Schumer (NY), Cory Booker (NJ), and Ron Wyden (OR) promote a bill to *federally legalize marijuana*. Interesting to note that they are all from states that have approved state legalization and are known to be blue for their liberal politics. It's as good as dead on arrival in the Senate where even some Democrats will vote against it, if it ever makes it that far. Stoners best hope now lies in 2024, if they can make this a single issue election with young voters.

2022 On April 1st The House of Representatives passes The Marijuana Opportunity, Reinvestment and Expungement (MORE) Act sponsored by Representative Jerry Nadler (D – NY) by a vote of 220 to 204 with two Democrats voting against it, and three Republicans voting for it. This push for complete federal legalization, while well-intended is doomed to failure. As to be expected, Jim Jordan (R – OH) threw our red herrings aplenty stating that they should be doing more important work. If you were rotting in jail on the strength of a bogus marijuana conviction for committing a nonviolent crime, you might reassess your stance, Jimbo. As usual, President Biden remains opposed (and clueless). This is the epitome of an April Fool's joke because the bill is as good as dead in the Senate. At present 63% of the nation is in favor of federal legalization, but the hardcore 37% of conservatives, along with their entrenched Republican Senators stand in the way. The only solution is the same as it has always been – vote them out. If you want to be free, you must vote them out!

Bibliography

Harry Jacob Anslinger and Will Ousler. *The Murderers*. Copyright 1961. Farrar, Straus, and Cudahy, New York. ASIN# B000JHQ581

Michelle Alexander. *The New Jim Crow: Mass Incarceration in the Age of Colorblindness*. Copyright 2012. New Press, New York. ISBN# 978-1-5955863-3-8.

Mary Appelhof. *Worms Eat My Garbage*. Copyright 1982, Second Edition 1997. Flowerfield Enterprises, Kalamazoo, MI. ISBN# 978-0-9778045-1-1.

Michael Backes. *Cannabis Pharmacy: The Practical Guide to Medical Marijuana*. Black Dog and Leventhal Publishers, Inc., New York, NY. ISBN# 978-1-57912-951-4.

Radley Balko. *The Rise of the Warrior Cop: The Militarization of America's Police Forces*. Copyright 2014. Public Affairs, New York. ISBN# 978-1-61039-211-2.

Bruce Barcott. *Weed the People: The Future Of Legal Marijuana In America*. Copyright 2015. Time Books, New York. ISBN# 978-1-61893-140-5.

Martin Booth. *Cannabis: A History*. Copyright 2003. Picador, New York. ISBN# 0-312-42494-7.

T.C. Boyle. *Budding Prospects*. Copyright 1984. Penguin Putnam Inc., New York. ISBN# 0-14-02.9996-3.

David Bradley. *The Chaneysville Incident*. Copyright 1981. Harper & Row New York. ISBN# 0-060-10491-0.

Emily Brady. *Humboldt: Life on America's Marijuana Frontier*. Copyright 2013. Grand Central Publishing: Hachette Book Group, New York. ISBN# 978-1-4555-0676-7.

Kathleen Norris Brenzel (editor). *Sunset Western Garden Book*. Copyright 2007. Menlo Park, CA Sunset Publishing Corporation. ISBN# 0-37603-916-7.

Jay Carter Brown. *Smuggler's Blues: The Saga of a Marijuana Importer*. Copyright 2007. ECW Press, Toronto, Ontario, Canada. ISBN# 978-1-55022-783-3.

Johnathan P. Caulkins, Angela Hawken, Beau Kilmer, Mark A.R. Kleiman. *Marijuana Legalization: What Everyone Needs to Know*. Copyright 2012. Oxford University Press, New York. ISBN# 978-0-19-991373-2

Jorge Cervantes. *Marijuana Horticulture: The Indoor/Outdoor Medical Grower's Bible*. Copyright 2006. Van Patten Publishing, Lake Forest Park, WN. ISBN# 978-1-878823-23-6.

Tommy Chong. *The I Chong: Meditations From the Joint*. Copyright 2006. Simon Spotlight Entertainment, New York. ISBN# 978-0-64198-657-4.

Robert Connell Clarke. *Hashish!* Copyright 1998, Second Edition 2010. Red Eye Press, Los Angeles. ISBN# 0-929349-05-9.

Robert Connell Clarke. *Marijuana Botany*. Copyright 1981. Ronin Publishing, Oakland, CA. ISBN# 978-0-914171-78-2.

Alfred Emile Cornebise. *The CCC Chronicles: Camp Newspapers of the Civilian Conservation Corps, 1933 - 1942.* Copyright 2004. McFarland & Company, Raleigh, NC. ISBN# 0-7864-1841-1.

Gretchen C. Daily and Katherine Ellison. *The New Economy of Nature: The Quest to Make Conservation Profitable.* Copyright 2002. Island Press/Shearwater Books, Washington, DC. ISBN# 1-55963-945-8.

Dave DeWitt. *Growing Medical Marijuana Securely and Legally.* Copyroght2013. Ten Speed Press, Berkeley, California. ISBN# 978-1-60774-428-3.

Tony Dokoupil. *The Last Pirate: A Father, His Son, and the Golden Age of Marijuana.* Copyright: 2014. Anchor Books, New York. ISBN# 978-0-307-73948-3.

Editors at Lane Publishing. *Sunset National Garden Book.* Copyright 1997. Menlo Park, CA Sunset Publishing Corporation. ISBN# 978-037-57603-9-6.

Steve Elliott. *The Little Black Book of Marijuana: The Essential Guide to the World of Cannabis.* Copyright 2014. Peter Pauper Press, Inc., White Plains, New York. ISBN# 978-1-4413-0611-1.

Doug Fine. *Too High To Fail: Cannabis and the New Green Revolution*. Copyright 2012. Gotham Books, New York. ISBN# 978-1-592-40761-3.

Steve Fox, Paul Armentano, & Mason Tvert. *Marijuana Is Safer: So Why Are We Driving People to Drink?* Copyright 2009. Chelsea Green Publishing Company, White River Junction, VT. ISBN# 978-1-60-358144-8.

Mel Frank. *Marijuana Grower's Insider's Guide*. Copyright 1993 (5th edition). Red Eye Press, Los Angeles. ISBN# 978-092-93490-0-8.

Carolyn Elizabeth Garcia. *Primo Plant: Growing Marijuana Outdoors*. Copyright 1998. Quick American Archives, Oakland, California. ISBN# 0-932551-27-0.

Greg Green. *The Cannabis Bible: The Definitive Guide to Growing Marijuana for Recreational and Medical Use* (2010 2nd edition). Green Candy Press, San Francisco, California. ISBN# 978-1931160582.

Robert Greenfield. *Timothy Leary: A Biography*. Copyright 2006. Harcourt, Inc., New York. ISBN# 978-0-15-100500-0.

Lester Grinspoon. *Marijuana Reconsidered*. Copyright 1971. Harvard University Press, Cambridge, MA. ISBN#

Johann Hari. *Chasing the Scream: The First and Last Days of the War on Drugs*. Copyright 2015. Bloomsbury, USA, New York. New York. ISBN# 978-1-62040-890-3.

Syndey J. Harris. *Winners and Losers*. Copyright 1973. Argus Communications, Allen, TX. ISBN# 0-91359-221-8.

Bibliography

Peter Hecht. *Weed Land: Inside America's Marijuana Epicenter and How Pot Went Legit.* Copyright 2014. University of California Press, Berkley, CA. ISBN# 978-0-520-27543-0.

Christian Hegeseth with Joseph D'Agnese. *Big Weed: An Entrepreneur's High-Stakes Adventures In The Budding Legal Marijuana Business.* Copyright 2015. Palgrave Macmillan Trade, New York. ISBN# 978-1-137-28000-8.

Jack Herer. *The Emperor Wears No Clothes.* Copyright 1973, 12th Edition 2010. Ah Ha Publishing, Austin, TX. ISBN# 978-187812-502-6.

Catherine Hiller. *Just Say Yes: A Marijuana Memoir.* Copyright 2015. Heliotrope Books, New York. ISBN# 798-1-942762-01-0.

Julie Holland M.D. (editor). *The Pot Book: A Complete Guide to Cannabis: Its Role in Medicine. Politics, Science, and Culture.* Copyright 2010. Park Street Press. Rochester, VT. Toronto, Canada. ISBN#: 978-1-59477-368-6.

John C. Krieg. *Environmental Cognizance: Towards the Year 2020.* Copyright 2005. Ivy House Publishing Group, Raleigh, NC. ISBN# 1-57197-436-9.

John C. Krieg. *EcoNation: America in Environmental Perspective.* Copyright 2005. Ivy House Publishing Group, Raleigh, NC. ISBN# 1-57197-451-2.

John C. Krieg. *Mobilizing the Green Revolution: Money and Manpower to Save the Planet.* Copyright 2006. Ivy House Publishing Group, Raleigh, NC. ISBN# 1-57197-468-7

Timothy Leary, Ralph Metzner, and Richard Alpert (Ram Dass). *The Psychedelic Experience: Based on the Tibetan Book of the Dead.* Copyright 1964. Citadel, New York. ISBN# 0-806-51652-6.

Martin A. Lee. *Smoke Signals: A Social History of Marijuana - Medical, Recreational, and Scientific.* Copyright 2012. Scribner, New York, London, Toronto, Sydney, New Delhi. ISBN# 978-4391-0261-9.

Alyson Martin and Nushin Rashidian. *A New Leaf: The End of Cannabis Prohibition.* Copyright 2014. The New Press. New York, London. ISBN# 978-1-59558-920-0.

Robert MacCoun and Peter Reuter. *Drug War Heresies: Learning from Other Vices, Times, and Places.* Copyright 2001. Cambridge University Press, New York. ISBN# 0-521-57263-0.

John McCaslin. *Weed Man: The Remarkable Journey of Jimmy Divine.* Copyright 2009. Thomas Nelson, Nashville, TN. ISBN# 978-1-59555-153-5.

Elise McDonough. *High Times Presents Marijuana for Everybody.* Copyright 2014. Chronicle Books, San Francisco. ISBN# 978-1-4521-2888-7.

Kenneth Morrow. *Marijuana Horticulture: A Comprehensive Guide to Cannabis Cultivation and Hashish Production.* Copyright 2016. Green Candy Press, San Francisco, California. ISBN# 978-1-937866—34-1.

Jeff Mowta. *Marijuana New School: Outdoor Cultivation.* Copyright 2007. Green Candy Press, San Francisco. ISBN# 978-1-931160-43-8.

Gabriel Nahas. *Marijuana - Deceptive Weed.* Copyright 1973. Elsevier Science Publishing, Amsterdam, Netherlands. ISBN# 0-720-44129- 3.

Gabriel Nahas. *Keep Off the Grass.* Copyright 1979. Paul Eriksson Publisher, Forest Dale, VT. ISBN# 0-707-82401-3.

Brian O'Dea. *High: Confessions of an International Drug Smuggler.* Copyright 2006. Other Press, New York ISBN# 978--1-59051-331-6.

S.T. Oner. *Marijuana: Outdoor Grower's Guide.* Copyright: 2007. Green Candy Press, San Francisco. ISBN# 978-1-931160-4-4.

Edward Padilla and Paul Wood. *Laurigancho.* Copyright 2012. Flying Rabbit Press, Pukalami, HI. ISBN# 978- 0- 970620-05-7.

Michael Pollen. *The Botany of Desire: A Plant's View of the World.* Copyright 2001. Random House, New York. ISBN# 978-0-37576-039-6.

Trish Regan. *Joint Ventures: Inside America's Almost Legal Marijuana Industry.* Copyright 2011. John Wiley and Sons, Inc., Hoboken, New Jersey. ISBN# 978-0-470-55907-9.

Roger Roffman. *Marijuana Nation: One Man's Chronicle of America Getting High: From Vietnam to Legalization.* Copyright 2014. Pegasus Books, New York. ISBN# 978-1-60598-546-6.

Ed Rosenthal with David Downs. *Beyond Buds: Marijuana Extracts: Hash Vaping, Dabbing, Edibles & Medicines.* Copyright 2014. Quick American, Piedmont, CA. ISBN# 978-1-93680-723-9.

Ed Rosenthal. *Ed Rosenthal's Marijuana Grower's Handbook. Ask Ed Edition*. Copyright2010. Quick American Publishing, Oakland, California. ISBN# 978-0-032551-46-7.

Jason Ryan. *Jackpot: High Times, High Seas, and the Sting That Launched the War on Drugs*. Copyright 2011. Lyons Press, Guilford, Connecticut. ISBN# 978-1-59921-976-9.

Nicholas Schou. *Orange Sunshine: The Brotherhood of Eternal Love and Its Quest to Spread Peace, Love, and Acid to the World*. Copyright 2010. Thomas Dunne Books, New York. ISBN# 978-0-312-60717-3.

D. J. Short. *Cultivating Exceptional Cannabis: An Expert Breeder Shares His Secrets*. Quick American Archives, Oakland, California. ISBN# 0-932551-59-9.

Soma. *Organic Marijuana Soma Style*. Copyright 2005. Quick American, Oakland, California. ISBN# 0-932551-68-8.

Subcool. *Dank 2.0: The Quest for the Very Best Marijuana Continues: Breeder's Tale*. Copyright 2011. Quick American Publishing, Piedmont, California. ISBN# 13-978-0-932551-53-5.

Larry "Ratso" Sloman. *Reefer Madness: A History of Marijuana*. Copyright 1979, Second Edition 1998. Saint Martin's Griffin, New York. ISBN# 0-312-19523-0

Tony Thompson. *Reefer Men: The Rise and Fall of a Billionaire Drug Ring*. Copyright 2007. Hodder and Stoughton Ltd, London. ISBN# 978-0-340-89933-5.

A.R. Torsone. *Herb Trader: A Tale of Treachery and Espionage in the Global Marijuana Trade*. Copyright 2009. Woodstock Mountain Press, New York. ISBN# 978-0-578-01292-6.

E.O. Wilson. *The Diversity of Life*. Copyright 1992. W.W. Norton & Co., New York. ISBN# 0-393-96479-5.

Clint Werner. *Marijuana Gateway to Health: How Cannabis Protects Us From Cancer and Alzheimer's Disease*. Copyright 2015. 978-0-98342-618-9.

Author Bio

John C. Krieg is a retired landscape architect and land planner who formerly practiced for over 40 years in Arizona, California, and Nevada. He is also retired as an International Society of Arboriculture (ISA) certified arborist and currently holds seven active categories of California state contracting licenses, including the highest category of Class A General Engineering for over 25 years. He has written a college textbook entitled *Desert Landscape Architecture* (1999, CRC Press). John has had pieces published in *A Gathering of the Tribes, Alternating Current, Blue Mountain Review, Clark Street Review, Conceit, Hedge Apple, Homestead Review, Indolent Books, Inlandia, Line Rider Press, LOL Comedy, Lucky Jefferson, Magazine of History and Fiction, Oddball Magazine, Palm Springs Life, Pandemonium, Pegasus, Pen and Pendulum, Raven Cage, Red Fez, Saint Ann's Review, Squawk Back, The Book Smuggler's Den, The Courtship of Winds, The Mindful Word, The Scriblerus, The Writing Disorder, True Chili, Twist & Twain*, and *Wilderness House Literary Review*. In conjunction with filmmaker/photographer Charles Sappington, Mr. Krieg has completed a two-part documentary film entitled *Landscape Architecture: The Next Generation* (2010). In some underground circles John is considered a master grower of marijuana and holds as a lifelong goal the desire to see marijuana federally legalized. Nothing else will do.

www.ingramcontent.com/pod-product-compliance
Lightning Source LLC
LaVergne TN
LVHW051825080426
835512LV00018B/2724